MW00913769

DUCASSE
FLAVORS OF
FRANCE

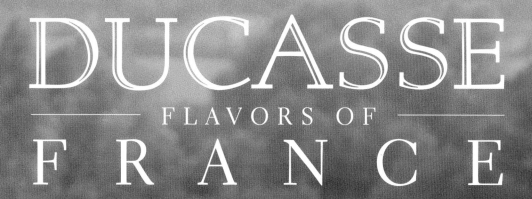

DUCASSE
— FLAVORS OF —
FRANCE

ALAIN DUCASSE

WITH LINDA DANNENBERG
PHOTOGRAPHS BY PIERRE HUSSENOT

ARTISAN
New York

The Publisher gratefully acknowledges
Stephanie Lyness and Judith Sutton,
who created the Appendix and whose
contribution to this work is evident
on every page.

Copyright © 1998 by Alain Ducasse

Photographs copyright © 1998 by Pierre Hussenot

All rights reserved. No portion of this book may be
reproduced—mechanically, electronically, or by any means,
including photocopying—without written permission
of the publisher.

This edition published in 2006 by Artisan
A Division of Workman Publishing Company, Inc.
225 Varick Street
New York, N.Y. 10014

The Library of Congress has catalogued the first edition as follows:
Library of Congress Cataloging-in-Publication Data
   Ducasse, Alain.
      Ducasse flavors of France / by Alain
      Ducasse; with Linda Dannenberg;
      photographs by Pierre Hussenot
         p.   cm.
       ISBN 1-57965-107-0 (1st ed.)
       1. Cookery, French. I. Dannenberg, Linda.
      II. Title. III. Title: Ducasse Flavors of France.
      TX719.D817 1998
      614.5944–DC21   98-6963
                  CIP

ISBN-13: 978-1-57965-319-4
ISBN 10: 1-57965-319-7

First edition, 1998
Second edition, September 2006

10 9 8 7 6 5 4 3 2 1

Printed in Singapore

Designer: Susi Oberhelman
Assistant Designer: Pat Tan
Production Director: Nancy Murray

FOR GWENAELLE

Mercredi 27 Août
BM
Artichauts violets cuits en barigoule
et d'autres crus, râpée de truffes
d'été et lard croustillant
Pavé de morue fraîche poêlé sur sa
peau, haricots coco, tomates et cèpes
Côte de veau rôtie en cocotte
oignons et blettes mijotés, jus
Fromages du plateau de Val
Vin Cuit
Selon
la Vieille Tradition
Provençale

CONTENTS

INTRODUCTION

MANY THINGS DREW ME TO MY MÉTIER, BUT PERHAPS THE
most compelling was that it was a pursuit that would lead me into a world of generosity, of conviviality, of
sharing. What you produce, the fruits of your labors, gives satisfaction, pleasure, even joy. It is also a pursuit
that is never dull. There is always something new to try—an ingredient, a technique, a combination of
elements or ingredients.

For me, very early on, the lure was irresistible. I knew that I wanted to be a chef at age twelve. I grew up
on a farm in Castelsarrazin in the Landes region of Southwest France, where my parents raised ducks and geese
for foie gras, my grandfather took care of our large vegetable garden, and my grandmother, a wonderful cook,
prepared every meal. It was a house full of delicious aromas—of stuffed chickens roasting over the fire, of cèpes
cooking in a pan with garlic, of cherry clafoutis baking in the oven. They waft through my memories still.

One weekend, my grandmother was preparing dinner, and on her menu were some thin, crisp *haricots
verts* from our garden. After she transferred the beans onto a platter, I sampled two or three and knew she had
left them on the stove a little too long. "Grandma," I said quietly, but feeling no timidity, "you've overcooked
the green beans." It was a small moment, but at the same time a sort of epiphany for me. "So," she said, "would
you like to do the cooking?" Yes, I thought to myself. Nothing from that point on could divert me.

My father attempted to dissuade me by arranging for a short apprenticeship in the kitchen of a
local restaurant, imagining that a hard, dreary interlude would wake me up to the realities of a chef's world.
On the contarary. . . .

I managed to talk myself into the kitchen of Michel Guérard in Eugénie-les-Bains, and later went on to
work for Roger Vergé, at the Moulin de Mougins in a hill town above the Riviera, but it wasn't until I arrived
in the kitchen of Alain Chapel in Mionnay, near Lyons, when I was twenty-one, that I truly became a chef
and at the same time found my most important mentor and the enduring principles that have defined my
cooking ever since.

Alain Chapel was a master who made me doubt myself and my calling every day by the standards that he
set and the perfection that he demanded. He represented an almost impossible ideal. Every move he made
showed his reverence for the products he worked with. He raised each to the quintessence of itself. There
was never a false note—no pretension, no contrivance—in his cuisine. When the finished dish was presented,
it had the appearance of simplicity and a casual grace that belied all the work and technical experience that
had gone into it.

I left Chapel after two years, filled with renewed confidence and enthusiasm. From the shoulders of this
giant I could see where I was going and at last had the mastery to go there. At its core, my cooking is about
clarity of taste, precision in execution, and respect for the product, which to me means retaining its original
flavor—at my restaurants a tomato will always taste like a tomato—and, when possible, its original shape. It's
actually harder to achieve this faux simplicity—where the essential nature of a product is revealed—than to
create a dish where the basic ingredient is hidden by sauces and cream. I use the best ingredients I can find. I
use as much of each element as I can—the trimmings, at times the skins, the shells, the baking juices, the pan
drippings, the heads, the cooking broth, all the by-products of the process—in order to reveal an ingredient's
precise taste. I also incorporate different preparations of the same product in a given dish, each revealing an
individual aspect of its flavor. For example, a dish might feature sliced raw artichokes, braised whole artichokes,

and paper-thin slices of fried artichokes; a dessert might feature grated raw pear, sautéed pear slices, and puréed and then frozen pear. The palate discerns different facets of the artichoke's or the pear's flavor in each incarnation. There is no such thing as genius in the kitchen; there is only the work—which is to respect the natural flavor of foods, to reveal their truest natures.

In my kitchens, a dish always begins with a product, never the other way around; I never decide I want to do a certain kind of dish and then look for the ingredients with which to compose it. The product determines its own destiny. Without the poultrymen of the Landes, the langoustine fishermen of Loctudy, the chanterelle gatherers from the Massif Central, the potato farmers of Noirmoutiers, without all these artisans who work with dedication and love and pride, the great kitchens of France could not exist. On all of my menus I honor many of the special products of France by highlighting their provenance in the titles of the recipes— lamb and salt cod from the Basque country, salmon from the Adour River, chickens from Bresse and the Landes, melons from Cavaillon, squab from the Alps of Haute-Provence, beef from Chalosse, red mullet from the Mediterranean.

French cuisine today is distinctly lighter than it was in the 1950s or 1960s, for example. Many of the accessories and extraneous decoration have been swept away, the dishes pared down to essentials. Instead of using heavy cream or egg yolks to create a rich sauce, as was often the case in old-style French cooking, we use the juices from meats and vegetables as the bases for their own sauces. And we pair many of our dishes with *sauces-à-manger*—essentially condiments—that have a touch of vinegar for acidity and enough texture and body that you can eat them with a fork. You'll find many such condiments within these pages: a marmalade made from caramelized endives; another of diced cèpes, chopped truffles, and shallots; a deep Burgundy-colored red wine and sour cherry sauce with the texture of a coarse purée; a mortar-crushed sauce made from Swiss chard, ham, capers, and lemon.

French gastronomy today is constantly evolving. Drawing on our savoir faire, our Escoffier base of traditional techniques and training, our professionalism, our diversity of products, our aesthetic sense, our culinary history, the many years we invest in our training, today's chefs are reinterpreting, revitalizing, and elevating classic French cooking every day. Each of us has his own style and leaves his mark, building stone by stone and layer by layer the evolving edifice that is French cuisine, in all its richness and diversity. For us, cuisine is a constant quest—to do better, develop techniques, find ways to extract more flavor, find superb new ingredients from small artisans, juxtapose flavors, refine the balance of harmony and opposition in flavors.

For me, French cuisine is endlessly fascinating, and being a chef is more than a career. Both animate and impassion me. Both allow me to continuously grow and to give of myself. In this book, I hope to share with you my love and reverence for the grand traditions of French cuisine, as well as the recipes that interpret, in a very personal way, this venerable cuisine. This is the first publication in which there are recipes from the three settings that describe my universe—Monaco, Moustiers, and Paris. They reflect the different styles and ingredients of these three kitchens. Every day I am astounded and seduced anew by the various pleasures each location affords. Some of the recipes are simple, others more complex, but all can be accomplished if you have the time and patience to do them the way they should be done. Some, based on olive oil, are more Mediterranean or Latin in feeling; others take their inspiration from a northern sensibility and are more akin to classic French cuisine; others are simply captured memories from childhood that have found a home in my cooking today. All revere and honor the products within. I hope that you will find this a book to savor, and that French cuisine will be for you, as it is for me, a daily celebration and joy.

ALAIN DUCASSE

THE KITCHENS OF ALAIN DUCASSE

Alain Ducasse has received more press coverage in the last couple of years than most chefs receive in a lifetime. In the spring of of 1998, he was awarded the *Michelin Guide's* ultimate accolade—three stars twice over, for both his Louis XV restaurant in Monte Carlo and the Restaurant Alain Ducasse in Paris—making him the world's only "six-star" chef. He has been the object of an extraordinary amount of international attention—attention he courts but seems to shun at the same time.

Chef Ducasse is a man of the world, sophisticated and urbane, but he's also reserved, not entirely comfortable in the limelight. At the Bastide in Moustiers, in Provence, he has a third restaurant. It's there, among the fig trees and almond groves and his beautiful vegetable garden, that he's most at home. He'd like to be able to linger, to take the time to savor the country life, but in Chef Ducasse there is always an urgency to press ahead.

Logging in countless air miles among restaurants every week, working "nine days a week," as he likes to say, his daily life would exhaust mere mortals. "Time is short, time is precious," he says, "and there are many things to accomplish." Yet despite the constraints of too little time and too much to do, we were able to meet in many towns, over many meals, and in many kitchens to work together on this, the first book to document the food of Alain Ducasse's three kitchens.

"A night at the opera" is how Ducasse sometimes describes the setting of the Louis XV restaurant in Monte Carlo. The restaurant is in a grand palace hotel, where the style is flamboyant, gilded, baroque, effusive. Here, in a luminous region permeated by a Latin sensibility, the mood and menu are a direct reflection of this

southern paradise. The most beautiful hand-cultivated, hand-raised, or line-caught products all come straight to the restaurant door every morning. The menu celebrates this fertile region with innumerable vegetable dishes—over half the menu is vegetable-based—and fish and shellfish fresh from the sea. The cuisine is lavishly, lovingly Mediterranean, with flavors and fragrances from all over the south, including Italy. A roasted langouste accompanies white beans cooked two ways—in a compote and puréed—with a sauce of the lobster's corral; cannelloni is stuffed with bitter greens and served atop mesclun salad and sautéed artichokes; a lemon tartlet is garnished with citrus fruit and wafer-thin orange "chips"; a fresh apricot tart is served with pistachio ice cream.

I spent most of my Louis XV evenings in the kitchen, observing, with ever-growing admiration, chef de cuisine Frank Cerutti and his brigade turning out plate after picture-perfect plate. Before a dish is whisked upstairs to the dining room, there will be a cluster of three or four chefs bent over the dish like a trauma team, working quickly, working precisely, one chef placing the hot garnish, another a cold garnish, a third adding an artistic swirl of sauce, all within a matter of seconds.

Paris is a different tale, sophisticated, reserved, luxurious, demanding, a city of eclectic tastes, and Restaurant Alain Ducasse, in the 16th arrondissement, offers another take on perfection. It is more northern in spirit and ingredients, and its state-of-the-art kitchen, presided over by chef Jean-François Piège, is characterized by an intense, stringent professionalism. The cuisine—refined and precise—is *classique contemporaine*, a synthesis of classic French cuisine and contemporary tastes and know-how. It is on the Paris menu that you find elegant interpretations of *pâté en croûte, canard à l'orange, pithiviers aux truffes, baba au rhum*. It's in Paris that many ingredients from the old French kitchen—sweetbreads, kidneys, cockscombs, foie gras—appear, though fewer ingredients are used in any given dish. The goal is flavors that are clear, tastes that are pure, sauces that are light, a cuisine that's classic in inspiration but in touch with its times.

The farmhouse kitchen in Moustiers Sainte-Marie, a sixteenth-century village in Provence, where Chef Ducasse turned a fortified seventeenth-century farmhouse into an intimate, dreamlike country inn, is presided over by Benôit Witz, a talented young chef from Alsace who worked with Chef Ducasse in the kitchen of the Louis XV for five years. Benôit turns out meals that are so fresh, so full of deep, rich flavors, and of such variety that, when I ate there every day, sometimes twice a day, for two weeks, I never tired of the cooking.

There are no printed menus at the Bastide, just a blackboard listing the day's choices. One day, the blackboard menu might offer a choice between a sautéed fillet of cod, cooked skin-side only, with a fennel confit, or a spit-roasted duck with roasted figs and potatoes; another day, a creamy risotto with cèpes or a roast beef with sautéed chanterelles and shallot confit. Every day I tried and every day I failed to resist the Bastide's enticing desserts—lighter-than-air *macarons* made with fresh ground almonds and filled with sugared mascarpone cream; caramelized grape and fresh fig tartlet with honey ice cream; vanilla, coffee, and chocolate *pots de crème* with crackly orange tile cookies on the side. And, as if one dessert was not indulgence enough, a surprise second dessert—often a rustic peach or strawberry or apple-almond tart—always arrived as I was nibbling the last crumbs of the first. Then, with coffee or tea, a basket of freshly made madeleines, *cannelés*—little molded cakes from the southwest—and chocolate shortbread cookies.

In good weather (which was every day but two during my sojourn here) breakfast, lunch, and dinner are served on the tree-shaded stone terrace overlooking the valleys and farmland of the Moustiers countryside. From the terrace you can see the old stone barn, a short walk downhill, where photographer Pierre Hussenot and I, with the generous help of Ducasse's amiable caretaker, René, mucked out a stable, strewed fresh lavender and then a sheet of plastic over the floor, and set up a small "studio" where many of the glorious dishes in this book were photographed. Nearby is a romantic *colombier*, or dovecote, while behind a band of cypresses lies a swimming pool with warmed azure water. It is in this bucolic setting that Ducasse enjoys alfresco lunches, full of laughter and bonhomie among friends. "The noise and the spectacle of life in the city are far away from here," Ducasse commented one

morning, "while the magic of nature, the gardens, the lavender fields, the animals, the sweet air, and spectacular sights such as the Gorges du Verdon, are all around us. The Bastide for me is a place apart, a little world completely conceived to enhance one's sense of well-being."

Alain Ducasse hoped that I would eventually be able to sample everything on all three menus. Although I went a long way toward eating my way through them, my goal remained unfulfilled. Just when I thought I was about to accomplish this gastronomic hat trick, the season and the menus would change, setting me back substantially. But what was true of all the meals was the impression of simplicity and at the same time the extraordinary sophistication of the cuisine, and the purity and depth of flavor he manages to achieve in each dish. With the wizardry of a Merlin, Alain Ducasse has created three decidedly different worlds, each with its own cuisine, atmosphere and philosophy. For most men, this would be accomplishment enough. But when you search his intelligent eyes, you see he's already thinking, What's next?

Perhaps he will develop the ultimate lidded casserole, or design a sensational kitchen chair, or conjure up yet another beguiling country inn or the quintessential Paris bistro (he's working on them all). I can't wait to see what this startlingly talented man will come up with—what flavors he will unearth, what pleasures he will devise, what designs he will realize. Nothing, it seems, is beyond his realm.

LINDA DANNENBERG

The restaurants of Alain Ducasse: The photographs on pages 2 through 6 were taken at La Bastide de Moustiers, near the Gorges du Verdon in Provence; the photographs on pages 8, 12, and 13 are of the Louis XV in Monte Carlo and its environs; and the photographs on the facing page and below were taken in the dining rooms and in the kitchen at the restaurant Alain Ducasse in Paris.

[Amuses-Bouches]

"For me, the best hors d'oeuvres reveal something about the meal you're going to share, about the region you're in, even about your hosts. This first chapter offers a sampling of hors d'oeuvres taken from the three settings that define my culinary universe, each of which has a personality all its own."

IN MONTE CARLO, THE SETTING IS OPULENT BUT
the ambiance has a certain easiness and Latin *esprit*. Here we
offer tartines that can be likened to a little bit of Mediterranean sun
atop toasted slices of baguette. In Moustiers, which is casual and
relaxed, with lots of country charm, little pots of spreads are brought
to the table as guests sit down. In Paris, sophisticated and urbane,
diners are served our *Tapas à la Française*, which include *feuilletés*—
tiny stuffed puff pastries—and other colorful mouthfuls. They are
more formal, more "schooled," than the tartines; yet this does not
mean the experience in Paris is in any way more special. What we
do in the south may seem less serious, easier, but it really is not.
Sometimes that which seems most simple demands the most effort.

FENNEL "MARMALADE"

Serves 4

THIS CHUNKY FENNEL COMPOTE, redolent of thyme, garlic, and basil, tastes like the essence of Provence. Serve with a basket of Garlic Toasts (page 233), alone or with other such savory condiments as tapenade (see page 62) and eggplant caviar (see page 31). (The fennel "marmalade" is pictured on page 19.)

1 tablespoon olive oil

2 medium fennel bulbs, trimmed, outer layer peeled off, cored, and chopped into large dice

1 garlic clove, lightly crushed

1 branch fresh thyme

Coarse sea salt, preferably fleur de sel

2 fresh basil leaves, crushed in your hands

Extra-virgin olive oil

Heat the 1 tablespoon olive oil in a medium skillet over medium heat. Add the fennel, garlic, and thyme and stir to combine, then reduce the heat to medium-low and cook, stirring often to keep the fennel from browning, until it is very tender, about 20 minutes. Remove the garlic and thyme, season to taste with salt, and stir in the basil leaves.

Spoon the fennel into small earthenware pots or a small glass jar and cover with extra-virgin olive oil. Refrigerate until ready to serve. (You can store the fennel "marmalade" in the refrigerator for up to a week.)

[*Barbajuans au Potiron*]

GOLDEN-FRIED PUMPKIN PURSES

Makes 20 purses

CALLED "UNCLE JOHNS" IN THE MONEGASQUE DIALECT, these little fried pouches are filled with pumpkin, leeks, rice, and Parmesan cheese. Like their Italian cousins—the *tortelli di zucca* from Lombardy—they are prepared like ravioli, but the similarity ends there. The dough, though not a pasta dough, is very thinly rolled and made with olive oil. The *barbajuans* are fried to a golden crispness rather than boiled or baked, and they are served with apéritifs rather than as a first course.

FOR THE PASTRY

2 cups plus 2 tablespoons
   all-purpose flour

¼ cup olive oil

1 teaspoon fine sea salt

1 large egg

½ cup ice-cold water

FOR THE FILLING

¼ cup olive oil

2 pounds fresh pumpkin, cut into
   3 or 4 large chunks, seeded, and
   strings removed

1¼ teaspoons fine sea salt

½ cup Arborio rice or other risotto rice

4 slim leeks (white and tender green
   parts only), cut lengthwise in half,
   rinsed well, patted dry, and minced

2 large eggs

¾ cup freshly grated Parmigiano-
   Reggiano cheese (about 6 ounces)

¼ teaspoon freshly ground black pepper

About 6 cups peanut oil, for frying

Coarse sea salt, for sprinkling

TO MAKE THE PASTRY: Combine the flour, olive oil, and salt in the bowl of a food processor or a large bowl. Process for about 8 seconds, or mix, until the mixture resembles coarse cornmeal. Add the egg and water and pulse 6 to 8 times, or mix briskly, until the dough forms a smooth ball. Remove from the bowl and knead for a minute between the palms of your hands (flour your palms once or twice if the dough is sticky). Form the dough into a disk, wrap in plastic wrap, and refrigerate for 1 hour.

TO MAKE THE FILLING: Preheat the oven to 400°F. Line a baking sheet with aluminum foil, then grease well with 1 tablespoon of the olive oil.

Place the pumpkin chunks skin side down on the sheet, drizzle with 2 tablespoons of the olive oil, and season with ½ teaspoon of the salt. Bake for about 1½ hours, until the flesh of the pumpkin is very soft when pierced with the tip of a knife or a fork. Let the pumpkin cool on the baking sheet.

Scrape the pumpkin flesh into a large bowl and mash until smooth. Set aside.

In a small saucepan, bring 1½ cups of water to a boil over high heat. Add ¼ teaspoon of the salt and the rice, reduce the heat to medium-low, and cook until the rice is half-done, about 10 minutes. Drain and set aside.

Heat the remaining 1 tablespoon olive oil in a medium skillet over medium heat. Add the leeks and cook just until they are translucent, but not browned, about 4 minutes. Transfer to the bowl with the pumpkin, then add the rice, eggs, half of the Parmesan, the remaining ½ teaspoon salt, and the pepper. Mix with a wooden spoon, slowly adding the remaining Parmesan, until well blended, 1 to 2 minutes. Set aside.

TO ASSEMBLE THE PURSES: Using a pasta machine, roll out the dough to a $\frac{1}{16}$-inch thickness. Or, on a floured work surface, roll out the dough with a floured rolling pin into a rectangle approximately 13 by 22 inches and $\frac{1}{16}$ inch thick. (The dough must be ultrathin, and this is a challenge if working with a rolling pin; make sure both your rolling pin and your work surface are well floured.)

Position the dough so that a short side faces you. Then, filling in the bottom half of the rectangle, spoon 20 walnut-size mounds of filling evenly spaced over the dough, about $1\frac{1}{2}$ inches apart. (If you're working with a narrower, machine-rolled dough rectangle, you'll need to make ten rows of two. If you're working with a 13- by 22-inch dough rectangle, make four rows of five mounds.)

Moisten the dough slightly around each mound, then carefully lift the top half of the dough with a spatula and fold it over the bottom half, making sure the edges of the dough meet on all sides. Gently press the dough together around each mound of filling with your fingertips. Cut the individual purses apart, then press the edges with the tines of a fork to seal. (A slightly easier method of forming the purses—practical if you are not adept at working with dough—is to cut the rolled-out dough into 20 individual rectangles approximately $4\frac{1}{2}$ by $2\frac{1}{2}$ inches. Place a walnut-size mound of filling in the center of the right half of each. Very slightly moisten the edges of each rectangle, then fold the left half over the right and press all four sides closed with the tines of a fork to seal.)

If you are not going to cook the purses immediately, place them on a lightly floured baking sheet, cover with plastic wrap, and refrigerate for up to 3 hours.

TO COOK THE PURSES: Just before serving, heat the oil in a large deep frying pan over medium-high heat to between 325° and 350°F. Cook the purses 5 or 6 at a time, turning them once or twice, until they puff up and turn light golden brown, about 2 minutes. Remove them with a slotted spoon and place on a baking sheet lined with a double layer of paper towels. Immediately sprinkle with coarse salt. Serve hot on a warmed platter or in a basket lined with a napkin.

MARINATED MUSHROOMS ON A BED OF PURÉED SPRING PEAS

Serves 10 as an appetizer

THE MUSHROOMS ARE QUICKLY COOKED and then cooled in a marinade of white wine, chicken stock, vinegar, lemon juice, and butter. They are then served over a bed of puréed fresh peas. Choose the smallest, whitest mushrooms you can find, and small fresh peas. (The mushrooms are pictured on page 18.)

FOR THE PEA PURÉE

6 tablespoons extra-virgin olive oil

3 cups shelled small fresh peas (about 2 pounds peas in the pod)

2 teaspoons fine sea salt

¼ cup Chicken Stock (page 229)

FOR THE MUSHROOMS

1½ pounds small white mushrooms

Juice of 1 lemon, plus a few drops

6 tablespoons dry white wine

3 cups Chicken Stock (page 229)

1 tablespoon white wine vinegar

2 tablespoons unsalted butter

1 teaspoon fine sea salt

½ teaspoon freshly ground black pepper

3 tablespoons extra-virgin olive oil

TO PREPARE THE PEA PURÉE: In a wide shallow saucepan, heat 1 tablespoon of olive oil. Add the peas, 1 teaspoon of the salt, and ¼ cup chicken stock and bring to a boil. Cover, reduce the heat, and simmer until tender, 3 to 5 minutes. Remove from the heat and set the pan in a bowl of ice-cold water to cool.

Transfer the peas with their liquid to the bowl of a food processor and add the remaining 1 teaspoon salt and the 5 tablespoons olive oil. Process for 6 to 8 seconds, scrape down the sides of the bowl, and then process until the mixture forms a smooth purée. Press the mixture through a fine sieve into a small bowl, cover with plastic wrap, and refrigerate.

TO PREPARE THE MUSHROOMS: Trim the mushroom stems to ½ inch from the caps. Rinse. If the mushrooms are larger than button-size, cut into quarters. Toss the mushrooms with a few drops of lemon juice to prevent darkening.

Pour the white wine into a large nonreactive saucepan and bring to a boil over medium-high heat. Lower the heat to medium and simmer for about 45 seconds, until reduced by half. Add the chicken stock and vinegar and bring to a boil. Stir in the remaining lemon juice and the butter, then stir in the mushrooms. Return to a boil, cover the pan, and cook for 3 minutes. Remove from the heat and stir in the salt and pepper. Set aside to cool, covered, in the pan, then transfer to a bowl and refrigerate until ready to serve, or up to 3 hours.

TO FINISH THE DISH: With a slotted spoon, transfer the mushrooms from the marinade to a clean bowl. Transfer 2 tablespoons of the marinade to a small bowl and gradually whisk in the olive oil to emulsify. Pour over the mushrooms and toss to coat.

Spoon the chilled pea purée into ten small vodka glasses. Remove the mushrooms from the dressing with a slotted spoon and arrange on top of the purée, slightly pressing the mushrooms into the purée. Serve immediately with small spoons.

FRENCH TAPAS

Although the word *tapas* describes the little nibbles served at stand-up bars throughout Spain, the word and concept have been adopted and given a French accent at the small, sleek Le Bar of the Restaurant Alain Ducasse in Paris. Here is a "tasting menu" of Le Bar's bite-size hors d'oeuvres.

[*Mille-Feuilles d'Omelettes*]

MULTILAYERED OMELETTE

Serves 6 to 8

THIS COLORFUL OMELETTE MILLE-FEUILLES (literally "a thousand layers") is really a stack of five thin omelettes, each with a different filling—Parmesan cheese, parsley, onions and red peppers, tapenade, and diced tomato. The stack is compressed under a weighted plate while it chills and then sliced into cubes.

1 tablespoon olive oil

1 medium onion, finely chopped

10 large eggs

Fine sea salt and freshly ground black pepper

¼ cup freshly grated Parmigiano-Reggiano cheese

½ cup chopped fresh flat-leaf parsley

1 red bell pepper, roasted (see page 249), peeled, seeded, and diced very small

¼ cup tapenade, homemade (see page 62) or store-bought

1 medium tomato, peeled, seeded, and diced small

5 tablespoons unsalted butter

Heat the olive oil in a small skillet over medium heat, then add the onion and cook for 2 to 3 minutes, until softened and translucent but not browned. Set aside.

In each of five small mixing bowls, combine 2 eggs with a pinch each of salt and pepper and whisk until frothy. Whisk the Parmesan into the first bowl. Whisk the chopped parsley into the second. Stir the red pepper and sautéed onion into the third bowl. Whisk the tapenade into the fourth bowl. Stir the tomato dice into the fifth bowl.

In a medium nonstick skillet, cook the omelettes one at a time: For each, melt 1 tablespoon of butter over medium heat. Add the egg mixture and cook until just cooked through and soft but not runny. Leave the omelettes flat; do not fold. Stack the omelettes on a large round serving plate or stainless steel tray, alternating the colors. Place a large plate or stainless steel tray on top of the omelette stack and weight it down with two cans of soup (or two cans of a similar weight) so that the layers compress. Refrigerate for about 1 hour.

Cut the omelette stack into ¾-inch squares and secure each one with a wooden toothpick. Serve immediately.

[*Feuilleté de Duxelles de Champignons, Jambon, et Gruyère*]

PUFF PASTRIES WITH DUXELLES, HAM, AND GRUYÈRE

Makes 36 hors d'oeuvres

One 9- by 9-inch sheet puff pastry
(about 8 ounces)

1 large egg yolk, beaten, for glaze

FOR THE FILLING

2 tablespoons unsalted butter

1/2 pound white mushrooms, stems
discarded, wiped clean, and cut into
very small dice

1/2 cup finely chopped baked ham

1/2 cup finely chopped Gruyère cheese

2 tablespoons heavy cream

Fine sea salt and freshly ground black
pepper

Preheat the oven to 350°F.

Using a cookie cutter or a bottle cap, cut out 1-inch circles from the dough; you should have 36 pastry circles. (Reserve the scraps for another use.) Place the circles on a baking sheet and brush the tops lightly with the beaten egg. Bake in the center of the oven until the circles puff up and turn golden brown, 12 to 14 minutes. Gently cut each pastry crosswise through the center and set aside on the baking sheet. Leave the oven on.

TO PREPARE THE FILLING: Melt the butter in a medium skillet over medium heat. Add the mushrooms and cook, stirring frequently, until they soften and begin to give up their moisture but do not brown, 3 to 4 minutes. Stir in the ham and cheese and cook until the cheese softens and begins to melt, 1 to 2 minutes. Add the cream and stir well, then season with salt and pepper to taste. Remove from the heat.

Spoon about 1½ teaspoons of the mushroom mixture onto the bottom half of each pastry puff and cover with the top half. Return the filled pastries to the oven for 3 to 4 minutes to heat through. Serve immediately.

[*Feuilleté de Morue en Brandade*]

PUFF PASTRIES WITH SALT COD AND POTATO PURÉE

Makes 36 hors d'oeuvres

One 9- by 9-inch sheet puff pastry (about 8 ounces)

1 large egg yolk, beaten, for glaze

FOR THE FILLING

1 small all-purpose potato (about 6 ounces), peeled and cut into ½-inch slices

2 cups crème fraîche

1 pound salt cod, soaked for 3 days to desalt (see page 249)

2 cups milk

1 star anise

1 garlic clove, lightly crushed

1 branch fresh thyme

1 tablespoon chopped fresh flat-leaf parsley

Freshly ground black pepper

2 tablespoons extra-virgin olive oil

Preheat the oven to 350°F.

Using a cookie cutter or a bottle cap, cut out 1-inch circles from the dough; you should have 36 pastry circles. (Reserve the scraps for another use.) Place the circles on a baking sheet and brush the tops lightly with the beaten egg. Bake in the center of the oven until the circles puff up and turn golden brown, 12 to 14 minutes. Gently cut each pastry crosswise through the center and set aside on the baking sheet.

TO PREPARE THE POTATO PURÉE: Combine the potato and crème fraîche in a medium saucepan and heat over medium heat until just below a boil. Reduce the heat to low and cook, stirring frequently so that the potato slices do not stick to the pan, until they disintegrate and the mixture forms a purée, 35 to 40 minutes.

MEANWHILE, PREPARE THE SALT COD: About 15 minutes before the potato purée is done, drain the cod, rinse under cold water, and pat dry. Combine the milk, star anise, garlic, and thyme in a large saucepan or a deep skillet, and add the cod. Bring the milk to a gentle boil over medium heat, cover, and poach until the cod is tender, 7 to 10 minutes. Drain the cod and set aside to cool slightly.

Flake the cod, add it to the potato purée, along with the parsley, and stir until the mixture is smooth and you can no longer see pieces of cod in it. Add pepper to taste and the olive oil, stir to blend, and remove from the heat.

Spoon about 1½ teaspoons of the cod and potato mixture onto the bottom half of each pastry and cover with the top half. Return the filled pastries to the oven for 3 to 4 minutes to heat through. Serve immediately.

[*Feuilleté aux Épinards*]

PUFF PASTRIES WITH SPINACH AND COMTÉ CHEESE

Makes 36 hors d'oeuvres

One 9- by 9-inch sheet puff pastry
(about 8 ounces)

1 large egg yolk, beaten, for glaze

FOR THE FILLING

2 tablespoons unsalted butter

½ pound baby spinach, tough stems
removed

2 tablespoons heavy cream

½ cup grated Comté, aged Fontina, or
Gruyère cheese

Fine sea salt and freshly ground black
pepper

Preheat the oven to 350°F.

Using a cookie cutter or a bottle cap, cut out 1-inch circles from the dough; you should have 36 pastry circles. (Reserve the scraps for another use.) Place the circles on a baking sheet and brush the tops lightly with the beaten egg. Bake in the center of the oven until the circles puff up and turn golden brown, 12 to 14 minutes. Gently cut each pastry crosswise through the center and set aside on the baking sheet. Leave the oven on.

TO PREPARE THE FILLING: Melt the butter in a medium skillet over medium heat. Add the spinach and cook, stirring frequently, until soft and wilted, about 3 minutes. Stir in the cream, then add the cheese and stir well to combine. Season to taste with salt and pepper and remove from the heat.

Spoon about 1½ teaspoons of the spinach mixture onto the bottom half of each pastry and cover with the top half. Return the filled pastries to the oven for 3 to 4 minutes to heat through. Serve immediately.

TARTINES

RUSTIC IN SPIRIT, these savory mouthfuls are traditional *amuses-bouches* at the Louis XV. Five variations of tartines follow; they can be served alone or in colorful combination. An assortment of tartines is pictured on pages 16–17.

[*Tartines au Caviar d'Aubergine*]

EGGPLANT CAVIAR TOASTS

Makes 20 tartines

1 small eggplant (about 1¼ pounds), sliced lengthwise in half

½ teaspoon fine sea salt

¼ teaspoon freshly ground black pepper

3 tablespoons extra-virgin olive oil

3 oil-packed anchovy fillets

1 tablespoon red wine vinegar

1 tablespoon tapenade, homemade (page 62) or store-bought

½ baguette (about 6 inches long), cut into twenty ¼-inch rounds

Preheat the oven to 375°F.

Using the tip of a sharp knife, cut a fine cross-hatch design in the cut surfaces of the eggplant, cutting all the way down through the flesh but taking care not to cut the skin. Place skin side down on a baking sheet. Season with the salt and pepper, then drizzle 2 tablespoons of the olive oil over the tops.

Bake for 20 to 25 minutes, until the flesh is very soft and offers no resistance when pierced with the tip of a small sharp knife. Transfer the baking sheet to a wire rack to cool.

Scoop out the flesh from the eggplant and place in the bowl of a food processor. Add the anchovy fillets, vinegar, the remaining 1 tablespoon olive oil, and the tapenade. Process for 6 to 8 seconds, until well blended. Transfer to a small bowl, cover loosely with plastic wrap, and refrigerate for at least 1 hour.

Preheat the broiler. Arrange the baguette slices on a baking sheet and place under the broiler. When the tops are browned, transfer to a platter.

Spread each tartine with about 1 teaspoon of the eggplant mixture, mounding each portion into a slight dome shape, and serve immediately.

FROMAGE BLANC AND BABY FAVA BEAN TOASTS

Makes 20 tartines

FRESH GOAT CHEESE, such as Montrachet, or a fresh sheep cheese, such as brébis from the French Pyrenees, may be substituted in these toasts.

½ baguette (about 6 inches long), cut into twenty ¼-inch rounds

5½ ounces fromage blanc or fresh goat cheese, such as Montrachet

1 tablespoon mild extra-virgin olive oil

1 teaspoon fine sea salt

½ pound fresh young fava beans, shelled and skinned; or substitute shelled baby lima beans

Freshly ground black pepper

Preheat the broiler. Arrange the baguette slices on a baking sheet and place under the broiler. When the tops are browned, transfer to a platter.

Combine the goat cheese, olive oil, and salt in a medium bowl and beat with a wooden spoon until smooth and blended. Spread on the baguette slices, mounding the mixture into a slight dome shape. Place the beans on end in the cheese, using 3 or 4 beans per tartine. Give a single turn of the peppermill to each tartine. Serve immediately.

[*Tartines aux Crevettes*]

SHRIMP TOASTS

Makes 20 tartines

½ baguette (about 6 inches long), cut into twenty ¼-inch rounds

3 tablespoons Garlic-Shallot Butter (page 233)

20 large shrimp (about 1½ pounds), peeled and deveined

½ teaspoon fine sea salt

¼ teaspoon freshly ground black pepper

2 medium shallots, minced

Preheat the broiler. Arrange the baguette slices on a baking sheet and place under the broiler. When the tops are browned, transfer to a platter.

In a large skillet set over medium heat, heat the garlic-shallot butter until just bubbling. Season the shrimp with the salt and pepper and add to the pan together with the shallots. Cook, stirring occasionally and turning the shrimp once, until cooked through and no longer translucent, about 3 minutes total.

Place 1 shrimp on each tartine, drizzle a few drops of the butter over each one, and serve immediately.

SUN-DRIED TOMATO AND BLACK OLIVE TOASTS

Makes 20 tartines

½ baguette (about 6 inches long), cut into twenty ¼-inch rounds

½ pound sun-dried tomatoes packed in oil, drained and finely minced

4 fresh basil leaves, finely minced

¼ teaspoon fine sea salt

¼ teaspoon freshly ground black pepper

40 Niçoise or other small brine-cured black olives, pitted and slivered

Preheat the broiler. Arrange the baguette slices on a baking sheet and place under the broiler. When the tops are browned, transfer to a platter.

Combine the tomatoes, basil, salt, and pepper in a bowl and stir briskly with a wooden fork until the mixture forms a rough paste.

Spread about 1 teaspoon of the mixture on each tartine, mounding each portion into a slight dome shape. Garnish the top of each tartine with a few black olive slivers, pressing the ends lightly into the tomato mixture so that the slivers point up or out. Serve immediately.

FRESH ANCHOVY AND SWEET RED PEPPER TOASTS

Makes 20 tartines

10 fresh anchovies (about ½ pound), filleted and meticulously boned

Fine sea salt and freshly ground black pepper

2 tablespoons olive oil

½ baguette (about 6 inches long), cut into twenty ¼-inch rounds

1 red bell pepper, roasted (see page 249), peeled, seeded, and cut into thin julienne

Preheat the broiler. Roll up the anchovy fillets and arrange them seam side down and just touching each other in an ovenproof dish. Season with salt and pepper and drizzle with 1 tablespoon of the olive oil. Broil for 3 to 4 minutes, until lightly browned. Remove and set aside.

Arrange the baguette slices on a baking sheet and toast under the broiler until lightly golden.

Meanwhile, season the roasted pepper strips with salt and pepper and drizzle with the remaining 1 tablespoon olive oil.

Arrange the toasts on a serving platter, place 2 or 3 strips of pepper on each slice, and top with a rolled anchovy fillet. Serve immediately.

[*Le Potager*]

VEGETABLES

"One of the most powerful memories of my childhood is of helping my grandfather in his big *potager*. In his hands, the melons and squashes and tomatoes, the perfect little radishes, the slim carrots were sensual objects, nature's works of art. That's the way I think of them to this day."

IN MANY RESTAURANTS IN FRANCE, VEGETABLES
are treated as second-class citizens—used as garnishes, tossed
into salads, or relegated to secondary roles in meat or fish dishes.
At the restaurant in Monte Carlo and at the Bastide in Moustiers,
almost 50 percent of our menus are based on vegetables and
fruits. We feature tomatoes, peppers, eggplant, fennel, Swiss chard,
lettuces, olives, basil, and melons—the bounty of the south.

In Moustiers, we grow 185 different types of vegetables, herbs,
and fruits. We planted a salad garden, an aromatic herb garden, a
root garden, a berry patch, and a wild garden where tomatoes grow
among the sunflowers. In Monte Carlo, we are blessed with beautiful
local produce supplied by the region's best artisanal growers. In

Paris, we take advantage of the city's great markets and buy produce that comes from the four corners of France. I am constantly searching for the best produce, and for dedicated people interested in growing only the best. Because we don't have the same access to just-picked produce, we focus more on slow-cooked root vegetables—carrots, turnips, small potatoes, salsify—and vegetables that have a subtle bitter quality, like endives and watercress.

This chapter is one of the largest in the book. The recipes reflect my fascination with the ways vegetables work, and cook, together: how they combine, complement, or contrast in meaningful and flavorful combinations, prepared in many different ways—raw, baked, braised, sautéed, steamed, marinated, grilled. Sometimes

several methods of preparation—marinated and then braised, blanched and then baked, for example—work together to form the dish. I am especially fond of pairing raw and cooked versions of a single vegetable on one plate. To experience the two together—a confit of tomatoes paired with raw tomatoes and a viniagrette of tomato pulp—is to marvel at the amazingly transformative power of fire.

Essential to preparing a great dish is finding impeccable ingredients. Stems and tops should be very green, the body of the vegetable should almost have a glow; it should be firm, crisp, vibrant—so full of freshness that you have the impulse to eat it raw.

A profound respect for the seasons, for the natural, true taste of things, is deep and abiding. This is what governs my cooking.

BROCCOLI SOUP WITH A CRÈME FRAÎCHE FROTH

Serves 4 as a first course

A RAGOUT OF GIROLLES AND CHIVES topped with tiny golden croutons and bits of bacon greet you at the bottom of a bowl of this satin-smooth soup. A fluffy dollop of crème fraîche spreads over the surface of the soup to create a cappuccinolike froth.

FOR THE SOUP

1½ pounds broccoli, cut into florets (stalks reserved for another use)

1½ cups Chicken Stock (page 229)

3 tablespoons extra-virgin olive oil

8 tablespoons (1 stick) unsalted butter, cut into ½-inch slices

1 teaspoon fine sea salt

Freshly ground black pepper

FOR THE GARNISH

4 tablespoons unsalted butter

3 slices soft white bread, crusts removed and cut into ¼-inch cubes

2½ ounces slab bacon or pancetta, cut into thin julienne strips

2 tablespoons olive oil

¾ pound small girolle mushrooms, trimmed and cleaned (see page 238), and, if larger than ½-inch wide, cut into halves or quarters, or 1 pound shiitake mushrooms, stems discarded, cleaned, and cut into ½-inch cubes

¼ cup chopped fresh chives

Fine sea salt and freshly ground black pepper

½ cup crème fraîche

4 sprigs fresh chervil

TO PREPARE THE BROCCOLI: Bring a medium pot of salted water to a boil. Add the broccoli and cook until tender, about 6 minutes. Drain and plunge into a bowl of ice-cold water. Cool for 1 minute, then drain again and thoroughly dry the broccoli by gently squeezing each floret between two layers of a clean linen or cotton towel. Place the broccoli in the bowl of a food processor and process, scraping down the sides once or twice, to a smooth purée. Set aside.

TO PREPARE THE GARNISH: Melt 2 tablespoons of the butter in a medium skillet over medium heat and cook the bread cubes, stirring frequently, until golden brown, 5 to 7 minutes. Transfer the croutons to paper towels to drain; reserve.

Brown the bacon in a nonstick skillet, then drain on paper towels. Chop into small pieces; set aside.

Heat the olive oil and 1 tablespoon of the remaining butter in a large skillet over medium heat. Add the mushrooms, stirring to coat with the fat, and cook, stirring, until they begin to give off their juices, 2 to 3 minutes. Add the remaining 1 tablespoon butter, stirring rapidly to blend. Stir in the chives and salt and pepper to taste. Remove from the heat and set aside.

In a chilled bowl, whisk the crème fraîche until it forms soft peaks; set aside.

TO FINISH THE SOUP: In a large saucepan, combine the chicken stock, broccoli purée, olive oil, and butter and bring to a boil over medium-high heat, stirring frequently. Remove from the heat and pour into the bowl

of a food processor. Add 3 tablespoons of the whipped crème fraîche and season to taste with the salt and pepper. Process to a smooth purée. Reheat the soup in the saucepan, then transfer to a warmed soup tureen.

To serve, place a large spoonful of the mushroom ragout in the center of each warmed soup bowl. Sprinkle 1 tablespoon of the croutons and 1 tablespoon of the chopped bacon around the ragout. Spoon a dollop of the whipped crème fraîche on top of the mushrooms. Carefully ladle in the soup. Garnish each serving with a sprig of chervil. Serve immediately.

PUMPKIN SOUP WITH GIROLLES

Serves 4 as a first course

AT THE LOUIS XV, bowls with sautéed tiny girolle mushrooms are presented to diners before the velvety pumpkin soup is ladled in. Crisp lardons are then sprinkled on top, followed by a finishing touch of whipped cream crowned with chervil.

FOR THE SOUP

3 tablespoons olive oil

1 pound fresh pumpkin, peeled, seeded, and cut into 1-inch cubes

1 small onion, minced

2 cups Chicken Stock (page 229)

6 tablespoons unsalted butter

1/2 teaspoon fine sea salt, or to taste

1/4 teaspoon freshly ground black pepper, or to taste

1/2 cup heavy cream, lightly whipped until it just forms soft peaks

1/2 cup heavy cream, whipped until it holds firm peaks (optional)

FOR THE GARNISH

1 tablespoon olive oil

1/2 pound small girolle mushrooms, trimmed and cleaned (see page 238)

1 medium shallot, finely minced

2 tablespoons unsalted butter

2 tablespoons finely chopped fresh chives

3 ounces slab bacon or pancetta, cut into 1/2-inch cubes (about 1/2 cup)

4 leafy sprigs fresh chervil

TO PREPARE THE PUMPKIN: In a large skillet, heat the olive oil over medium-high heat. Add the pumpkin and onion and stir to coat with oil. Reduce the heat to medium-low and cook until the pumpkin begins to soften and the onions are translucent but not brown, about 5 minutes. Pour in 1 cup of the chicken stock, or enough to cover the pumpkin slices, and continue cooking until the pumpkin is very soft, about 10 minutes. Remove from the heat and let cool slightly, then pass through a food mill (or press through a strainer with the back of a spoon) into a medium bowl. Reserve.

TO PREPARE THE GARNISH: Heat the olive oil in a medium skillet over medium heat. Stir in the girolles and shallot and cook, stirring frequently, until mushrooms give off their liquid and it evaporates. Stir in 2 tablespoons of the butter to coat the mushrooms, then add the chives. Stir to combine and remove from the heat.

Put the bacon cubes in a small saucepan and cover with cold water. Bring to a boil over high heat, reduce the heat to medium-low, and simmer for 1 minute to blanch and remove some of the salt. Drain and rinse briefly in cold water. Drain again and pat the lardons dry.

Sauté the lardons in a small skillet until they are brown and crisp. Transfer to paper towels to drain.

TO FINISH THE SOUP: In a large saucepan, combine the pumpkin mixture with the remaining 1 cup chicken stock and stir to combine. Bring the mixture to a gentle boil, then stir in the 6 tablespoons of butter, salt, pepper, and lightly whipped cream. Pour the mixture into the bowl of an electric mixer and beat on medium speed until smooth and creamy. Adjust the seasoning to taste.

Pour into a warmed soup tureen. Divide the girolle mushroom mixture among four warmed soup plates. Spoon in the pumpkin soup. Sprinkle on the lardons, then, if you wish, place a dollop of whipped cream in the center of each serving. Garnish with the sprigs of chervil. Serve immediately.

TRUFFLED POTATO SOUP WITH LEEKS, FOIE GRAS, AND GNOCCHI

Serves 4 as a first course

CLASSICALLY, a *parmentier* is prepared simply, with potatoes, leeks, and cream, but in this version, each spoonful is enhanced with bits of foie gras, light potato gnocchi, and chopped truffles.

FOR THE SOUP

8 tablespoons (1 stick) unsalted butter

1 onion, halved and thinly sliced

4 leeks (white part only), cut lengthwise in half, rinsed well, and thinly sliced

1 pound all-purpose potatoes (about 2 medium), peeled, quartered lengthwise, and thinly sliced

Fine sea salt

4 cups Chicken Stock (page 229)

Freshly ground black pepper

Coarse sea salt, preferably fleur de sel

3 to 4 ounces black truffles, chopped

1/3 cup heavy cream, whipped to soft peaks

1/4 pound foie gras confit or terrine, cut into small cubes

Potato Gnocchi (recipe follows)

2 tablespoons fresh chervil leaves

TO PREPARE THE SOUP: Melt 2 tablespoons of the butter in a large saucepan over medium heat. Add the onion, 2 of the leeks, the potatoes, and salt to taste. Cook, stirring frequently, until the onions begin to soften and turn translucent but do not brown, 4 to 5 minutes. Pour in the chicken stock, stirring to combine. Adjust the seasoning to taste with salt and pepper and simmer for 20 minutes. Remove from the heat, then transfer the soup, in batches, to a blender or a food processor and purée. Strain into a bowl and set aside.

Melt 1 tablespoon of the butter in a medium skillet over medium heat, then add the remaining leeks and a pinch of coarse sea salt and cook, stirring, until the leeks turn translucent but do not take on any color, 4 to 6 minutes. Stir in the truffles and remove the pan from the heat. Immediately add 1 tablespoon of the butter, stir until it melts, and set aside.

TO COOK THE GNOCCHI: Bring a large pot of salted water to a rolling boil. Add the gnocchi, in batches; as soon as they float to the surface, they are done. Transfer the gnocchi with a slotted spoon to a lightly oiled warm bowl.

Meanwhile, reheat the soup in a large saucepan over medium heat.

Spoon the leek and truffle mixture into the center of four warmed soup bowls. Stir the remaining 4 tablespoons butter into the soup, then whisk in the whipped cream. Gently stir in the foie gras and season to taste with salt and pepper.

Pour one ladleful of soup into each soup bowl, stirring to combine with the leek mixture. Divide the gnocchi among the four bowls, spooning soup over them to coat well. Then ladle more soup into each bowl so that it just covers the gnocchi. Garnish with the chervil leaves and serve immediately.

POTATO GNOCCHI

Makes about 80 gnocchi

Coarse sea salt or kosher salt

3 large all-purpose potatoes (about 10 ounces each)

2 tablespoons olive oil

Fine sea salt

1 to 1¼ cups all-purpose flour

1 large egg

Preheat the oven to 400°F.

Cover the bottom of a baking pan or small baking sheet with coarse salt and place the potatoes on top. Bake until the potatoes are tender, about 1 hour. If the tip of a sharp knife easily enters the flesh, the potatoes are done. Set aside to cool slightly.

Peel the baked potatoes, then press them through a fine strainer onto a lightly floured work surface. Drizzle the olive oil over the potatoes, add a small pinch of salt, and then sprinkle 1 cup flour, a little at a time, over the potatoes, mixing until blended. Make a well in the center of the mixture, then crack the egg into the well. Mix together with your fingertips, gathering the potato-flour mixture into the egg a little at a time, and adding more flour if the dough is very sticky. When the dough forms a smooth, slightly sticky ball, knead in another small pinch of salt. Cut the dough into four equal portions.

Clean the work surface. Lightly dust it with flour, and, one at a time, roll each portion of dough under your palms to form a long smooth sausage ½ inch thick. Cut each roll into ½-inch pieces. Roll each piece between your palms to form an oval, dusting your hands with flour as necessary. Mark the gnocchi by placing each piece, one by one, on the tines of a dinner fork, pressing down lightly in the center of the gnocchi, and then rolling it off the fork quickly to form the light groove design; place the finished gnocchi on a kitchen towel–lined baking sheet.

MEDITERRANEAN VEGETABLE TOURTE

Serves 6 as a first course

MANY RECIPES from the Louis XV reflect the influence of Italy on the cuisine of France's Mediterranean coast. The inspiration for this mixed vegetable tart comes from the Ligurian *Torta Pasqualina*, or Easter Torte. The pastry crust holds a filling of impeccably fresh garden vegetables and greens bound with Arborio rice, ricotta, Parmesan cheese, and egg. Served hot or at room temperature, it's a dish that weaves together many of the flavors of the Mediterranean.

FOR THE PASTRY

2½ cups all-purpose flour

1 teaspoon fine sea salt

¾ cup olive oil

2 large egg yolks

⅔ cup water

FOR THE FILLING

1 tablespoon uncooked Arborio or other risotto rice

4 tablespoons plus 1 teaspoon olive oil

10 zucchini blossoms, pistils removed and sliced crosswise into ½-inch slices

10 baby zucchini, cut into ½-inch slices

3 large Swiss chard leaves or ½ pound spinach, stems and tough ribs discarded, leaves shredded

½ cup shelled fresh peas, cut in half

2 medium onions, minced

3 small purple artichokes, trimmed (see page 248) and grated

4 lightly packed cups mesclun or mixed salad greens, shredded

5 spring onions (white part only), outer layer peeled off and thinly sliced, or 1 leek (white part only), rinsed well and thinly sliced

1 large egg, lightly beaten

½ cup freshly grated Parmigiano-Reggiano cheese

¾ cup ricotta cheese

Fine sea salt and freshly ground white pepper

1 large egg yolk, beaten, for glaze

Olive oil for brushing

TO MAKE THE PASTRY: In a bowl of a food processor, or a large bowl, combine the flour, salt, and olive oil. Process for about 10 seconds, or mix, until the mixture has a crumbly texture resembling coarse cornmeal. Add the egg yolks and water and pulse six or seven times, or mix briskly with your fingertips, until the ingredients just come together but the dough does not quite form a ball. Remove from the bowl and knead on an unfloured work surface until the egg is completely incorporated and the dough is smooth, supple, and slightly elastic, about 2 minutes. Divide the dough in half. Press each half into a disk, wrap with plastic film, and refrigerate for at least 1 hour, or overnight.

TO PREPARE THE FILLING: Bring a small pot of water to a boil, add the rice and 1 teaspoon of the olive oil, and cook for 9 minutes; drain.

Combine the zucchini blossoms and all the vegetables in a large bowl. Stir in the egg, Parmesan, ricotta, 1 teaspoon salt, ½ teaspoon pepper, the rice, and the remaining ¼ cup olive oil, mixing well with a wooden spoon. Adjust the seasoning.

Preheat the oven to 325°F. Remove the dough from the refrigerator and allow to warm slightly to become malleable.

TO ASSEMBLE THE TOURTE: On a well-floured work surface, roll out one piece of dough into a 15-inch circle about ¹⁄₁₆ inch thick. Place the dough in a lightly greased 10½- to 11-inch tart pan with a removable bottom or a focaccia pan and trim to leave a scant ¾-inch overhang. Spoon in the vegetable filling, then sprinkle salt and pepper to taste over the top. Fold the edges of the dough over the filling. Brush the dough "collar" with the egg yolk glaze. Roll out the remaining dough to a 15-inch circle and place over the filling. Press down all around the edge of the dough to seal, then trim the dough, leaving a 1-inch overhang. Fold this overlap over itself and make a decorative fluted edge with your fingers.

TO BAKE THE TOURTE: With the tip of a small sharp knife or a pair of kitchen scissors, cut five or six snippets in the top of the tart to allow steam to escape. Brush the top of the tart lightly with a little olive oil. Place in the center of the oven, increase the temperature to 350°F, and bake for 45 to 60 minutes, until the top of the tart is rich golden brown. Transfer to a wire rack and brush the top of the tart again with olive oil. Serve warm or cold, accompanied by a crisp garden salad.

Variations: For an herb filling, add 2 to 3 tablespoons chopped fresh flat-leaf parsley or 1 teaspoon chopped fresh rosemary, sage, or summer savory. Around each serving, drizzle some pan drippings from a roast chicken if you have it, or a bit of chilled fruity extra-virgin olive oil.

SUGGESTED WINE

A LIVELY CHENIN BLANC, SUCH AS A VOUVRAY SEC LE MONT
1995 FROM DOMAINE HUET, OR A WASHINGTON STATE HOGUE
CHENIN BLANC 1996, FROM THE COLUMBIA VALLEY

TART OF YOUNG LETTUCES AND TOMATO CONFIT

Serves 6 as a first course

A THREE-LAYERED TART: slightly bitter crisp greens dressed lightly in olive oil and salt on the bottom, a baked crust in the center, and tomato confit on top. The tomato confit, subtly scented with garlic, is strewn with lightly cooked zucchini skin, basil leaves, and shavings of aged Parmigiano-Reggiano. (Prepare the tomato confit early in the day or a day ahead.)

FOR THE PASTRY CRUST

1¾ cups plus 2 tablespoons all-purpose flour

12 tablespoons (1½ sticks) unsalted butter, cut into bits, slightly softened

1 teaspoon fine sea salt

2 large egg yolks

1 large egg yolk, beaten with 1 teaspoon water, for egg glaze

FOR THE TOPPING

¼ pound mixed arugula, mesclun, and frisée, tough stems discarded

¼ cup extra-virgin olive oil

1 teaspoon fine sea salt

Tomato Confit (page 232)

½ small zucchini, skin sliced off in wide ⅛-inch-thick strips and cut into 1½-inch lengths

5 or 6 fresh basil leaves

2 ounces Parmigiano-Reggiano cheese, sliced with a peeler into shavings (about ½ cup)

Small fresh thyme sprigs for garnish

TO MAKE THE PASTRY: Combine the flour, butter, and salt in a food processor or medium bowl. Process for 10 to 12 seconds, or work together with your fingertips, until the mixture resembles coarse meal. Add the egg yolks and pulse 12 to 14 times, or mix briskly with your fingertips, until the dough just comes together. Remove the dough from the processor or bowl, knead it for about 2 minutes between the palms of your hands, and form it into a ball. Press into a disk, wrap in plastic wrap, and refrigerate for at least 2 hours, or overnight.

TO BAKE THE CRUST: Preheat the oven to 375°F. Line a baking sheet with kitchen parchment. Remove the dough from the refrigerator and allow to soften at room temperature until it is just malleable enough to work with.

On a well-floured work surface, roll out the dough with a floured rolling pin into a circle 11 inches across and ⅛ inch thick. Carefully lift up the dough, draping it over the rolling pin, and transfer it to the baking sheet. Prick the dough in several places with a fork. Bake in the center of the oven for 20 minutes, or until golden brown. Remove the baking sheet from the oven and brush the egg glaze evenly over the top of the crust. Return to the oven and bake for 5 minutes longer. Let cool on a wire rack, then transfer the crust to a serving plate, lifting up the kitchen parchment and gently sliding the crust off it; work with care, since the crust is quite crumbly.

TO ASSEMBLE THE TART: Toss the lettuces together with 2 tablespoons of the olive oil and the sea salt. Spread evenly over the cooled crust. Arrange the tomatoes, cut side down and slightly overlapping, in concentric circles, starting at the outside edge and working toward the center.

Heat the remaining 2 tablespoons olive oil in a small skillet over medium heat. Add the zucchini "strips" and cook, without coloring, until shiny and barely warm, about 1 minute. Remove to a plate. Swirl the basil leaves around in the oil to coat and remove to the plate. Stand the zucchini strips up among the tomatoes and garnish with the Parmesan shavings, 3 or 4 pieces of garlic from the tomato confit, the basil, and a few sprigs of thyme. Serve immediately (do not refrigerate before serving).

"This tart is so simple, with each of its various elements
frank and identifiable. I love dishes with lots
of flavor, but where no one element dominates another."

SUGGESTED WINE
A FLAVORFUL, SLIGHTLY SPICY RED WINE, SUCH AS
CHÂTEAU DE CALISANNE 1989 CUVÉE PRESTIGE,
COTEAUX D'AIX-EN-PROVENCE, OR A NAPA VALLEY MERLOT,
SUCH AS STAG'S LEAP WINE CELLARS 1994

LITTLE STUFFED VEGETABLES

Serves 4 as a main course, 6 as a first course

THESE COLORFUL, plump stuffed eggplant, zucchini, and tomatoes can be eaten hot, at room temperature, or chilled. Serve one or two as a hearty appetizer, all three as a satisfying main course. They also make a fine addition to a buffet table or a picnic. In addition to the vegetables called for here, you could also use sweet onions or red or yellow bell peppers. The dish was inspired by an 1892 recipe from Lucien Tendret, a French lawyer, author, and committed gastronome, who once wrote, "Gourmandism is the only passion that does not leave behind any remorse, sorrow, or suffering." The truffles, though optional, add a wonderful, earthy flavor and aroma to the stuffing.

4 nicely rounded baby eggplants (about 6 ounces each), cut lengthwise in half

Fine sea salt and freshly ground black pepper

1/2 cup olive oil

1 tablespoon plus 1 teaspoon unsalted butter

3/4 pound boneless skinless chicken breasts, cut into 2-inch chunks

2/3 pound boneless leg of lamb, cut into 2-inch chunks

1/2 pound boiled ham, cut into chunks

4 small shallots, finely minced

1 large garlic clove, lightly crushed

1/4 pound large white mushrooms, stems discarded, caps wiped clean and finely minced

2 ounces black truffles, coarsely chopped (optional)

3/4 cup freshly grated Parmigiano-Reggiano cheese

1/2 cup fresh flat-leaf parsley leaves, coarsely chopped

4 nicely rounded medium zucchini, if available, or longer, thinner zucchini (about 6 ounces each)

4 round firm medium tomatoes (about 6 ounces each), ideally with short stems

8 pieces Tomato Confit (page 232), finely chopped

Juice of 1 medium lemon

1/2 cup Chicken Stock (page 229)

4 tablespoons unsalted butter, melted

FOR THE VINAIGRETTE

Juice of 1/2 lemon

1/2 teaspoon fine sea salt

3 tablespoons extra-virgin olive oil

5 cups mesclun

1 tablespoon extra-virgin olive oil

TO PREPARE THE EGGPLANT: Preheat the oven to 350°F.

Put the eggplant cut side up in a lightly greased ovenproof dish, sprinkle with salt and pepper, and drizzle each eggplant half with 1 teaspoon of the olive oil. Bake the eggplant for 20 minutes, or until tender. Remove the pan to a wire rack and cool slightly, then scoop out most of the eggplant pulp, leaving just enough to form a firm shell. Chop the eggplant flesh, then set aside with the shells.

MEANWHILE, COOK THE CHICKEN AND LAMB: Heat 2 tablespoons of the olive oil and 2 teaspoons of the butter in a large skillet over medium-high heat. Add the chicken and lamb, season with salt, and cook just until golden brown on all sides, about 4 minutes. The meat should still be raw inside; if it overcooks, the stuff-

ing will be dry instead of tender and juicy. Transfer the chicken and lamb to a cutting board. With a sharp knife, finely mince the chicken and lamb with the ham. Place in a large bowl and set aside.

TO COOK THE MUSHROOMS: In a small skillet, heat 1 tablespoon of the oil and the remaining 2 teaspoons butter over medium heat. Add the shallots and cook for 1 minute. Add the garlic, sprinkle with salt, and cook for about 1 minute. Add the mushrooms, stirring to combine, then add another 1 tablespoon olive oil, stir, and cook for another minute. Add the truffles, if using them, and cook for 1 minute, stirring to coat well in the oil. Transfer the mixture to the bowl containing the meat. Season with salt and pepper, add the Parmesan and parsley, and mix well with a wooden spoon.

TO PREPARE THE ZUCCHINI AND TOMATOES: If they are very thick, first blanch the zucchini. Plunge them into a large pot of boiling salted water for 1 minute. Drain and immediately rinse under cold water. With round zucchini, cut about one quarter of each zucchini off to make a "cap" and reserve; with long zucchini, working with each zucchini in a horizontal position and starting 1 inch from the end, cut about one quarter of the upper part off to make a "cap," stopping 1 inch short of the other end; reserve. Scoop out the flesh of the zucchini, leaving enough to form a firm shell. Chop the zucchini flesh, then set aside with the shells.

Cut off the top quarter of each tomato for the "caps"; scoop out the seeds and flesh and discard, or save for another use. Set aside the tomatoes and caps.

TO BAKE THE VEGETABLES: Preheat the oven to 350°F. Lightly grease a large baking pan at least 1½ inches deep.

Divide the stuffing mixture equally among three bowls. Mix the reserved zucchini flesh into the first bowl, the eggplant flesh into the second, and the tomato confit into the third. Fill the zucchini with the zucchini stuffing, top with their caps, and set in the baking pan. Fill the eggplants with the eggplant stuffing, top with their caps, and set in the baking pan. Fill the tomatoes with the remaining stuffing, top with their caps, and set in the baking pan. Pour the lemon juice and chicken stock around the vegetables, then pour over the remaining 4 teaspoons olive oil and the melted butter. Bake for 20 minutes, or until the edges of the vegetables are well browned. Remove from the oven and set the pan on a wire rack.

If there is a lot of stock left in the bottom of the baking pan, spoon this into a small saucepan and boil over medium heat until the liquid reduces by half, 3 to 4 minutes. Keep warm over low heat.

TO MAKE THE VINAIGRETTE: Place the lemon juice and salt in a small bowl and whisk together until the salt dissolves. Add the olive oil and whisk to blend. Place the mesclun in a salad bowl, pour the vinaigrette over, and toss to coat the leaves.

Mound the salad in the center of four individual plates. Arrange one zucchini, one tomato, and two eggplant halves around the salad on each plate. Spoon the cooking juices over the vegetables, sprinkle with salt and pepper, drizzle with the olive oil, and serve.

SUGGESTED WINE

A BOLD RED WINE WITH A LONG FINISH, SUCH AS A
CLOS D'IÈRE 1993 CUVÉE 2, CÔTES DE PROVENCE,
OR A CHATEAU SOUVERAIN CABERNET SAUVIGNON 1994,
FROM SONOMA'S ALEXANDER VALLEY

FALL VEGETABLES AND FRUITS

Serves 4 as a first course

THE LAVISH EFFORTS involved—the vegetables are braised, then marinated, and finally sautéed—result in a succulent savory casserole that's spicy with pepper and juniper berries and sweet and sour with cherry nectar and vinegar; each vegetable gives the sweet-and-sour a slightly different twist. The chestnuts, cooked with salt pork, are particularly wonderful, salty and satisfying. Begin preparations at least 7 hours ahead of serving, since the vegetables must marinate for 6 hours.

FOR THE MARINADE

¼ cup sour cherry nectar (see page 247)

¼ cup sour cherry vinegar

5 strips lime zest, sliced with a
    vegetable peeler

Juice of 1 lime

1½ cups Chicken Stock (page 229)

10 juniper berries

30 black peppercorns

30 coriander seeds

7 tablespoons olive oil

4 small white turnips, green tops
    trimmed to 1 inch, outer two layers
    peeled off, and halved

2 small purple artichokes, trimmed
    (see page 248) and halved

4 medium carrots, peeled and cut on the
    diagonal into 1-inch pieces

1 cardoon stalk or large celery stalk,
    peeled and cut on the diagonal into
    3-inch pieces

4 small cèpe (porcini) mushrooms,
    trimmed and wiped clean
    (see page 238)

4 medium fennel bulbs, trimmed, outer
    layer peeled off, cored, and quartered
    lengthwise; one quarter coarsely
    chopped and reserved

4 spring onions (white part only), outer
    layer peeled off

About 4 cups Chicken Stock (page 229)

8 chestnuts

4 crisp Savoy cabbage leaves, ribs
    discarded, sliced into triangles

1 tablespoon Chicken Jus (page 230) or
    rich chicken or veal pan drippings

1 dried fennel branch or ¼ teaspoon
    fennel seed

6 tablespoons unsalted butter

¾ pound seedless green grapes

Fine sea salt and freshly ground
    black pepper

1 medium Granny Smith apple,
    peeled, quartered, cored, and sliced
    paper-thin

¼ pound girolle mushrooms, trimmed
    and cleaned (see page 238), very
    thinly sliced

4 teaspoons rich, fruity extra-virgin
    olive oil

Juice of ½ lemon

TO PREPARE THE MARINADE: Combine all the ingredients in a large bowl. Set aside.

TO PREPARE THE VEGETABLES: In a large heavy-bottomed casserole, ideally cast iron, heat ¼ cup of the olive oil over medium heat. Add the turnips, artichokes, carrots, and cardoon and cook for 2 minutes, stirring frequently. Add the porcini mushrooms and the fennel quarters and cook, shaking the pan from time to time, for 1 minute. Stir in the onions, and add enough chicken stock so that there is about ½ inch covering the bottom of the casserole. Cover and cook until all the vegetables are tender, about 12 to 15 minutes. Continue adding

stock as the vegetables cook, so that there is always about ½ inch of stock covering the bottom of the casserole. Check the vegetables frequently, as some will be done before others; as soon as a vegetable offers no resistance to the tip of a small sharp knife, remove with a slotted spoon and place in the marinade. When all the vegetables are cooked, let cool, then cover the bowl with plastic wrap and refrigerate for 6 hours. Transfer the braising juices to a bowl, cover, and refrigerate.

TO PREPARE THE CHESTNUTS: With a sharp knife, carefully make a small slit in the flat side of each chestnut. Put the chestnuts into a small saucepan with just enough water to cover and bring to a boil. Cook for 3 minutes, then remove from the heat and set aside to cool slightly. Drain, reserving the cooking liquid, peel, and set aside. Strain the cooking liquid and set aside.

MEANWHILE, COOK THE CABBAGE: Bring a medium pot of water to a boil. Plunge in the green cabbage leaves and blanch for 1 minute, then remove with a slotted spoon and transfer to a bowl of ice-cold water to stop the cooking. Set aside.

TO COOK THE CHESTNUTS: In a medium saucepan, combine the chestnuts with 1 cup chicken stock, the chicken jus, fennel, and the reserved chopped fennel. Heat to boiling over medium heat, then reduce the heat to medium-low, cover, and cook, stirring frequently, until the chestnuts are tender, browned, and glazed with sauce, 10 to 15 minutes.

MEANWHILE, COOK THE GRAPES: Melt 2 tablespoons of the butter in a medium skillet over medium-high heat. Add half of the grapes and cook, stirring frequently, until they have a caramelized appearance—they should be shiny all over and golden brown over at least half their surface. Remove to a plate and repeat with another 2 tablespoons butter and the remaining grapes. Set aside.

TO FINISH THE DISH: Drain the vegetables and set aside. In a large heavy-bottomed saucepan set over medium heat, heat the remaining 2 tablespoons butter with the remaining 3 tablespoons olive oil. When the butter has melted, add the marinated vegetables, stir to coat with the butter and oil, and cook, stirring frequently, for 2 minutes. Lay the cabbage leaves on top of the vegetables. Cook for 5 minutes, shaking the pan frequently to prevent sticking. Add the grapes and cook for 4 minutes longer, shaking the pan frequently.

Meanwhile, reheat the reserved vegetable braising juices.

Add the reserved chestnut cooking liquid and braising juices to the saucepan and cook until the vegetables caramelize lightly, taking on a nice golden color, about 3 minutes longer. Season to taste.

Arrange the apple and girolle slices, overlapping them, on the bottom of four soup plates. Drizzle 1 teaspoon of extra-virgin olive oil over each serving, then sprinkle on a few drops of lemon juice and a pinch of salt. Divide the vegetable mixture among the plates (the heat from the cooked vegetables will slightly cook the mushrooms and apple), then scatter on the grapes. Serve immediately.

❝I love the rustic and savory combination of fall fruits and vegetables slowly cooked together in a casserole. The sweetness of the fruits and the earthiness of the vegetables complement each other like partners in a good marriage.❞

SUGGESTED WINE

A RUSTIC, SOFT RED WINE, SUCH AS A PINOT NOIR D'ALSACE
BURLENBERG 1990, OR A COLUMBIA CABERNET
FRANC YAKIMA VALLEY RED, WILLOW VINEYARD, DAVID
LAKE SIGNATURE SERIES 1994

GARDEN VEGETABLES SLOW-COOKED IN A CAST-IRON POT

Serves 4 as a first course

YOUNG ROOT VEGETABLES mixed with asparagus, Swiss chard, and artichokes yield an earthy flavor with a slight edge of bitterness, brightened by the fresh lemon in the hot vinaigrette. In the fall, you might substitute chestnuts, celery, fennel, and leek for the spring onions, zucchini blossoms, asparagus, and radishes and replace the lemon juice with aged red wine vinegar.

½ cup olive oil

8 small carrots, peeled, and tops trimmed to ½ inch

8 small turnips, greens trimmed to ½ inch, outer two layers peeled off

8 small red radishes, root ends trimmed off and tops trimmed to ½ inch

4 spring onions, greens trimmed to 3 inches

2 crisp young Swiss chard leaves, green parts and white ribs separated and ribs peeled

2 to 3 cups Chicken Stock (page 229)

16 tiny artichokes, trimmed (see page 248; it is not necessary to remove the chokes) and quartered

4 small zucchini blossoms, pistils removed

8 asparagus spears, trimmed on the diagonal to 3 inches and peeled

1 cup shelled fresh peas

1⅛ teaspoons coarse sea salt, preferably fleur de sel

Juice of ½ lemon

Freshly ground white pepper

In a large cast-iron casserole, heat 3 tablespoons of the olive oil over medium-high heat. Add the carrots, turnips, radishes, spring onions, and the Swiss chard ribs, stir well, and cook for 3 to 4 minutes. Add ¼ cup of the chicken stock and cook, stirring frequently, until the vegetables are lightly browned but still firm, 8 to 10 minutes. (When you prick the vegetables with the tip of a sharp knife, you should feel a slight resistance.) Add more chicken stock to the pot as it evaporates, adding enough each time to just moisten the vegetables and cover the bottom of the pan. Add the artichokes and zucchini blossoms and cook, gently stirring occasionally, for another 7 minutes, again adding just enough chicken stock from time to time to moisten.

Add the asparagus tips, the Swiss chard leaves, the peas, ¼ cup more chicken stock, 2 tablespoons of the olive oil, and 1 teaspoon of the salt, stirring to combine. Cook, adding the chicken stock only as needed, until all the ingredients are meltingly tender. Remove from the heat. Squeeze in the lemon juice, then add the remaining 3 tablespoons olive oil and ⅛ teaspoon sea salt and pepper to taste. Stir well and serve immediately.

Note: Several paper-thin slices of black truffle or paper-thin slices of raw vegetables such as radishes, asparagus, fennel, or artichoke, would be lovely on top.

SUGGESTED WINE

A NICELY PERFUMED WHITE WINE, SUCH AS A DOMAINE DE CHAUSSE 1994, CÔTES DE PROVENCE, OR A WASHINGTON STATE COVEY RUN GEWÜRZTRAMINER, FROM CELILO VINEYARD

SALAD OF BRAISED AND RAW ARTICHOKES WITH PASTA AND PARMESAN CRISPS

Serves 4 as a first course

THIS DISH, more a salad than a pasta, sets raw artichoke, black pepper, and arugula against smooth, cool pasta and braised artichoke hearts. Olive oil adds richness and silky texture; the fragile, savory Parmesan crisps, shaped while hot into "tuiles," are salty and nutty.

The salad is built on a base of arugula mixed with thinly sliced raw artichoke hearts, flavored with olive oil. The pasta shapes are draped over the lettuce and vegetables, topped with braised artichokes, and garnished with more of the raw artichoke slices. Each salad is served with two to three Parmesan crisps.

FOR THE PASTA

2½ cups all-purpose flour

3 large eggs

2 tablespoons olive oil

1 teaspoon fine sea salt

12 small purple artichokes, trimmed (see page 248)

6 tablespoons olive oil

2 cups plus 3 tablespoons Chicken Stock (page 229)

Coarse sea salt, preferably fleur de sel, and freshly ground black pepper

1 tablespoon fresh lemon juice

¼ pound arugula, tough stems discarded

2 tablespoons fruity extra-virgin olive oil

Lacy Parmesan Crisps (page 233)

TO MAKE THE PASTA DOUGH: In the bowl of a mixer equipped with a dough hook, combine all the pasta ingredients. Knead until the mixture becomes a smooth, silky, and homogeneous dough. Remove from the bowl, shape into a ball, wrap in plastic wrap, and refrigerate for at least 2 hours.

TO PREPARE THE ARTICHOKES: Quarter 8 of the artichokes. Heat 2 tablespoons of the olive oil in a deep medium skillet over medium heat. Add the quartered artichokes, stirring to coat with the oil. Cook just until the artichokes begin to soften and give off some of their moisture, about 3 to 4 minutes, then pour in 2 cups of the chicken stock (the stock should come almost to the top of the artichokes) and season with salt and pepper. Cook, stirring occasionally, until the artichokes are tender, about 15 minutes. Stir in 1 more tablespoon of olive oil, remove from the heat, and, with a slotted spoon, transfer the artichokes to a bowl; set aside.

Using a mandoline or a sharp knife, carefully slice the remaining 4 artichokes paper-thin. Place the artichokes in a small bowl, add 1 tablespoon of the olive oil, the lemon juice, a pinch of coarse sea salt, and a good turn of the peppermill, and toss well. Reserve in the refrigerator.

TO PREPARE THE PASTA SHAPES: With a pasta machine, roll out the dough to a ⅛-inch thickness. Cut the pasta sheet into triangles, circles, rectangles, or other geometrical shapes about 2 inches in diameter; prepare four or five shapes per serving.

Bring a large pot of salted water with 1 tablespoon of the olive oil to a rolling boil. Add the pasta shapes a few at a time and cook until tender, 2 to 3 minutes, then transfer to a bowl using a slotted spoon. Moisten the pasta with the remaining 3 tablespoons chicken stock, then drizzle on the remaining 1 tablespoon olive oil and gently coat the pasta shapes by turning them over carefully once or twice with your hands. Set aside.

In a medium bowl, combine the arugula, half of the raw artichoke slices, and salt to taste. Drizzle the extra-virgin olive oil over the salad, season with pepper, and toss well to coat. Divide the salad among four serving plates, then arrange the pasta shapes over the salads. Top with the cooked artichoke quarters, followed by the remaining raw artichoke slices, and crown each with 2 or 3 Parmesan crisps. Serve immediately.

"In carrying out these recipes, precision is very important—
precision and appreciation for what you're doing—and a
desire to make the dish beautiful . . . to ensure the unique taste of
each product so that we can appreciate it to its fullest."

SUGGESTED WINE

AN OPEN, SLIGHTLY TANNIC WHITE WINE, SUCH AS A CONDRIEU
LA CÔTE 1996 Y. CUILLERON, OR A BRANDER SAUVIGNON BLANC
1996 CUVÉE NATHALIE, FROM SANTA YNEZ VALLEY

[*Cocotte Verte*]

COCOTTE OF YOUNG SPRING VEGETABLES

*Serves 4 as a first course or light meal,
6 to 8 as an accompaniment*

THOUGH STUDDED WITH TINY NEW POTATOES, this light, bright vegetable casserole is primarily green. Cooked sequentially, each springtime vegetable retains its flavor and texture, the whole bound by a smooth, light base of olive oil and chicken broth. Because the potatoes and onions are browned in olive oil, they add a layer of golden caramelized flavor to what would otherwise be a simple bright, fresh green taste, set off by the slight bitterness of the lettuces. The vegetables are served with lots of the buttered chicken stock they're cooked in. For variation, substitute, or add, Swiss chard greens, baby spinach, or sugar snap peas, adding them at the same time as the asparagus and lettuce.

8 firm green asparagus stalks, peeled, tough parts removed

6 tablespoons olive oil

12 tiny new potatoes (all the same size), washed and halved

8 spring onions (white part only), outer layer peeled off

3 cups shelled fresh peas (about 2 pounds peas in the pod)

1 cup shelled fresh baby lima beans

12 crisp red-leaf lettuce leaves, ribs only

1¾ cups Chicken Stock (page 229)

Coarse sea salt and freshly ground black pepper

2 cups mesclun or arugula, tough stems discarded

20 fresh flat-leaf parsley leaves

Bring a large pot of salted water to a boil over high heat. Plunge in the asparagus and cook until al dente, about 4 minutes. Carefully remove with tongs or a slotted spoon and transfer to a bowl of ice-cold water to stop the cooking. Drain, pat dry, and set aside.

In a medium cast-iron casserole, heat 5 tablespoons of the olive oil over medium heat. Add the potatoes and cook, stirring frequently, until golden brown, about 7 minutes. Add the spring onions and cook, stirring frequently, until they are golden brown, about 4 minutes. Stir in the peas and cook for 3 minutes, shaking the pan from time to time and stirring occasionally. Add the lima beans, stir to coat with oil, and cook for 3 minutes.

Add the asparagus and lettuce to the casserole, gently stirring to combine, then add the chicken stock. Bring to a simmer and cook, uncovered, until all the vegetables are just cooked through, 5 to 7 minutes.

Season with salt and pepper to taste, then place the mesclun and parsley on top of the vegetables, drizzle with the remaining 1 tablespoon of olive oil, and remove the casserole from the heat. Bring the casserole to the table and serve immediately, serving some of the sauce with the vegetables.

SUGGESTED WINE

A PERFUMED RED OR WHITE WINE, SUCH AS A CLOS ST. JOSEPH ROUGE 1993, CÔTES DE PROVENCE, OR A DAVIS BYNUM SAUVIGNON BLANC, RUSSIAN RIVER 1996, VALLEY SHONE FARM VINEYARD SELECTION FROM CALIFORNIA

RIVIERA SALAD, LIKE A NIÇOISE

Serves 4 as a first course

THIS COMPOSITION OF CONTRASTING COLORS, textures, and flavors is a favorite on the menu of the Louis XV. Each vegetable is meticulously prepared: Some are chopped into a tiny dice or sliced ultrathin; some are individually dressed with a sherry wine vinaigrette, others left bare; and half the artichoke slices are crisply fried, the other half left raw. The salad is topped with red-rimmed slices of radish and set off with toasts spread with rich black tapenade, each holding a tiny half quail egg. Use a slightly fruity olive oil for this.

½ medium seedless (hothouse) cucumber, peeled and cut into ½-inch dice

Fine sea salt

1 medium red bell pepper, roasted (see page 249), peeled, seeded, and cut into ¼-inch strips

1 sprig fresh thyme

1 garlic clove, lightly crushed

½ cup extra-virgin olive oil

FOR THE TAPENADE

7 ounces Niçoise olives, pitted

1 tablespoon capers, drained and coarsely chopped

¼ teaspoon fresh lemon juice

½ garlic clove

1 tablespoon sherry vinegar

Pinch of fine sea salt

Freshly ground black pepper

¼ cup extra-virgin olive oil

FOR THE VINAIGRETTE

1 tablespoon sherry vinegar

Fine sea salt and freshly ground black pepper

¼ cup extra-virgin olive oil

12 thin slices baguette, toasted

½ garlic clove

4 quail eggs, hard-boiled (5 minutes), shelled, and halved lengthwise (or use 2 small hen's eggs: boil for 10 minutes, shell, and quarter)

8 medium Niçoise olives, a thick slice cut off each and remainder reserved for another use

4 small purple artichokes, trimmed (see page 248), halved, and sliced paper-thin

2 cups peanut oil

1 celery heart, trimmed, sliced paper-thin, and reserved in cold water

¼ pound mesclun

4 tomatoes, peeled, seeded, and quartered

8 small spring onions (white part only), outer layer peeled off and sliced paper-thin

8 anchovy fillets packed in oil

4 ounces solid white tuna packed in oil

8 fresh basil leaves, cut into chiffonade

8 small red radishes, trimmed and sliced paper-thin

Fresh lemon juice

Place the cucumber in a colander and sprinkle with 1 tablespoon salt; set aside for about 10 minutes so that the cucumber gives off its water. Wipe as much salt off as you can with a kitchen cloth or paper towels and reserve.

In a small bowl, combine the roasted pepper with the thyme, garlic clove, and 1 tablespoon of the olive oil; set aside.

TO MAKE THE TAPENADE: Combine the olives in a blender or mini-food processor with the capers, lemon juice, garlic, sherry vinegar, salt, pepper to taste, and the olive oil. Blend to a thick paste, then transfer to a small bowl and set aside.

TO MAKE THE VINAIGRETTE: Combine the vinegar in a small bowl with a pinch of salt, pepper to taste, and the olive oil. Stir vigorously with a fork to blend; set aside.

TO PREPARE THE TOASTS: Rub the baguette slices lightly on one side with the ½ garlic clove, then spread with a thin layer of the tapenade; reserve a bit of the tapenade for the dressing. Garnish 8 of the slices with half a quail's egg, and place a slice of olive on top of each egg. Set all the slices aside on a plate.

TO PREPARE THE ARTICHOKES: Drain the artichoke slices on paper towels and pat thoroughly dry. Heat the peanut oil in a large deep skillet over medium-high heat. When the oil is very hot (375°F), carefully put in half of the artichoke slices. Fry until the artichokes are light golden brown, about 2 minutes. Remove with a slotted spoon to several layers of paper towels and season immediately with a pinch of salt. Combine the remaining artichoke slices with 1 tablespoon of the vinaigrette in a small bowl and toss to coat.

In another small bowl, toss the cucumber with 1 tablespoon of the vinaigrette. Drain the celery heart and pat dry. In a third small bowl, toss with another tablespoon of vinaigrette. (Reserve the remaining vinaigrette for another use.)

TO ASSEMBLE THE SALAD: Arrange the ingredients on four serving plates in the following sequence: first the mesclun, then the red pepper, tomatoes, cucumber, raw artichoke slices, celery heart, spring onions, anchovy fillets, tuna, and basil leaves. Scatter the radish slices and the fried artichoke slices over the top and sprinkle with a few drops of lemon juice. Arrange 3 tapenade toasts on the side of each plate (2 with quail eggs, 1 plain).

In a small bowl, stir together the remaining 7 tablespoons olive oil and the remaining tapenade, then transfer to a sauceboat. Serve the salad immediately, passing the sauceboat at the table.

SUGGESTED WINE

A SIMPLE RED, WHITE, OR ROSÉ, SUCH AS A CLOS BERNARDE
BLANC 1994 DOMAINE DE LA BERNARDE, CÔTES
DE PROVENCE, OR A JOSEPH PHELPS GRENACHE ROSÉ 1996
CALIFORNIA VIN DU MISTRAL, FROM THE NAPA VALLEY

FORK-MASHED POTATOES WITH OLIVE OIL AND PARSLEY

Serves 4 as an accompaniment

USE BEAUTIFUL, FIRM POTATOES with uniform color and smooth, thin skin; the finest unsalted butter you can find; an extra-virgin olive oil whose taste you love; crisp, fresh parsley; and fine sea salt, preferably Guérande from Brittany. Since these potatoes, cooked on a bed of coarse salt to keep them moist, are fork-mashed, not whipped or puréed, you can truly taste the potato's flavor and feel its fine, grainy texture as you eat. An almost universal accompaniment, these potatoes go particularly well with roast or grilled beef, roast chicken, or a poached or baked meaty fish such as turbot or halibut.

1 cup or more coarse sea salt or
   kosher salt

2 pounds medium all-purpose potatoes
   (about 5), washed and dried

2 tablespoons unsalted butter, softened

3 tablespoons extra-virgin olive oil

Fine sea salt

1 tablespoon finely chopped fresh flat-
   leaf parsley

Preheat the oven to 375°F.

    Layer the coarse salt evenly over the bottom of a baking pan. Arrange the potatoes side by side on the salt. Bake until the tip of a knife slides easily through a potato, 45 to 55 minutes. Remove from the oven and let cool briefly, until the potatoes are cool enough to handle.

    Peel the potatoes and put them into a warmed bowl. Mash them coarsely with a fork, then add the butter and continue mashing until the potatoes are well mixed with the butter but still have some texture. (They shouldn't be the consistency of smooth whipped potatoes.) Drizzle in the olive oil, add salt to taste, and stir just until the ingredients are blended; do not overwork. Spoon into a warmed serving bowl or onto warmed individual plates, sprinkle with the parsley, and serve immediately.

SAUTÉED PUMPKIN SLICES CRUSTED WITH CRACKED SZECHUAN PEPPERCORNS

Serves 4 as an accompaniment

THIN SLICES OF PUMPKIN are generously coated (the term *panée* means breaded) with cracked Szechuan peppercorns, sprinkled with sea salt, and sautéed in olive oil. The mild spiciness and crunch of the pepper contrasts with the smooth, almost nutty flavor of the pumpkin. Serve with roast veal, duck, or venison.

One 2- to 3-pound nicely rounded
  pumpkin

¼ cup cracked Szechuan peppercorns

Fine sea salt

About ⅓ cup olive oil

Preheat the oven to 200°F.

Cut out the stem of the pumpkin. Halve the pumpkin lengthwise and remove the seeds and strings. Following the pumpkin's natural segmentation, cut it lengthwise into ¾-inch slices; cut off the peel.

Spread the pepper over a large flat plate. Press both sides of the pumpkin slices into the pepper so that slices are well covered, then sprinkle with salt.

Heat 2 tablespoons of olive oil in a large skillet over medium heat. Lay several pumpkin slices in the pan, side by side so that they do not overlap, lower the heat to medium-low, and cook until each side has browned lightly and the tip of a knife passes easily through the flesh, about 8 minutes on each side. Remove the pumpkin slices to an ovenproof platter and keep warm in the oven. Repeat with the remaining slices, adding oil to the pan as necessary. Serve warm.

GLAZED COOKED AND RAW ASPARAGUS WITH BUTTER AND PARMESAN

Serves 4 as a first course or accompaniment

THIS IS A RICH YET EXQUISITELY SIMPLE DISH that can be at its best only if every ingredient is of top quality. The asparagus must be fresh and in season, firm, brightly colored, and crisp, with almost a glow in the center of the stalk. If you can find butter from Normandy, use it; for Parmesan, use only Parmigiano-Reggiano, with its full, ripe flavor. The asparagus is not actually *rôtie*, or roasted, but rather sautéed in butter until it has a gilded, roasted appearance. The sprinkling of chopped raw asparagus at the end adds crunch and a slightly nutty taste to a dish of silken textures and flavors.

40 medium green asparagus spears (about 2 pounds), trimmed to about 5 inches and peeled, plus tips only of 4 medium asparagus spears, coarsely chopped

1 tablespoon fine sea salt

6 tablespoons unsalted butter

1/2 cup freshly grated Parmigiano-Reggiano cheese

Freshly ground black pepper

4 teaspoons fruity extra-virgin olive oil, chilled

TO COOK THE ASPARAGUS: Using kitchen string, tie the asparagus spears together in bunches of five. Bring a large pot of water, with the salt, to a rapid boil. Plunge in the asparagus bunches and cook until the tip of a knife can pierce a stalk without resistance, about 4 minutes. Remove the asparagus and pat the bunches dry, then carefully untie the strings.

Melt 3 tablespoons of butter in each of two large skillets over medium heat (if you have just one large frying pan, cook in two batches). When the butter is white and bubbly, lay the asparagus in the pans in a single layer. Roll the stalks around so that each gets well covered with butter and cook for 2 minutes or so, until they take on a shiny, "gilded" look. Sprinkle on the Parmesan and remove from the heat.

TO FINISH THE DISH: Divide the asparagus among four warmed serving dishes, then scatter the chopped asparagus tips over the cooked asparagus. Sprinkle a pinch of freshly ground pepper over each serving, then drizzle 1 teaspoon of chilled olive oil in a thin filament around the edge of each plate. Serve immediately.

Variations: Instead of drizzling olive oil onto the serving plates, substitute a thin filament of highly reduced pan drippings from a roast, punctuated around each plate by 6 tiny Niçoise olives. Or garnish each plate with 4 fresh morel mushrooms that have been sautéed in butter with minced shallots.

WHITES AND GREENS OF SWISS CHARD WITH TOMATOES

Serves 6 as an accompaniment

A RAGOUT OF TOMATOES and young leeks is topped with the whites of the chard that have been braised in chicken stock and butter and the greens of the chard that have been wilted in olive oil and garlic.

2 pounds crisp Swiss chard	1½ teaspoons fine sea salt
Juice of 1 lemon	4 plum tomatoes, peeled, seeded, and cut into large dice
6 slim young leeks (white and pale green parts only)	¼ teaspoon freshly ground black pepper
5 tablespoons olive oil	1 tablespoon rich, fruity extra-virgin olive oil
1 cup Chicken Stock (page 229)	1 garlic clove, peeled
4 tablespoons unsalted butter	

TO PREPARE THE VEGETABLES: Carefully separate the white and green parts of the Swiss chard. Remove and discard the most prominent veins from the green parts, then slice the remaining greens into thin julienne strips and reserve. Peel the outside layer of the white stalks, carefully removing the fibers. Cut the stalks on the diagonal into 2-inch pieces. Fill a large mixing bowl three-quarters full of cold water, stir in the lemon juice, and place the Swiss chard stalks in the water to keep them from discoloring.

Peel off the outside layers of the leeks, rinse well to remove all traces of sand, and pat dry. Slice them on the diagonal into three pieces each.

TO COOK THE VEGETABLES: Heat 2 tablespoons of the olive oil in a medium skillet over medium-high heat. Drain the Swiss chard stalks and pat dry, then place in the skillet and stir to coat with oil. Add the chicken stock, butter, and ½ teaspoon salt and stir to combine. Cook, covered, over medium heat for 5 minutes. Uncover and cook for 10 minutes more over high heat, or until the liquid has evaporated.

Meanwhile, in a second skillet set over medium-high heat, heat 2 tablespoons of the olive oil, then stir in the leeks. Add the tomatoes, sprinkle with ½ teaspoon salt and the pepper, and stir them into the leeks. Cook over high heat until all the liquid evaporates, 8 to 10 minutes. Remove the pan from the heat and drizzle the fruity olive oil over the tomato mixture.

Heat the remaining 1 tablespoon olive oil in a medium skillet over medium heat. Poke the tines of a fork through the garlic clove. Add the Swiss chard greens to the pan and stir them with the "garlic fork" just until they begin to wilt, about 1 minute. Remove from the heat, sprinkle with the remaining ½ teaspoon salt, and set aside.

Spread the tomatoes over the bottom of a warmed serving platter. Arrange the Swiss chard stalks over the tomatoes and garnish the top with the chard greens. Serve immediately.

[*Artichauts à la Barigoule*]

PROVENÇAL-STYLE ARTICHOKES BRAISED IN WINE WITH OLIVE OIL

Serves 4 as an accompaniment

THE LOVELY VIOLET ARTICHOKES of Provence are halved and braised, then served bathed in their white wine broth flavored with olive oil, prosciutto, and fennel. A splash each of sherry wine and balsamic vinegars at the end brightens the broth.

FOR THE BROTH

6 fresh basil leaves

1 sprig fresh thyme

1 bay leaf

2 teaspoons coriander seeds

2 teaspoons black peppercorns, coarsely crushed

1½ tablespoons olive oil

½ medium onion, peeled and chopped

1 medium carrot, peeled and cut into small dice

4 garlic cloves, peeled

½ medium fennel bulb, timmed, tough outer layer peeled off, cored, chopped

1 celery stalk, peeled and chopped

Fine sea salt and freshly ground black pepper

1 cup dry white wine

FOR THE ARTICHOKES

¾ cup olive oil

16 small purple artichokes, trimmed (see page 248), leaving 1½-inch stems, and cut in half

¼ pound thickly sliced prosciutto di Parma or other cured ham, cut into large dice

Fine sea salt and freshly ground black pepper

1 cup dry white wine

4 large fresh basil leaves

2 teaspoons aged balsamic vinegar

1 tablespoon sherry vinegar

1½ tablespoons thick, fruity extra-virgin olive oil

TO PREPARE THE BROTH: Tie the basil leaves, thyme, bay leaf, coriander seeds, and peppercorns together in a small square of cheesecloth. Set aside.

In a medium saucepan, heat the olive oil over high heat. Add the onion, carrot, and garlic, reduce the heat to medium, and cook without coloring, stirring frequently, until the vegetables begin to give off moisture and the onions begin to turn translucent, about 3 minutes. Add the fennel and celery, season with salt and pepper, and cook, stirring often, until the vegetables begin to brown lightly, about 8 minutes. Pour in the white wine and simmer until the liquid reduces by half, then add just enough water to cover the vegetables, about 2½ cups. When the liquid begins to simmer, add the herb pouch, reduce the heat to low to keep the broth at a bare simmer, and cook for 1 hour. Remove from the heat, strain the broth into a bowl, and set aside.

TO COOK THE ARTICHOKES: In a wide saucepan, heat the olive oil over medium-high heat, then add the artichokes and prosciutto and stir to combine. Add just a small pinch of salt (since the prosciutto is already quite salty) and pepper to taste, pour in the wine, and stir to mix. Bring to a simmer and cook until the liquid reduces by half. Add the reserved broth. The broth should just cover the artichokes; if it does not, add just

enough water to cover. Add 3 of the basil leaves, cover the pot, reduce the heat to medium-low so the liquid remains at a gentle simmer, and cook for 25 minutes.

Remove the artichokes from the pan with a slotted spoon and place in a warm serving dish together with some of the prosciutto (about 1 tablespoon per serving). Discard the basil.

TO FINISH THE DISH: Bring the liquid remaining in the pan to a boil over medium-high heat, then add the balsamic vinegar and sherry vinegar. Bring to a boil again, then pour in the olive oil, stir well, and season with pepper to taste. Cook, shaking the pan frequently, until the surface of the sauce is covered with tiny bubbles. Cook for only 30 seconds longer, then immediately remove the pan from the heat and pour the sauce over the artichokes. Thinly slice the remaining basil leaf, sprinkle over the artichokes, and serve immediately.

SUGGESTED WINE

A SLIGHTLY TANNIC WHITE WINE, SUCH AS A BELLET
BLANC CHÂTEAU DE BELLET 1996, OR A BOEGER SAUVIGNON
BLANC 1996, FROM EL DORADO, CALIFORNIA

POLENTA WITH CÈPES

Serves 4 as an accompaniment or first course

POLENTA IS POPULAR IN NICE and the surrounding hills of the Riviera backcountry, reflecting the strong influence of Northern Italy on the cooking of the region. The polenta cooks up full of flavor in a rich chicken broth smoothed with olive oil and is crowned by a savory, aromatic ragout of cèpes, prosciutto, garlic, and shallots.

FOR THE POLENTA

1 quart Chicken Stock (page 229)

1 teaspoon fine sea salt

$\frac{1}{2}$ teaspoon freshly ground black pepper

$1\frac{1}{3}$ cups polenta (or coarse cornmeal)

$\frac{1}{4}$ cup extra-virgin olive oil

FOR THE CÈPES

$\frac{1}{4}$ cup goose or duck fat, or extra-virgin olive oil

2 pounds fresh cèpe (porcini) mushrooms (about 8 medium cèpes), stems trimmed to 1 inch, wiped clean (see page 238), and cut into $\frac{1}{4}$-inch slices

1 garlic clove, crushed

1 shallot, finely chopped

2 slices prosciutto di Parma or other cured ham (about 2 ounces total), sliced into fine strips

1 cup Veal Jus (page 231) or duck or veal pan juices

Fine sea salt and freshly ground black pepper

1 tablespoon chopped fresh flat-leaf parsley

TO PREPARE THE POLENTA: Oil the bottom and sides of a large cast-iron skillet. Add the chicken stock, salt, and pepper and bring to a rolling boil. Remove from the heat and add the polenta, tossing it in little by little in a light "rain" of grains and stirring constantly with a wooden spoon to avoid lumps. Continue stirring, adding the olive oil bit by bit, until the polenta is very smooth, about 5 minutes. Cover the polenta with a piece of oiled kitchen parchment paper and place the pan over very low heat. Let the polenta cook for about 1 hour, stirring often. At the end of the cooking time, the polenta should be very smooth and still just thin enough to be pourable.

MEANWHILE, PREPARE THE CÈPES: About 15 minutes before the polenta has finished cooking, heat 3 table-spoons of the fat or olive oil in a large cast-iron skillet over medium heat. Add the cèpes and garlic, stir to coat them with fat, and sauté until the mushrooms release their juices and turn light golden brown, 8 to 10 minutes. Remove the cèpes to a plate and set aside. In the same skillet, heat the remaining 1 tablespoon fat or olive oil over medium heat, then add the shallots and cook just until the shallots begin to give off a little moisture,

about 2 minutes. Add the cèpes, prosciutto, and veal jus and stir well with a wooden spoon to combine. Simmer for 2 to 3 minutes, until the mixture is heated through. Season to taste, scatter on the parsley, and remove from the heat.

Divide the polenta among four heated plates, spoon the cèpes ragout over, and serve immediately.

SUGGESTED WINE

A TANNIC BUT NOT OVERLY STRONG RED WINE, SUCH
AS A MONDEUSE DE SAVOIE 1995, M. GRISARD,
OR A BUENA VISTA HAYWOOD 1994 (ROCKY TERRACE),
FROM CALIFORNIA'S CARNEROS REGION

[*Gratin de Cèpes*]

GRATIN OF CÈPES

Serves 4 as a first course or accompaniment

HERE'S A LOVELY WAY TO PREPARE FRESH CÈPES using both stems and caps, ham, shallots, parsley, and a light topping of Parmesan. Serve it with slices of toasted country bread.

2 pounds cèpe (porcini) mushrooms (about 8 medium), trimmed and wiped clean (see page 238)

5 tablespoons olive oil

1 medium shallot, cut into small dice

2 tablespoons unsalted butter

¼ pound prosciutto di Parma or other cured ham, cut into small dice

2 tablespoons fresh flat-leaf parsley leaves, torn into bits

1 tablespoon pan drippings from a roast or 1 small black truffle, chopped, or 1 large garlic clove, minced (optional)

Fine sea salt and freshly ground black pepper

½ cup freshly grated Parmigiano-Reggiano cheese

TO PREPARE THE MUSHROOMS: Separate the caps and stems. Chop the stems into small dice and slice the caps into ⅓-inch slices.

Heat 3 tablespoons of the olive oil in a large skillet over medium heat. Add the shallot and chopped mushroom stems and stir to coat with oil, then stir in the butter, ham, and parsley. Cook until the mushroom stems soften and the shallots begin to look translucent, about 4 minutes. If you wish, just before you take the mixture off the heat, add the pan drippings, truffle, or minced garlic, stir well, and cook for about 1 minute. Remove the pan from the heat and set aside.

In a cast-iron or other heavy-bottomed skillet, heat the remaining 2 tablespoons oil over medium heat. Add the sliced cèpes, stirring to coat them with oil, and reduce the heat to medium-low. Season with salt and pepper to taste and cook, stirring occasionally, until the cèpes have softened, released their liquid, and begun to brown, about 5 minutes. Remove from the heat.

TO FINISH THE GRATIN: Preheat the broiler. Divide the cèpe-and-ham mixture among four gratin dishes or shallow ovenproof serving dishes, about 5 inches in diameter. Divide the cèpe slices equally among the dishes, arranging the slices over the cèpe-and-ham mixture so that they slightly overlap, then sprinkle the Parmesan evenly over the tops. Place the dishes under the broiler for about 30 seconds, until the Parmesan just starts to color. Serve immediately.

SUGGESTED WINE

A MATURE RED WINE WITH LOTS OF VOLUME, SUCH AS A
DOMAINE RABASSE CHARAVIN CUVÉE ESTEVENAS 1990
CAIRANNE OR A ROCHIOLI PINOT NOIR 1994 BLACK RESERVE,
FROM CALIFORNIA'S RUSSIAN RIVER VALLEY WEST

[*Pommes de Terre Boulangère*]

POTATO AND LEEK GRATIN

Serves 6 as an accompaniment

AS CHICKEN STOCK REDUCES around potatoes, the starch from the potatoes binds it into a thick, buttery sauce. You must use a homemade chicken stock rich with natural gelatin for this recipe; commercial stock lacks gelatin, without which the sauce won't thicken. The name of this classic, homey side dish derives from the tradition of the baker's wife, as well as other women of the village, using the still-hot bread oven at the end of the day to cook the family dinner.

7 tablespoons unsalted butter, softened

2¼ pounds evenly shaped all-purpose potatoes (about 6 medium)

5 medium leeks, white part sliced on the diagonal into 1½-inch pieces, light green part thinly sliced

3 tablespoons olive oil

1 pound onions (about 3 medium), sliced

Fine sea salt

¼ teaspoon fresh thyme leaves

Freshly ground white pepper

1½ to 1¾ cups Savory Chicken Broth (page 229)

Preheat the oven to 400°F. With 3 tablespoons of the softened butter, generously grease a medium earthenware or ceramic baking dish, such as a 3-inch-deep 12-inch oval dish.

Peel the potatoes and reserve in a large bowl of cold water to prevent discoloration.

Place the leeks in a large bowl of cold water and soak for several minutes to remove any grit between the layers. Remove from the water and pat thoroughly dry. Set aside.

TO COOK THE ONIONS: Heat 2 tablespoons of the olive oil in a medium skillet over medium heat. Add the onions, season with salt, and cook, stirring, for 1 minute. Add the leek greens and stir to coat with the oil. Cover the pan and cook until the onions and leeks are soft and translucent, 4 to 6 minutes; shake the pan often to make sure they do not brown. Add the thyme and a pinch of white pepper, stir to combine, and remove from the heat. Transfer the onion mixture to the buttered baking dish and spread evenly over the bottom.

TO ASSEMBLE THE GRATIN: Remove the potatoes from the water and pat dry. Cut into ¼-inch-thick slices. Season the potatoes and leeks with 1 teaspoon salt and ½ teaspoon white pepper. At a short end of the pan, arrange a row of leeks, from top to bottom, standing on end and tilted at a slight angle. Arrange a row of potatoes next to the leeks, positioned in the same way. Continue across the pan, alternating leeks and potatoes, until all the vegetables are used up. (You'll have four rows of leeks and four of potatoes.) Dot the remaining 4 tablespoons butter by teaspoonfuls over the potatoes and leeks. Bring the chicken broth to a boil and pour over the vegetables, to come three quarters of the way up the potatoes.

TO BAKE THE GRATIN: Place in the center of the oven and bake for 25 minutes. Lower the oven temperature to 375°F and bake for about another 45 to 50 minutes, until the top of the potato-leek mixture is nicely browned and the potatoes are tender. (The potatoes are done when they offer no resistance when pierced with the tip of a sharp knife.) If the vegetables darken too much in the first 25 minutes, cover loosely with aluminum foil. Remove from the oven and let stand for 10 minutes.

Drizzle the remaining 1 tablespoon of olive oil over the top and serve.

[La Mer]

SHELLFISH AND FISH

"Marine flavors from throughout the spectrum mesh beautifully when well combined. I often pair fish or lobster with shellfish and make a sauce from the shellfish broth. What you must seek to preserve is the authentic taste of an ingredient and its environment."

IN FRANCE, WE ARE ENORMOUSLY FORTUNATE

to be bounded by two very different seas, the Mediterranean and the Atlantic, the waters of which yield a great diversity of fish and shellfish. I have loved fish ever since I was a child, growing up on a farm. There, meat was our "daily bread," and fish, especially salmon, was the special-occasion treat. You might say to me, "Salmon is a banal fish, something you see on every menu," but for me it has always meant celebration. Every holiday, every special occasion, out of the kitchen would come this beautiful, succulent fish caught by local fishermen in the River Adour. The best quality today, of course, is wild salmon. But wild or farmed, the essential is that the fish be of an irreproachable freshness. Today, fish and shellfish

dominate among the appetizers and the main courses on my menus in both Monte Carlo and Paris.

I love the pure taste of the sea—that distinctive, slightly iodized marine flavor of a sea bass or turbot, the delicately sweet, subtly briny flavor of a lobster—but it can come through only when fish or shellfish is cooked and presented simply and without artifice. The one thing all the recipes in this chapter have in common is the simplicity of preparation of the seafood itself, usually at the last minute, just before serving. It is with the accompaniments that the *tours de main* come into play. We honor the seafood by staying true to its unique taste and texture, by cooking it simply and lightly, and by spooning on the sauce and arranging the garnish with great restraint.

SPINY LOBSTER WITH A RHUBARB-GINGER CHARDONNAY SAUCE

Serves 4

THE SPINY LOBSTER POACHES in a wonderfully aromatic court bouillon perfumed with lemon balm, vanilla, ginger, and Szechuan peppercorns. The court bouillon is then transformed into a delicate, fresh-flavored sauce.

14 tablespoons (1¾ sticks) unsalted butter

3 stalks rhubarb, trimmed and sliced diagonally into 2-inch pieces

1 vanilla bean, split

⅓ cup Szechuan peppercorns

¼ pound fresh lemon balm

1 tablespoon thinly sliced ginger

1 bottle (750 ml) Chardonnay

1 cup water

½ teaspoon fine sea salt, or to taste

Two 1½-pound spiny lobsters (rock lobsters) (see page 243)

FOR THE VEGETABLE JULIENNE

5 tablespoons unsalted butter

1 medium carrot, peeled and sliced into thin julienne

1 tablespoon finely julienned black truffle

2 leeks (white part only), split lengthwise, rinsed well, and sliced into thin julienne

2 large white mushrooms, stems removed, wiped clean, and sliced into thin julienne

½ medium onion, sliced into thin rings

TO PREPARE THE COURT BOUILLON: Melt 1 tablespoon of the butter in a large pot over medium heat. Add the rhubarb, vanilla bean, pepper, lemon balm, and ginger and stir to combine. Pour in all but ½ cup of the wine. Add the water and salt and bring to a boil, then reduce the heat and cook at a low boil for 25 minutes.

Strain the court bouillon and return to the pot. Bring to a boil, add the lobsters, and return to a full boil. Cover and cook until just cooked through, about 10 minutes. With tongs, transfer the lobsters to a cutting board to cool slightly.

Strain the court bouillon into a clean pot, set over low heat, bring to a boil, and reduce by half. Remove from the heat and set aside.

TO PREPARE THE LOBSTERS: Preheat the oven to 200°F.

Turn each lobster on its back and, using a sharp knife or kitchen scissors, cut down the center of the tail shell. Leaving the tail attached to the body, carefully remove the tail shell. Remove the intestinal tract that runs the length of the tail. With a large sharp knife, split each lobster lengthwise and remove the small stomach pouch. Place the lobsters in a buttered baking dish.

Melt 3 tablespoons of the butter and brush the lobsters generously with the butter to prevent them from drying out. Put them in the oven to keep warm.

TO PREPARE THE VEGETABLE JULIENNE: One at a time, sauté each of the vegetables separately in a small skillet: Melt 1 tablespoon of the butter over low heat. Add the carrots and sauté just until they soften,

3 to 4 minutes; just before they finish cooking, add 1 teaspoon of the truffle to the pan. Transfer to a plate and repeat with the leeks and then the mushrooms, using 1 tablespoon butter for each and adding 1 teaspoon of the truffle at the end of cooking. Melt the remaining 2 tablespoons butter, add the onion to the skillet, and cook, stirring, until lightly browned, about 8 minutes. Transfer to a medium skillet, add the other sautéed vegetables and 1 tablespoon of the court bouillon, cover, and set over very low heat to keep warm.

TO FINISH THE DISH: Bring the court bouillon to a boil over medium heat, then whisk in the remaining 10 tablespoons butter, about 1 teaspoon at a time, until the sauce emulsifies. Reduce the heat to low and stir frequently until it stops boiling, then stir in the reserved ½ cup Chardonnay. Strain the sauce over the julienned vegetables and adjust the seasoning to taste.

To serve, divide half the julienned vegetables among four warmed soup plates. Place a lobster half in each plate and spoon on the remaining vegetables. Ladle on some of the sauce, transfer the remaining sauce to a sauceboat, and serve on the side.

SAUTÉED LANGOUSTINES ON A BED OF CRISP VEGETABLES

Serves 4 as a first course

A HANDFUL OF CRISP, marinated raw vegetables—baby fava beans, cucumber, radishes, celery, and Boston and romaine lettuce—mixed with tomato confit form a bed for this light, bright salad. A pleasantly tart shrimp condiment adds a vibrant counterpoint to the quickly sautéed langoustines.

1 medium seedless (hothouse) cucumber, peeled and cut into small dice

2 tablespoons coarse sea salt or kosher salt

FOR THE SHRIMP SAUCE

¼ pound small shrimp, peeled

1 tablespoon olive oil

Fine sea salt and freshly ground black pepper

1 tablespoon sherry vinegar

¼ cup balsamic vinegar

4 pieces Tomato Confit (page 232)

8 radishes, trimmed and sliced paper-thin

⅓ cup shelled fresh baby fava beans, tough skin removed

1 celery stalk with leaves, peeled and sliced paper-thin on the diagonal, leaves reserved

4 branches fresh dill, stems discarded, leaves chopped

5 to 6 firm Boston lettuce leaves, ribs removed and sliced diagonally into 2-inch pieces (leaves reserved for another use)

1 small head romaine lettuce, separated into leaves, and torn into small pieces

FOR THE VINAIGRETTE

2 tablespoons truffle juice

2 tablespoons fresh lemon juice

Fine sea salt and freshly ground black pepper

1 cup olive oil

2 tablespoons olive oil

16 langoustines (about 4 pounds), peeled (see page 243)

Fine sea salt and freshly ground black pepper

Put the cucumber in a colander and toss with the salt. Let stand for 30 minutes, until the cucumber has released most of its water.

MEANWHILE, MAKE THE BASE FOR THE SHRIMP SAUCE: Combine the shrimp and olive oil in a mini-food processor or a blender and process until ground, 30 to 40 seconds. Season with salt and pepper. Add the sherry vinegar and balsamic vinegar and purée. With a wooden spoon, press the ground shrimp through a fine strainer into a bowl. Adjust the seasoning and set aside.

Rinse the cucumber well under cold water, pat dry, and transfer to a salad bowl. Add the tomato confit, radishes, fava beans, cucumber, celery, dill, the Boston lettuce ribs, and the romaine leaves.

TO PREPARE THE VINAIGRETTE: Place the truffle juice in a small bowl. Whisk in the lemon juice and season with salt and pepper. Whisk in the olive oil until emulsified. Spoon 5 tablespoons of the dressing over the salad and toss well. Set aside to marinate for 4 to 5 minutes. Transfer the remaining dressing to a sauceboat.

TO COOK THE LANGOUSTINES: In each of two large skillets, heat 1 tablespoon of olive oil over high heat. Add half of the langoustines to each pan, season with salt and pepper, and sauté, turning once or twice, until lightly browned, 2 to 3 minutes. Transfer to a warmed plate and cover loosely to keep warm.

TO FINISH THE DISH: Heat 2 tablespoons of the reserved ground shrimp in a small frying pan over medium heat. Whisk in 1 tablespoon of the vinaigrette and cook, stirring, until the ground shrimp are just warmed through and pink, about 1 minute. Remove from the heat.

Divide the salad among four serving plates. Arrange 4 langoustines in the center of each plate and season with salt and pepper. Spoon the sauce onto the plate to dip the langoustines in. Serve immediately with the remaining vinaigrette on the side.

SUGGESTED WINE

A WHITE WINE WITH A HINT OF HERBS, SUCH AS A DOMAINE DE LA COURTADE BLANC 1993 CÔTES DE PROVENCE, OR A MARKHAM SAUVIGNON BLANC 1996, FROM THE NAPA VALLEY. FOR THE RECIPE ON PAGE 84, A BIG CHARDONNAY, SUCH AS ST. AUBIN BLANC 1995, DOMAINE LARUE, OR NAPA'S TREFETHEN 1994.

[*Vol au Vent aux Cuisses de Grenouilles, Écrevisses, et Champignons*]

PUFF PASTRY SHELL WITH FROG'S LEGS, CRAYFISH, AND MUSHROOMS

INDIVIDUAL PUFF PASTRY cases are overstuffed with poached pike quenelles; sautéed girolle mushrooms; black truffles; sautéed frog's legs; littleneck clams that have been opened in a white wine–shallot broth; crayfish that have been poached, shelled, and sautéed; and slices of raw cèpes. All are bound with an ivory-colored sauce made by cooking together shallots, garlic, mushroom stems, parsley, frog's legs, white wine, and a pike fish bouillon, then straining the broth, thickening it with cream and butter, and seasoning with clam juice. The plates are finished by spooning some of the sauce around the filled pastry cases. Into this sauce are swirled drops of a green sauce made by boiling, blending, and straining spinach, watercress, and parsley.

SHELLFISH SALAD WITH WHITE BEANS AND ARUGULA

Serves 4 as a first course

THE ELEGANT SIMPLICITY OF THIS DISH, which can also be served as a light main course, requires quite a bit of behind-the-scenes labor and a broad array of ingredients, but the result—as much a ragout as a salad—is well worth the effort. (You can prepare the court bouillon the night before if you like; the octopus should be frozen overnight to tenderize it.) The baby squid, langoustines, octopus, lobster, and two kinds of clams are cooked separately, then combined with tender white beans and chilled briefly. The cool seafood mixture is presented on a crisp bed of arugula, topped with warm sautéed lobster and langoustines.

1 small octopus (about 1 pound)

FOR THE WHITE BEANS

½ cup white beans, such as Great Northern, picked over, rinsed, soaked overnight in cold water to cover, and drained

1 bouquet garni

1 onion, cut in half

1 large carrot, peeled and cut into 3 pieces

½ garlic bulb

Fine sea salt

FOR THE COURT BOUILLON

4 cups water

1 bouquet garni

1 onion, chopped

1 carrot, peeled and chopped

1½ cups dry white wine

½ teaspoon fine sea salt

1 teaspoon black peppercorns

½ cup white wine vinegar

1 bouquet garni

1 tomato, peeled, seeded (seeds reserved), and diced

FOR THE SEAFOOD

Two 1½-pound spiny lobsters (rock lobsters) (see page 243)

7 to 8 tablespoons olive oil

36 littleneck or cherrystone clams, scrubbed, soaked for 1 minute in a bowl under cold running water, and drained

1 medium shallot, finely chopped, plus ½ shallot, finely chopped, if using the razor clams

¼ cup dry white wine, plus ¼ cup if using the razor clams

8 razor clams, scrubbed, soaked for 1 minute in a bowl under cold running water, and drained (optional)

4 large langoustines, shelled (see page 243)

6 ounces baby squid, or cleaned small squid bodies without tentacles

½ cup Chicken Stock (page 229)

½ cup chopped fresh flat-leaf parsley

8 tablespoons (1 stick) unsalted butter, cut into bits

Fine sea salt and freshly ground black pepper

Juice of 1 lemon

¼ pound arugula, trimmed and torn into small pieces

Seal the baby octopus in a freezer bag and freeze overnight to tenderize the flesh.

THE NEXT DAY, remove the octopus from the freezer and set aside to thaw.

TO PREPARE THE WHITE BEANS: Place the beans, bouquet garni, onion, carrot, and garlic in a large pot and add cold water to cover by about 1 inch. Bring to a boil over high heat, reduce the heat to medium, and cook until the beans are tender, about 1½ hours. When the beans are almost cooked, season with salt. Drain the beans, discard the onion, carrot, garlic, and bouquet garni, and set aside.

MEANWHILE, PREPARE THE COURT BOUILLON: Combine all the ingredients except the vinegar in a large saucepan and bring to a boil over high heat. Reduce the heat to medium-low and simmer for 5 minutes. Add the vinegar and simmer for 15 minutes longer. Remove from the heat and let cool, then transfer to a bowl.

TO PREPARE THE OCTOPUS: Combine 2 cups of the court bouillon, the bouquet garni, and the reserved tomato seeds in a pot and bring to a boil over medium heat. Add the octopus, cover, reduce the heat, and simmer until tender, 45 minutes to 1 hour. Check the pot occasionally to make sure at least ½ inch of liquid always covers the bottom of the small pot, adding water if necessary. Remove from the heat and let cool.

Peel the skin from the octopus and scrape out and discard the head and viscera. Slice the tentacles of the octopus into thin rings, cover, and set aside.

TO PREPARE THE SEAFOOD: Bring the remaining court bouillon to a boil in a large pot over high heat. Add the lobsters, cover, and cook for 9 minutes. Transfer to a cutting board to cool slightly.

In a large pot, heat 1 tablespoon of the olive oil over medium heat. Add the littleneck clams and one of the chopped shallots, stir well, and cook for 1 minute. Pour in the ¼ cup white wine, cover tightly, and cook, shaking the pot occasionally, until the clams have opened, about 5 minutes. Transfer the clams to a colander set over a large bowl, discarding any that have not opened, and let cool slightly. Strain the cooking liquid though a strainer lined with cheesecloth into a medium bowl and set aside.

Working over the colander, shuck half the clams. Transfer to a bowl, cover, and set aside. Transfer the remaining clams to another bowl and set aside. Strain the liquid remaining in the bowl through the cheesecloth-lined sieve, into the medium bowl; reserve.

If using the razor clams, wipe out the pot and heat 1 tablespoon of oil over medium heat. Add the razor clams and the remaining shallot, stir well, and cook for 1 minute. Pour in the remaining ¼ cup wine, cover tightly, and cook, shaking the pot occasionally, until the clams have opened, about 5 minutes. Transfer the clams to a colander set over a bowl, discarding any that have not opened, and let cool slightly. Strain the cooking liquid through the cheesecloth-lined sieve into the reserved clam broth.

Working over the colander, shuck the razor clams. Transfer to a bowl and set aside. Strain the liquid in the bowl into the clam broth.

Separate the lobster tails from the bodies (reserve the bodies for stock if desired). Turn each tail over and, using a sharp knife or kitchen scissors, cut down the center of the shell, without piercing the meat. Carefully remove the shell, then the intestinal tract. Cut each tail into 8 slices.

In a medium skillet, heat 1 tablespoon of the olive oil over medium-low heat. Add the lobster slices and cook, stirring frequently, just until they are barely cooked and begin to color slightly, 1 to 2 minutes. Transfer to an ovenproof platter, cover, and set aside.

In the same pan, heat 1 more tablespoon of the olive oil over medium-low heat. Add the langoustines and cook, stirring frequently, until just cooked through and starting to color slightly, about 5 minutes. Add to the platter with the lobster, cover, and set aside.

Preheat the oven to 200°F.

TO FINISH THE DISH: Combine the baby squid, littleneck and razor clams, and the baby octopus in a medium pot and add the reserved clam broth, the chicken stock, parsley, the cooked beans, and the diced tomato. Stir well and set over medium heat. Add the butter, 3 tablespoons of the olive oil, ½ teaspoon salt, and pepper to taste and cook, shaking the pan frequently, until the seafood is well coated and the sauce has thickened slightly and reduced by about one third. Adjust the seasoning and remove from the heat.

Transfer the seafood mixture to a small bowl and place in an ice bath to chill; stir occasionally. Stir in the lemon juice.

Meanwhile, place the plate of lobster and langoustines in the oven to warm through.

Scatter the arugula leaves over the bottom of 4 large soup plates. Divide the chilled seafood mixture among the plates and arrange the lobster slices and langoustines on top. Spoon any juices on the platter over the lobster and langoustines, drizzle the remaining 1 tablespoon olive oil over the top, and serve immediately.

SUGGESTED WINE

A BIG, SUNNY WHITE WINE, SUCH AS A CHÂTEAU SIMONE
BLANC 1992 PALETTE, OR A NAPA VALLEY FAR NIENTE
ESTATE BOTTLED CHARDONNAY 1995

ALAIN CHAPEL'S LOBSTER RAGOUT WITH POTATOES

Serves 4

A SIMPLE, REFINED STEW with distinctive, sunlit flavor, this ragout is a recipe from late chef Alain Chapel, who was inspired to create this dish after a trip to the remote Breton island of Sein. There he saw fishermen just back from the sea with their haul of lobsters boil up a big pot of seawater, putting in whatever shellfish they had on hand, and perhaps a piece of eel. Then they added potatoes and the lobsters' coral and served the whole thing up straight from the pot to accompany the hot grilled lobsters. In this version, the lobster is very briefly boiled, then sautéed in olive oil, giving a wonderful roasted flavor to the meat. This unusual technique produces such delicious results that you may never return to simply boiling or steaming lobster again!

1 pound littleneck clams, scrubbed, soaked for 1 minute in a bowl under cold running water, and drained

One ½-pound slice saltwater eel, skinned

½ bottle (about 2 cups) dry white wine, such as Muscadet

½ cup olive oil

6 baby spring onions (white and tender green parts only), diced

½ cup chopped onions

1 large carrot, peeled and diced

1 leek, trimmed, split lengthwise in half, rinsed well, and thinly sliced

2 tomatoes, peeled, cut into sixths, and seeded

⅓ cup celery leaves

6 garlic cloves, unpeeled

1¼ pounds tiny Yukon Gold potatoes

Four 1½-pound lobsters, preferably female

2 teaspoons fine sea salt

1 teaspoon freshly ground black pepper

2 tablespoons unsalted butter, softened

Preheat the oven to 375°F.

TO COOK THE CLAMS: Combine the clams, eel, and wine in a large saucepan and add enough cold water to just cover. Bring to a boil over medium-high heat, cover, reduce the heat to medium, and cook until the clams open, 5 to 10 minutes. Remove from the heat. Remove the clams and the eel, discarding any clams that have not opened. Strain the broth. Set the clams aside in a bowl, and reserve the eel with the clam broth.

TO PREPARE THE VEGETABLES: Heat 3 tablespoons of the olive oil in a large cast-iron or other heavy-bottomed oven-proof casserole over medium heat. Stir in the spring onions, chopped onions, carrot, leek, tomatoes, celery leaves, and garlic and cook just until the vegetables begin to soften, 2 to 3 minutes. Add the potatoes, the reserved clam broth and eel, and the salt and pepper and stir to combine. Cover and cook in the center of the oven for 45 to 50 minutes, until the vegetables are tender and the liquid has reduced and thickened.

MEANWHILE, PREPARE THE LOBSTERS: Fill a large stockpot with water and bring to a boil over high heat. To kill the lobsters quickly, plunge them into the boiling water, return the water to a boil, and cook for 1 minute. Remove the lobsters from the pot and let cool slightly.

Cut the lobsters into pieces: Cut off each claw and crack the shells. Cut off the tails and split them lengthwise, cutting them from the softer underside of the shell. Scoop out the coral, if any, from the bodies of the lobsters and mash with a tablespoon in a small bowl; reserve.

Heat the remaining 5 tablespoons olive oil in a large skillet over medium-high heat. Add the lobster claws and tails in batches and sauté, turning once or twice, until the tail meat is almost cooked through and the shells have turned a deep reddish-orange color, 2 to 3 minutes. Remove from the heat.

TO FINISH THE DISH: About 10 minutes before the ragout is cooked, stir in the reserved coral, if any, and the butter, cover, and return to the oven. After 5 minutes, add the lobster claws and tails and the reserved clams, cover, and return to the oven for 5 minutes. Bring the casserole to the table and serve directly from it.

SUGGESTED WINE

A BIG CHARDONNAY, SUCH AS A POUILLY FUISSÉ "LES CARRONS" 1992,
R. DENOGENT, OR A MONDAVI CHARDONNAY RESERVE 1995, FROM THE NAPA VALLEY.
FOR THE RECIPE ON PAGE 94, HERMITAGE BLANC 1995, B. FAURIE, OR HAMILTON
RUSSELL 1997 "WALKER BAY" CHARDONNAY, FROM SOUTH AFRICA.

SPIT-ROASTED LOBSTER WITH CARAMELIZED SALSIFY AND ALMONDS

Serves 4

SWEET, TENDER LOBSTER MEAT is combined with braised and caramelized salsify, with its delicate flavor reminiscent of artichokes, and topped by roasted almonds. The lobster is spit-roasted, which leaves the meat extremely succulent. (You can oven-roast it if you don't have a spit or rotisserie set-up.)

10 salsify

Juice of 1 lemon

8 tablespoons (1 stick) unsalted butter, plus 1 tablespoon if desired

1 tablespoon olive oil

About ¾ cup Chicken Stock (page 229)

Fine sea salt and freshly ground black pepper

1 cup sliced blanched almonds

3 tablespoons balsamic vinegar

Four 1½-pound lobsters

2 tablespoons Cognac

1 shallot, finely chopped

5 branches fresh flat-leaf parsley, stems removed, leaves chopped

TO PREPARE THE SALSIFY: Peel the salsify. Slice 3 salsify on the diagonal into ⅛-inch slices. Place in a bowl of cold water, and add half the lemon juice. Cut the remaining salsify into 4½-inch-long bâtonnets (see page 248).

Heat 4 tablespoons of the butter and the olive oil in a medium skillet over medium heat. Add the salsify bâtonnets and cook until they begin to soften, without coloring, about 3 minutes. Add just enough chicken stock to come to the top of the salsify and cook, shaking the pan and turning the salsify with a spatula occasionally, until tender when pierced with a knife, 6 to 8 minutes; add additional stock if necessary to keep the salsify moist. Season with salt and pepper, transfer to an ovenproof platter, cover, and set aside.

Melt 1 tablespoon of the butter in a heavy skillet over medium heat. Drain the sliced salsify, pat dry, and add to the pan. Cook, stirring, until lightly browned. Add the almonds and cook, stirring frequently, until the salsify caramelizes, turning a deep, shiny brown, about 6 minutes. Season with salt and pepper, pour in the vinegar, and stir to scrape up all the browned bits from the bottom and sides of the pan. Remove from the heat and set aside.

TO PREPARE THE LOBSTERS: Preheat the spit or preheat the oven to 425°F.

Bring a lobster pot or other large pot of water to a rolling boil. To kill the lobsters quickly, plunge them into the boiling water, return the water to a boil, and cook for 1 minute. Remove from the pot and pat dry. Set the lobsters into the spit "cage" and roast for 10 minutes. Or place on a baking sheet and roast in the oven for 10 minutes. Remove to a cutting board and let cool slightly.

Preheat the oven (or reduce the temperature) to 200°F.

With a sharp knife, cut off the lobster claws and tails. Reserve the coral, if any, and set aside in a bowl. Cut the heads into large pieces and place in a blender. Add ½ cup of the chicken stock, 2 tablespoons of the butter, and 1 tablespoon of the Cognac and blend at high speed until the shells are pulverized and the mixture is well blended. Strain the sauce through a fine strainer into a bowl, pressing on the solids to extract all the liquid, and set aside.

Crack the claws and remove the meat. Split the tail shells, remove the meat, and cut each tail lengthwise in half. Transfer the lobster to a heatproof bowl and place in the oven, along with the salsify sticks, to keep warm.

TO FINISH THE SAUCE: Melt the remaining 1 tablespoon butter in a medium skillet over medium heat. Add the shallots and cook, stirring, until they soften, about 2 minutes. Stir in the remaining 1 tablespoon Cognac, scraping up any browned bits stuck to the bottom of the pan, then pour the reserved lobster sauce through a fine strainer into the pan and stir to combine. Cook until the sauce reduces by one quarter, then add the coral, if you have it; do not let the sauce boil after adding the coral. If you would like the sauce a little richer, swirl in 1 more tablespoon of butter. Adjust the seasoning to taste, then stir in 1 teaspoon of the remaining lemon juice, or more to taste, and the parsley. Remove from the heat.

Divide the salsify bâtonnets among four warmed serving plates. Arrange 2 lobster tail pieces and 2 claws on each plate and scatter on the caramelized salsify and almonds. Drizzle on the sauce and serve immediately.

RISOTTO WITH CUTTLEFISH AND SAUTÉED SQUID

Serves 4

INFLUENCED BY ITALY'S PROXIMITY, this delicately briny risotto from Southeast France is studded with cuttlefish and topped with sautéed squid.

5 tablespoons fruity extra-virgin olive oil

½ pound small squid, cleaned, tentacles cut off and discarded (or saved for another use), bodies cut into ¼-inch slices

Fine sea salt and freshly ground black pepper

½ cup dry white wine

6 tablespoons unsalted butter

3 tablespoons chopped fresh flat-leaf parsley

4 cups Chicken Stock (page 229) or water

1 cuttlefish (about 1 pound), cleaned, tentacles cut off and saved for another use, body cut into small dice

1 medium onion, finely chopped

1 cup Arborio or other risotto rice

1 cup heavy cream, whipped to soft peaks

½ teaspoon fresh lemon juice

TO PREPARE THE SQUID: Heat 1 tablespoon olive oil in a large skillet over medium-high heat. Add the squid and cook, stirring, until juices reduce and lightly caramelize, 1 to 1½ minutes. Season with salt and pepper, add 1 tablespoon of the wine, 2 tablespoons butter, and parsley. Stir to melt the butter; set aside.

TO PREPARE THE RISOTTO: Bring the chicken stock to a boil; reduce the heat and keep at a low boil. Heat 2 tablespoons of the olive oil and 2 tablespoons of the butter in a large deep cast-iron or other heavy pot over medium heat. Add the cuttlefish, onion, and rice and stir to coat well with the oil and butter. Reduce the heat to low and cook, stirring constantly, until the onions are pale golden, about 5 minutes. Stir in the remaining white wine and cook, stirring, until all the wine has been absorbed. Pour in 1½ cups of the boiling chicken stock and cook, stirring constantly, until the stock has been absorbed. Add another ½ cup stock and continue to cook, stirring and adding ½ cup more stock each time the rice has absorbed the liquid, until the rice is barely cooked through but not mushy, about 18 minutes. You may not need all the stock.

Meanwhile, warm the squid over low heat without boiling.

Stir the remaining 2 tablespoons each butter and olive oil and the whipped cream into the risotto, then stir in the lemon juice. Season to taste and remove from the heat. Divide the risotto among four warmed soup plates, garnish with the squid, spooning their juices over them, and serve immediately.

Variation: In Italy and the Basque country, this risotto is traditionally colored jet black with cuttlefish ink, which is added with the whipped cream.

[
SUGGESTED WINE

A POTENT WHITE OR RED WINE, SUCH AS A CHATEAUNEUF-DU-PAPE BLANC 1994, CHÂTEAU DE LA GARDINE, OR A RED TAURASI 1990 MASTROBERARDINO CAMPANIE, FROM ITALY
]

[*Coquilles Saint-Jacques Poêlées, Crème de Laitue*]

SAUTÉED SEA SCALLOPS
WITH LETTUCE-BUTTER SAUCE

LETTUCE LEAVES ARE BLANCHED IN CHICKEN STOCK JUST TO WILT, then refreshed in cold water to keep their bright color, and finally puréed. Peppercorn-infused chicken stock is thickened with a bit of cornstarch, boiled, strained, and combined with the lettuce purée. Brown butter is whisked in and the sauce is spooned over the bottom of the plate. Scallops, seared in butter, are placed in the lettuce-butter sauce and topped with slices of white or black truffle (depending on which is in season). A sprinkle of coarse sea salt and a drizzle of olive oil (if the truffle is black) or beurre noisette (if white) complete the dish.

SCALLOPS STEAMED IN THEIR SHELLS

Serves 4 as a first course

STEAMING PERFECTLY FRESH SCALLOPS in their shells reveals their delicately sweet flavor as no other cooking technique can, while it keeps their creamy flesh moist. You'll need spoons to scoop up the scallop-infused butter sauce, or you can drink it right from the shell. To accompany this delicate dish, serve a simple salad of baby greens tossed lightly in balsamic vinaigrette.

In France, scallops are sold live in their shells. Here you'll have to buy scallop shells to make this dish. Since the puff pastry is only for sealing the shells, you can use a store-bought variety.

FOR SEALING THE SHELLS

1 pound puff pastry

2 large egg yolks, beaten with
   1 teaspoon water, for glaze

12 large very fresh sea scallops
   (about 1¼ pounds)

4 tablespoons salted butter

24 sea scallop shells

5 cups coarse sea salt or kosher salt

Preheat the oven to 425°F.

On a floured surface, roll out the puff pastry very thin, ¹⁄₁₆ to ⅛ inch thick. Cut the pastry into 1- by 13-inch strips.

Set each scallop in the center of a shell. Place 1 teaspoon butter on top of each scallop and cover with a second shell. Seal each double shell with a strip of puff pastry, cutting and piecing the pastry as necessary (you'll need a strip about 18 inches long to seal each shell). Encircle the edges completely to leave no gaps, and press firmly to be sure the dough adheres to the shell. Glaze the tops and sides of the dough with egg wash.

Spread the salt evenly in two 12- by 17-inch jelly-roll pans. Nestle the shells in the salt and bake for 13 minutes. Serve immediately, arranging 3 scallop shells on each warmed dinner plate.

Variations: Place a tiny bed of one of the following in each scallop shell before adding the scallops:

Trim the root ends from 3 medium leeks, and trim off all but the bottom 4 inches of each. Split the leeks lengthwise in half, rinse well, and cut into 2-inch-long julienne strips. Cook, covered, in 1½ tablespoons salted butter with ¼ teaspoon coarse sea salt over low heat until very soft but not brown, about 15 minutes.

Or, trim the stems from 4 ounces oyster or white mushrooms and wipe clean. Slice the caps. Cook in 1½ tablespoons salted butter over medium-high heat until tender but not browned, about 3 minutes. Sprinkle with a few grains of coarse sea salt.

SUGGESTED WINE

A BRIGHT, LIVELY WHITE WINE, SUCH AS A
MACON CLESSÉ BLANC 1989, DOMAINE J. THEVENET, OR
A WOODWARD CANYON CHARDONNAY 1995, FROM OREGON

GRILLED SCALLOPS WITH BLACK TRUFFLES AND BROWN BUTTER

Serves 4 as a first course

SERVED ON A BED OF SLIGHTLY BITTER GREENS, sweet, briny scallops, each stuffed with a slice of truffle, are complemented by the smooth, nutlike flavor of the browned butter. The scallops are grilled briefly, just to mark them, then finished in the oven so they cook evenly. (If necessary, use a grill grid or vegetable basket to keep the scallops from falling through the grate. If you don't have a grill, sear the scallops in a hot skillet over medium-high heat until lightly browned on both sides.)

1 medium black truffle

24 sea scallops (1½ to 2 pounds)

FOR THE VINAIGRETTE

2 tablespoons balsamic vinegar

2 tablespoons sherry vinegar

¼ teaspoon fine sea salt

6 tablespoons extra-virgin olive oil

½ pound (2 sticks) unsalted butter

2 tablespoons extra-virgin olive oil

FOR THE SALAD

1 small head radicchio, leaves separated and tough center ribs trimmed

2 cups (about 3 ounces) mesclun

2 cups (about 3 ounces) oak leaf lettuce, tough center ribs trimmed

2 cups (about 3 ounces) lamb's lettuce, stems trimmed

Coarse sea salt and freshly ground black pepper

1 small bunch fresh chives, cut into 1½-inch pieces

1 small handful fresh chervil leaves

TO PREPARE THE SCALLOPS: Using a truffle slicer, mandoline, or a very sharp knife, cut 24 very thin slices from the truffle. Set the remaining uncut truffle aside. Using a very sharp knife, slice the scallops horizontally almost but not all the way in half. Slide a truffle slice into the center of each scallop and press closed. Set aside.

TO PREPARE THE VINAIGRETTE: In a medium bowl, combine the vinegars with the salt and whisk to dissolve the salt. Gradually add the olive oil, whisking to emulsify. Set aside.

TO MAKE THE BEURRE NOISETTE: Melt the butter in a medium skillet over medium heat and cook until nut-brown and fragrant. Strain through a strainer lined with cheesecloth into a small saucepan. Set aside.

Preheat the oven to 400°F. Oil a baking dish large enough to hold the scallops in a single layer, or oil a baking sheet. Heat the grill until hot.

Brush the scallops lightly with the olive oil. Grill, turning once, just long enough to mark them on both sides. Transfer to the oiled baking dish and set aside.

TO PREPARE THE SALAD: Combine all the lettuces except the lamb's lettuce in a salad bowl. Whisk the vinaigrette again, then pour over the salad and toss well. Arrange the lamb's lettuce in a slightly overlapping border around the edges of each of four serving plates. Arrange an airy "bouquet" of the salad in the center of each plate, leaving about a 1½-inch ring between the lamb's lettuce and the salad.

Place the scallops in the oven and bake for about 1 minute, just until heated through. Rewarm the beurre noisette over medium heat.

Arrange 6 scallops on each plate, in the space between the lettuces. Season each scallop with a pinch of coarse sea salt and one turn of the pepper mill, then drizzle the brown butter over them. Grate the remaining truffle over the scallops, scatter on the chives and the chervil, and serve immediately.

SUGGESTED WINE

A RICH, UNCTUOUS WHITE WINE, SUCH AS A
CHÂTEAU BELLERIVE 1985 QUARTS DE CHAUME OR A
WASHINGTON HILLS SEMILLON CHARDONNAY,
COLUMBIA VALLEY VARIETAL SELECT, FROM WASHINGTON

[*Huîtres Belon dans Leur Jus Crémé, Crépinette Grillée*]

BELON OYSTERS WITH CREPINETTE SAUSAGES

BELON OYSTERS are shelled and poached in their own juices. Thin slices of carrots and onions and julienned leeks are gently cooked in butter, then simmered until tender in white wine with whole black peppercorns and orange peel tied in cheesecloth.

The oyster-poaching liquid and the white wine vegetable broth are combined and reduced to intensify the flavors. Then cream is added to the sauce to thicken and enrich. A drop of lemon juice is whisked in and seasonings adjusted.

The hot oysters and vegetable garnish are spooned over lamb's lettuce in the bottom of a soup plate. The oysters are coated with the cream sauce, and carrot slices and chervil are sprinkled over. Flat sausages made with sweetbreads and black truffles, wrapped in lacy crepinette, lightly coated in bread crumbs, and gently grilled, are served as a side dish.

SAUTÉED SALT COD WITH PROVENÇAL VEGETABLES

Serves 4

SALT COD, POPULAR ALL ALONG THE MEDITERRANEAN COAST, and especially in the port of Marseilles, is cooked very simply here, meunière-style, dredged in flour and sautéed in butter, then served atop an array of Provençal vegetables and sliced potatoes. The colorful vegetables—red, yellow, and green peppers, leeks, fennel, and garlic—cook slowly, almost like a sweet jam, to the consistency of a compote. The sauce is like a reduced bouillabaisse with fewer tomatoes and no saffron. (The salt cod has to soak for three days.)

FOR THE COD

1 pound salt cod with skin

2 cups milk

3 star anise, sliced into julienne strips

FOR THE FISH BROTH

2 tablespoons olive oil

1 large onion, thinly sliced

Fine sea salt

5 cloves garlic, unpeeled and crushed

½ fennel bulb, trimmed, outer layer peeled off, cored, and sliced

2 branches dried fennel or ½ teaspoon fennel seed

2 small tomatoes, quartered

2 pounds rockfish or other inexpensive white-fleshed fish, cleaned

½ bunch fresh basil

8 white peppercorns

Zest from 1 lemon, removed with a vegetable peeler in 4 strips

FOR THE VEGETABLES

6 to 8 tablespoons olive oil

9 garlic cloves, crushed

2 small onions, halved and sliced

2 medium leeks, split lengthwise, rinsed well, and sliced into julienne strips

2 small fennel bulbs, outer layer peeled off, trimmed, cored, and sliced into julienne strips

1 medium green bell pepper, cored, seeded, and sliced into julienne strips

1 medium red bell pepper, cored, seeded, and sliced into julienne strips

1 medium yellow bell pepper, cored, seeded, and sliced into julienne strips

Fine sea salt and freshly ground black pepper

2 small all-purpose potatoes (about ¾ pound), peeled and cut into ¼-inch slices

1 cup all-purpose flour

¼ cup olive oil

3 tablespoons unsalted butter

Skin of 1 lemon, sliced into twists

2 tablespoons fruity extra-virgin olive oil

THREE DAYS BEFORE YOU INTEND TO SERVE THE DISH: Place the cod in a large pot of cold water to cover. Let soak in the refrigerator for about 72 hours, changing the water three times during each 24-hour period.

TO PREPARE THE FISH BROTH: Heat the olive oil in a medium pot over medium heat. Add the onion, season with salt, and cook, stirring frequently, until translucent, about 5 minutes. Add the garlic and the fresh and dried fennel and cook, without coloring, about 5 minutes. Add the tomato quarters and cook until they melt, 3 to 5 minutes. Add the rockfish, basil stems, peppercorns, and lemon zest. Pour in enough water to cover, and bring to a simmer. Reduce the heat to low and cook for 20 minutes.

Strain the broth through a fine strainer into a bowl. You should have about 4 cups; if there is more, reserve for another use.

TO BLANCH THE COD: Drain the cod and set aside. In a large deep skillet, heat the milk to 180°F, or slightly below the boiling point; do not let it boil. Add the star anise, then add the cod, skin side down, and cook for 2½ minutes. (If necessary, cut the cod in half so it fits in the skillet.) Turn and cook for another 2½ minutes. Drain the cod, place skin side up on a clean kitchen towel, and pat dry.

TO PREPARE THE VEGETABLES: Heat 1 tablespoon of the olive oil in a large skillet over medium heat. Add the garlic and onions and cook, stirring occasionally, until the onions are translucent, about 3 minutes; if the onions start to color, add 1 more tablespoon olive oil. Stir in the leeks and cook until wilted, about 2 minutes. Stir in the fennel and cook until slightly softened, about 2 minutes. Add the green, red, and yellow pepper strips; if the pan seems dry, add 1 more tablespoon of olive oil, stirring well to combine. Season with salt and pepper to taste. Add 2 cups of the fish broth, stir well, cover, reduce the heat to low, and simmer gently, stirring occasionally, until the vegetables are meltingly tender and have the consistency of a compote, 30 to 35 minutes. Keep warm over very low heat until ready to serve.

MEANWHILE, PREPARE THE POTATOES: In a large skillet, heat 5 tablespoons of the olive oil over medium heat. Add the potatoes and stir to coat with oil. Season with salt and cook, stirring often, until nicely browned, about 10 minutes. Pour in the remaining 2 cups fish broth and simmer until the potatoes are very tender, 15 to 20 minutes. Remove from the heat, cover loosely, and set aside.

TO FINISH THE DISH: Dredge the cod in the flour, turning several times to coat well; pat off any excess. Heat the olive oil in a large skillet over medium heat. Place the fish skin side down in the pan and cook until the skin is lightly browned, about 3 minutes. Add the butter and heat until it starts to foam. Baste the fish with the oil and butter and cook until the skin is very crisp, another 2 minutes or so. Turn the fish over and cook just until golden brown, about 2 minutes. With a slotted spatula, transfer to paper towels to drain.

Using a slotted spoon, transfer the vegetable mixture to a warmed large platter, leaving the cooking juices in the pan. Spread the vegetables evenly over the bottom of the platter and cover with the potato slices. Reduce the cooking juices over medium heat until syrupy, 2 to 4 minutes.

Arrange the cod on top of the potatoes, spoon the sauce over, and garnish with the lemon twists. Drizzle on the fruity olive oil and serve immediately.

SUGGESTED WINE

A POWERFUL AND TANNIC RED WINE, SUCH AS A
CHÂTEAU LA TOUR LEVEQUE NOIR ET OR 1990, CÔTES
DE PROVENCE, OR A WASHINGTON STATE CHÂTEAU
STE. MICHELLE MERLOT, COLUMBIA VALLEY RESERVE 1993

[*Stockfisch: Delicat Ragoût de Tripettes aux Piquillos,
Olives de Nice, et Saucisse Perugina, Morue Pochée Puis Effeuillée*]

RAGOUT OF SALT COD WITH RED PEPPERS, OLIVES, AND SAUSAGES

THIS ELEGANT NIÇOISE STEW is made by gently cooking *tripettes* that have been soaked for 1 week in water and then gently cooked in olive oil with onion, red pepper, garlic, tomato, and dried, ground, fragrant Basque pepper. Salt cod, soaked separately for several days, is then poached in milk scented with star anise and dried fennel branch. Just before serving, the dish is seasoned with olive oil, sherry vinegar, salt and pepper, fresh parsley leaves, and tiny Niçoise olives. The poached fish, shredded and gently mixed with olive oil and a pinch of Basque pepper, garnishes the ragout. Each plate is then completed with small, sautéed, garlicky Perugina sausages.

SALMON WITH BÉARNAISE REDUCTION SAUCE

Serves 4

THE SAUCE IS ACTUALLY the partial preparation of a béarnaise sauce—the reduction of vinegars with herbs and shallots, into which, classically, one would incorporate egg yolks and clarified butter. But the reduction sauce is distinctive enough on its own to serve with the salmon without its rich, classical finish. Serve with a very simple garnish, such as a salad of endive tips. (If you don't have a grill, sear the salmon in a lightly oiled large heavy skillet over medium-high heat.)

FOR THE SAUCE

2 shallots, finely minced

¼ cup sherry vinegar

¼ cup white wine vinegar

2 sprigs fresh tarragon, 1 left whole, 1 crushed with the back of a knife and coarsely chopped

1 sprig fresh flat-leaf parsley

1 tablespoon white peppercorns, finely crushed

4 tablespoons unsalted butter

Four 1- to 1¼-inch-thick salmon steaks (about 8 ounces each), skin left on

1 tablespoon olive oil

1 tablespoon coarse sea salt, preferably fleur de sel

Preheat a grill until hot. Preheat the oven to 375°F. Lightly oil a baking sheet.

TO PREPARE THE SAUCE: Combine the shallots, both vinegars, the tarragon sprig, parsley sprig, and the cracked peppercorns in a small skillet. Bring to a boil, then reduce the heat to medium-low and simmer until most of the liquid has evaporated but the shallots are still moist, about 8 minutes. Remove from the heat and set aside.

Melt the butter in a small skillet over medium heat and cook until a golden, nutty brown and fragrant. Strain through a fine-mesh strainer into a small bowl, cover, and refrigerate.

TO COOK THE SALMON: Brush the salmon lightly on both sides with the olive oil. Grill it, turning once, just until marked on both sides, about 1 minute on each side. Transfer to the greased baking sheet and sprinkle on 1½ teaspoons of the salt. Bake for 8 to 10 minutes, until just cooked through. Transfer the baking sheet to a wire rack to cool slightly. Very gently remove the large central bones from the salmon steaks by loosening them a bit first with the tip of a small sharp knife and then carefully pulling them out. Return the salmon on the baking sheet to the turned-off oven to keep warm.

TO FINISH THE DISH: Remove the sprigs of tarragon and parsley from the vinegar reduction and discard. Whisk the chilled browned butter into the reduction and warm over medium heat, whisking to blend well. Stir in the chopped tarragon and remove from the heat.

Spoon a small pool of the shallot-butter sauce into the center of each serving plate. Place the salmon on the sauce, sprinkle on the remaining 1½ teaspoons salt, and serve immediately.

BAKED SALMON FILLETS WITH ENDIVE "MARMALADE"

Serves 4

HERE AN ENDIVE "MARMALADE"—with its wonderful interplay of sweet, sour, and bitter flavors—accompanies a meltingly tender salmon fillet simply brushed with butter and lightly baked just until warmed through but still very rare in the center.

FOR THE ENDIVE MARMALADE

4 medium shallots, finely minced

¼ cup sherry vinegar

¼ cup white wine vinegar

1 sprig fresh tarragon

1 sprig fresh flat-leaf parsley

1 tablespoon white peppercorns, finely crushed

2 tablespoons unsalted butter

16 endives, trimmed, cored, and cut lengthwise into julienne strips

2 tablespoons sugar

1 teaspoon fine sea salt

Four 8-ounce center-cut salmon fillets, skin removed

2 teaspoons unsalted butter, melted

1 teaspoon coarse sea salt, preferably fleur de sel

1 teaspoon coarsely ground black pepper

Preheat the oven to 375°F. Line a baking sheet with kitchen parchment.

TO PREPARE THE MARMALADE: Combine the shallots, vinegars, tarragon, parsley, and white pepper in a small skillet. Bring to a boil, then reduce the heat and simmer until most of the liquid has evaporated but the shallots are still moist, about 8 minutes. Remove the tarragon and parsley; set the shallots aside.

Melt the butter in a large skillet over medium heat. Add the endive and stir until coated, then stir in the sugar and fine sea salt. Cook, stirring frequently, until the endive is soft and translucent, about 10 minutes. Stir in the shallots, remove from the heat, and set aside.

TO COOK THE SALMON: Set the salmon fillets on the baking sheet and brush with the melted butter. Sprinkle with the salt. Bake for 8 to 10 minutes, until the outside is firm to the touch and the center is just warmed through (the interior temperature should be 97°F).

Divide the endive marmalade among four serving plates, making a bed of endive in the center of each plate. Place a salmon fillet on each, sprinkle the black pepper over the salmon, and serve immediately.

SUGGESTED WINE

A CONCENTRATED RED WINE WITHOUT TOO MUCH TANNIN, SUCH AS A CHÂTEAU VANNIERE BANDOL 1995 OR A PARADIGM MERLOT 1994, FROM THE NAPA VALLEY. FOR THE RECIPE ON PAGE 107, A BORDEAUX-STYLE RED, SUCH AS A CHÂTEAU MEYNEY 1991 OR A COSENTINO MERLOT 1994 NAPA VALLEY RESERVE

GRILLED BASS WITH ARTICHOKE SAUCE AND RAW ARTICHOKE GARNISH

Serves 4

THIS RECIPE SHOWS OFF THREE DIFFERENT FLAVORS of artichoke: the nuttiness of the braised; the crunchy, bright taste of the raw; and puréed artichokes in a creamy, sweet sauce. The grilled fish is placed in a pool of puréed artichoke sauce. Braised, quartered artichoke hearts are sprinkled over the top along with lemony sliced raw artichoke hearts, and the whole dish is drizzled with olive oil.

1 European sea bass (about 3½ pounds), filleted, bones reserved (see page 241)

FOR THE FISH STOCK

2 tablespoons olive oil

2 branches dried fennel

¼ teaspoon coarsely ground black pepper

1 cup dry white wine

About ⅔ cup olive oil

2 large artichokes, trimmed to hearts (see page 248) and quartered

Coarse sea salt, preferably fleur de sel, and freshly ground black pepper

3 to 4 cups Chicken Stock (page 229)

Juice of 1 lemon, plus extra for sprinkling

12 small purple artichokes, trimmed (see page 248)

Cut off the fish head. With a heavy knife, split the head lengthwise in half. Chop the fish bones into 4-inch lengths. Soak the fish head and bones in cold water for 5 minutes; drain and pat dry.

TO PREPARE THE FISH STOCK: Heat the olive oil in a large pot. Add the fish bones and head and cook, stirring occasionally, until very lightly browned, 4 to 5 minutes. Add the fennel, pepper, wine, and just enough cold water to cover. Bring to a boil, reduce the heat to medium-low, and simmer for 25 minutes. Strain through a fine-mesh sieve into a bowl and set aside.

TO PREPARE THE ARTICHOKE SAUCE: Heat 1 tablespoon of the olive oil in a medium skillet over medium-high heat. Add the quartered artichoke hearts and cook, stirring, until lightly browned. Season with salt and pepper, add just enough chicken stock to cover, and simmer gently until the artichokes are tender, about 20 minutes. Drain the artichokes and reserve the cooking liquid.

In a blender, combine the cooked artichokes, ½ cup of the cooking liquid, 3 tablespoons of the olive oil, and salt and pepper to taste and purée until smooth; transfer to a medium saucepan and whisk in half the lemon juice and enough of the fish stock (⅓ to ½ cup) to thin it to the consistency of a crème anglaise; it should just coat the back of a wooden spoon. Set aside. Reserve any remaining fish stock for another use.

TO PREPARE THE BRAISED ARTICHOKES: Set aside 4 of the small artichoke hearts. Quarter the remaining 8 hearts. Heat 2 tablespoons of the olive oil in a deep medium skillet over medium heat. Add the quartered artichokes, season with salt and pepper, and cook for 2 minutes, stirring. Add just enough chicken stock to cover, bring to a simmer, and simmer until tender, about 15 minutes. Drain the artichokes, reserving the cooking liquid, and return to the skillet. Set the hearts and cooking liquid aside.

TO PREPARE THE RAW ARTICHOKES: With a mandoline or very sharp knife, cut the remaining 4 artichoke hearts into paper-thin slices. Combine in a bowl with the remaining lemon juice and 2 tablespoons olive oil, season with a pinch each of salt and pepper, toss gently, and set aside.

Meanwhile, preheat the grill.

TO COOK THE FISH: Season the sea bass with salt. Brush the grill with olive oil and cook the fish, turning once, until just done, 3 to 5 minutes per side.

Meanwhile, reheat the braised artichokes in their cooking liquid over medium heat. Reheat the sauce gently over low heat.

To serve, spoon the artichoke sauce into the center of four warmed serving plates. Place the sea bass fillets on top and garnish with the braised artichokes. Scatter on the raw artichoke slices, drizzle about 1 teaspoon of olive oil over each serving, and sprinkle on a few drops of lemon juice. Season with coarse salt and pepper, and serve immediately.

"*Loup* is the Mediterranean version of sea bass and
bar is the Atlantic version. But the success of these recipes
isn't dependent on a single type of fish."

SUGGESTED WINE

A FULL-BODIED, PERFUMED WHITE WINE, SUCH AS A
CHÂTEAU PAPE CLÉMENT BLANC 1994 PESSAC LÉOGNAN OR A
TYRELL'S VAT 47 1996 CHARDONNAY, FROM AUSTRALIA

BASS FILLETS BAKED IN PARCHMENT WITH FENNEL-TRUFFLE SAUCE

Serves 4

THIS IS A REALLY DELICIOUS and gorgeous-looking recipe, with its spectacular white and golden brown colors. The fish fillets are baked in the oven between two buttered sheets of parchment so that they stay very white and moist. They are placed on top of a bed of endive that has been caramelized and then braised in butter, chicken stock, and balsamic vinegar—the taste of the endive is so rich that it's almost meaty. The fish is glazed with a sauce that's mildly flavored with fennel and sprinkled with black truffles. The dish is enlivened with a tiny "salad" of raw endive seasoned with lemon and olive oil. The bitterness of the raw endive balances the richness of the cooked.

FOR THE SAUCE

1 tablespoon extra-virgin olive oil

1 European sea bass head, eyes removed, split lengthwise in half, soaked in cold water for 5 minutes, drained, and patted dry (see page 241)

1 medium onion, minced

½ fennel bulb, trimmed, outer layer peeled off, cored, and thinly sliced

1 branch dried fennel

3 garlic cloves, unpeeled

Zest of 1 lemon, removed in strips with a vegetable peeler

15 white peppercorns

2 cups Chicken Stock (page 229)

Fine sea salt and freshly ground black pepper

4 tablespoons unsalted butter

2 ounces black truffles, chopped

FOR THE ENDIVE

12 small slim endives (about 2 ounces each)

5 tablespoons unsalted butter

Fine sea salt

1 cup Chicken Broth (page 229)

3 tablespoons balsamic vinegar

Freshly ground black pepper

1 tablespoon extra-virgin olive oil

1 teaspoon fresh lemon juice

FOR THE FISH

Four 3-inch-square pieces European sea bass fillets, skin removed (see page 241)

Fine sea salt and freshly ground black pepper

Butter for greasing the parchment paper

TO PREPARE THE SAUCE: Heat the olive oil in a large heavy pot over medium-low heat. Add the fish head and cook, stirring once or twice, until lightly browned, 4 to 5 minutes. Add the onion and cook, stirring often, until translucent, 2 to 3 minutes. Add the fresh and dried fennel, the garlic, lemon zest, and white peppercorns and cook for 30 seconds. Pour in the chicken stock, raise the heat to medium, and bring almost to a boil. Reduce the heat to very low and cook, uncovered, stirring occasionally, for 40 minutes.

Remove from the heat and strain through a fine strainer into a small saucepan, pressing on the solids to release all the liquid. Bring to a boil over medium-high heat and cook until the liquid reduces by half (you should have ¾ to 1 cup). Add salt and pepper to taste and reduce the heat to medium-low. Stir in the butter and truffles and simmer until the sauce is smooth and syrupy, 5 to 7 minutes. Remove from the heat and set aside.

MEANWHILE, PREPARE THE ENDIVES: Remove the outer three leaves of each endive; wash the leaves, pat dry, and refrigerate. Slice the endives lengthwise in half, trim the bottoms, and remove the cores. Melt 4 tablespoons of the butter over medium heat in a skillet just large enough to hold the endives in a single layer. Place the endives cut side down in the pan and cook until lightly browned, nudging them gently with a spatula as necessary to keep them from sticking (but not so much that the leaves separate), 6 to 7 minutes. Season with salt, cover, and cook for 3 minutes. Turn the endives over, add the remaining 1 tablespoon butter, and cook until browned on the other side, about 5 minutes (be careful not to burn the endives). Pour in the chicken stock and balsamic vinegar, bring to a simmer, and cook until almost all of the liquid has evaporated but the endives are still moist, about 15 minutes. Season with salt and pepper to taste and set the pan aside.

TO BAKE THE FISH: Preheat the oven to 375°F. Cut eight 4-inch squares of kitchen parchment and butter one side of each sheet. Lay out 4 sheets, buttered side up, and place the bass fillets on top. Season lightly with salt and pepper. Place a second sheet, buttered side down, on top of each fillet and press down gently. Place the fillets in a large dry cast-iron or other heavy ovenproof skillet. Warm the fillets over medium-low heat for about 2 minutes. Then transfer the pan to the oven and bake for 8 to 12 minutes, depending on the thickness of the fillets, until gently resistant to the touch but not browned.

Meanwhile, cut off the top 1¼ inches from each of the reserved endive leaves (save the remainder for another use). Toss the endive tips with the olive oil, lemon juice, and salt and pepper to taste.

Reheat the truffle sauce and the cooked endive over low heat.

To serve, divide the cooked endive among four warmed plates, making a bed of endive in the center of each plate. Discard the parchment paper and place the bass fillets on top of the endive. Spoon the truffle sauce over the fillets and garnish with the raw endive. Serve immediately.

[
SUGGESTED WINE

A DISTINCTLY FRUITY, GOLDEN-HUED WHITE WINE, SUCH AS A
ROUSSANE "VIEILLES VIGNES" 1983, CHÂTEAU DE BEAUCASTEL
CHATEAUNEUF DU PAPE BLANC, FAMILLE PERRIN, OR AN ART
SERIES MARGARET RIVER CHARDONNAY 1986, FROM AUSTRALIA
]

SAUTÉED BASS "TOURNEDOS" WITH CRISP POTATO RAVIOLI

Serves 4

FOR THE "RAVIOLI" IN THIS DISH, savory stuffing is sealed between two wafer-thin slices of potato and then fried in olive oil. They are served with sautéed sea bass steaks that have been boned and tied into compact medallions to resemble *tournedos de boeuf.* The ravioli stuffing, light and delectable, is prepared from cèpe and white mushrooms, mixed fresh herbs, some cured ham, and a bit of calf's brain, which provides *velours*, a certain unctuousness The sea bass tournedos are drizzled with an aromatic and slightly acidic sauce, made from a reduced fish broth enriched with chicken jus and a touch of butter.

The ravioli also make appealing little cocktail party hors d'oeuvres on their own. They can be assembled up to 2 hours in advance; arrange them on a baking sheet lined with paper towels, cover with a layer of damp paper towels, and refrigerate until ready to cook.

½ set (1 lobe) calf's brains

FOR THE SAUCE BASE

1 tablespoon olive oil

1 European sea bass head, eyes removed, split lengthwise in half, soaked in cold water for 5 minutes, drained, and patted dry (see page 241)

1 European sea bass backbone, cut into 4-inch lengths, soaked in cold water for 5 minutes, drained, and patted dry (see page 241)

1 carrot, peeled and cut into large cubes

1 onion, cut into large dice

1 tomato, cut into large dice

1 celery stalk, cut into large dice

½ garlic bulb, peeled and chopped

3 tablespoons white peppercorns, coarsely ground

¼ cup sherry vinegar

¼ cup dry white wine

1 cup Chicken Jus (page 230) or roasting juices from a chicken

Four 9-ounce European sea bass steaks, about 1 inch thick (see page 241)

FOR THE RAVIOLI FILLING

2 teaspoons unsalted butter

1 tablespoon olive oil

½ cup very finely diced white mushrooms

½ cup very finely diced cèpe (porcini) mushrooms

1 shallot, very finely diced

¼ cup very finely diced prosciutto or other cured ham

½ cup mixed finely chopped fresh herbs: 2 tablespoons *each* basil, parsley, tarragon, and chervil

1 tablespoon freshly grated Parmigiano-Reggiano cheese

Coarse sea salt, preferably fleur de sel, and freshly ground black pepper

FOR THE RAVIOLI

1 pound large all-purpose potatoes (about 2)

1 tablespoon potato starch

2 teaspoons water

1 large egg

TO FINISH THE DISH

Fine sea salt

2 tablespoons white peppercorns, coarsely ground

3 tablespoons unsalted butter

1 to 2 tablespoons olive oil

4 cups olive oil, for deep-frying

TO PREPARE THE CALF'S BRAINS: Soak the brains in cold water to cover, changing the water several times, until the water remains clear, about 2 hours.

TO PREPARE THE SAUCE BASE: Heat the olive oil in a large heavy pot over medium heat. Add the fish head and bones and cook, stirring occasionally, until very lightly browned, 4 to 5 minutes. Add the carrot, onion, tomato, celery, and garlic and cook, stirring frequently, until the vegetables soften slightly, 3 to 4 minutes. Stir in the white pepper. Add the sherry vinegar and wine and cook, scraping up any browned bits stuck to the bottom and sides of the pan, until most of the liquid has evaporated but the vegetables are still moist, about 10 minutes. Stir in the chicken jus, reduce the heat to medium-low, cover, and cook for 30 minutes. Strain the sauce base through a fine sieve into a small saucepan; set aside.

MEANWHILE, PREPARE THE TOURNEDOS: To bone the fish steaks, with a small boning knife or paring knife, carefully cut through the skin and along each side of the backbone in the center of each steak. Following the curves of the steaks, cut away any small bones and the membranes that line the inside of the flaps of the steaks. You should have two boneless pieces of equal size from each steak; keep the halves of each steak together. Form each pair of fish pieces into tournedos by curling the narrow ends of each piece inward to make a compact oval. Cut four strips of parchment paper 1 inch wide and long enough to encircle the tournedos. Oil the strips of parchment and wrap them, oiled side in, around the tournedos. Fasten each strip of parchment securely with kitchen twine, forming a neat, compact shape. Cover the tournedos loosely with plastic wrap and refrigerate.

TO PREPARE THE RAVIOLI FILLING: Drain the calf's brains and carefully peel off as much of the very thin membrane that covers the surface as possible. Place the brains in a small saucepan, pour in enough cold water to cover by 2 inches, and bring to a simmer over medium-high heat. Simmer for 5 minutes; do not boil. Remove from the heat and cool to room temperature in the cooking liquid, then drain and pat dry.

Heat the butter in a medium skillet over medium heat until nutty brown and fragrant. Add 1 teaspoon of the olive oil and swirl to blend. Add the calf's brains and cook, lightly mashing with a fork, until they change color and are the consistency of loosely scrambled eggs, about 1 minute. Remove from the heat and set aside. Heat the remaining 2 teaspoons olive oil in a small skillet over medium heat. Add the white and porcini mushrooms and the shallot and cook until the mushrooms are dry, 3 to 5 minutes. Stir in the ham and cook for 15 to 20 seconds. Add the calf's brains and stir well to combine, then transfer to a bowl and let cool to room temperature.

When the stuffing is cool, add the chopped herbs, Parmesan cheese, a generous pinch of coarse salt, and pepper to taste and mix well. Cover and refrigerate.

TO PREPARE THE RAVIOLI: Peel the potatoes. Using a mandoline, slice them lengthwise into very thin slices, a scant 1/16 inch; they should be so thin as to be almost transparent and very flexible. You will need enough slices to make 32 potato circles. Using a 2-inch cookie cutter, cut 32 rounds from the potato slices.

In a small bowl, stir the potato starch and water with a fork to blend well. Add the egg and beat until well blended. Using a pastry brush, brush half of the potato circles with the egg yolk mixture. Place 1/4 teaspoon of the stuffing in the center of each of these circles. Cover with the remaining potato circles. Press the potato circles firmly together with your fingertips all around the edges of the ravioli to seal well.

TO FINISH THE DISH: Heat the olive oil in a large deep heavy skillet—cast-iron is ideal—to 350°F. Reduce the heat to medium-low.

Meanwhile, season both sides of the sea bass tournedos with salt and the white pepper. In a large, preferably nonstick, frying pan, heat 2 tablespoons of the butter over medium heat until foamy. Add 1 tablespoon olive oil, swirl the skillet to mix, and add the sea bass tournedos. Cook, turning once and basting frequently with the butter and oil, until the tournedos are very lightly browned on both sides, 2 to 3 minutes on each side; if there is not quite enough butter and oil to baste the fish and keep it moist, add 1 more tablespoon oil to the pan. Turn the tournedos onto their paper-wrapped sides, and cook for 2 to 3 minutes. Turn over to

the opposite paper-wrapped side and cook for 2 to 3 minutes, until just rare in the center. Remove the tournedos to a warm platter, and cover with aluminum foil to keep warm.

WHILE THE SEA BASS IS COOKING, FINISH THE SAUCE AND FRY THE RAVIOLI: Bring the sauce base to a boil over high heat and boil until reduced to about ⅓ cup. Remove the sauce from the heat and whisk in the remaining 1 tablespoon butter. Cover the pan to keep warm.

If necessary, reheat the olive oil to 350°F. Using a slotted spoon, lower as many of the ravioli as will float freely into the hot oil and fry until golden brown, about 2 minutes. Transfer the ravioli to a paper towel–lined plate, and sprinkle with salt. Cook the remaining ravioli in the same way, maintaining the oil temperature.

To serve, gently reheat the sauce if necessary. Remove the twine and paper from the tournedos and place one in the center of each warmed plate. Arrange the ravioli around the top of the plates and spoon some of the sauce over the tournedos.

SUGGESTED WINE

A POWERFUL, YET SUBTLY NUANCED WHITE WINE, SUCH AS A
CHÂTEAU PAPE CLÉMENT CHATEAUNEUF DU PAPE BLANC 1993,
OR A CHÂTEAU STE. MICHELLE CHARDONNAY, CANOE RIDGE 1995,
FROM WASHINGTON STATE'S COLUMBIA VALLEY

[*Blanc de Bar Grillé, Sauce Pilée au Mortier, Courgettes et Côtes de Blettes*]

GRILLED BASS FILLETS WITH A MORTAR-CRUSHED SAUCE, ZUCCHINI, AND SWISS CHARD

Serves 4

THE SAUCE FOR THE GRILLED BASS is more like a Mediterranean "salsa" than it is a traditional sauce. Light and fresh-tasting, it is fragrant with the flavors of fennel, garlic, tomatoes, lemon pulp, basil, spring onions, almonds, and some ham.

2 pounds Swiss chard

Juice of ½ lemon

FOR THE SAUCE

About ½ cup olive oil

3 medium white onions, thinly sliced

8 garlic cloves, unpeeled

Fine sea salt

1 large fennel bulb, trimmed, outer layer peeled off, cored, and sliced, plus 5 very small fennel bulbs, trimmed, outer layer peeled off, cored, and thinly sliced on the diagonal

Zest from ½ lemon, removed with a vegetable peeler in 4 strips

4 branches dried fennel or 1 teaspoon fennel seed

3 pounds rockfish or other inexpensive white-fleshed fish, cleaned

8 stems fresh basil (leaves reserved for another use)

15 white peppercorns

Freshly ground black pepper

2 thin lemon slices, plus 2 lemons, peeled, segments removed from membranes, seeded, and cut into small dice

¼ pound baked ham, sliced into very thin julienne

2 tablespoons unsalted butter

½ cup fresh almonds, shelled, skinned, and finely sliced, or ⅓ cup packaged sliced almonds

5 pieces Tomato Confit (page 232), lightly crushed with a fork

5 spring onions, white part reserved for another use, tender green part thinly sliced on the diagonal

20 small capers

FOR THE VEGETABLE GARNISH

6 tablespoons unsalted butter

2 to 3 cups Chicken Stock (page 229)

3 tablespoons olive oil

4 medium zucchini, skin sliced off in ¾-inch-wide and ⅛-inch-thick strips and cut into 3-inch lengths

FOR THE FISH

Four 8-ounce European sea bass fillets, skin removed (see page 241)

4 teaspoons extra-virgin olive oil

Coarse sea salt, preferably fleur de sel

TO PREPARE THE CHARD: Trim the chard. Cut off the stalks, peel them, and cut into 3- by ¾-inch rectangles. Place the stalks in a bowl of cold water and add the lemon juice. Cut 4 of the leaves into chiffonade and reserve for the sauce. Reserve the remaining leaves for another use.

TO PREPARE THE SAUCE BASE: Heat ⅓ cup olive oil in a medium pot over medium heat. Add the onions and garlic, season with salt, and cook, stirring frequently, until the onions are very soft and translucent, 7 to 8 minutes. Add the sliced fennel, the lemon zest, and the dried fennel and cook, stirring frequently, until all the vegetables are tender, 15 to 20 minutes.

Add the rockfish, basil stems, white peppercorns, ½ teaspoon salt, and a pinch of black pepper. Pour in just enough water to cover and bring to a simmer. Reduce the heat to low and cook for 40 minutes.

Strain the broth through a fine strainer into a clean saucepan, pressing gently on the solids to extract the broth. Add the lemon slices, bring to a boil over medium heat, and reduce the liquid by half. Strain into a large saucepan and set aside.

Meanwhile, combine half of the chiffonade of Swiss chard leaves, half the ham, and one quarter of the diced lemon in a mortar and crush to a coarse paste with the pestle. Set aside.

TO PREPARE THE GARNISH: Melt 5 tablespoons of the butter in a large saucepan over medium heat. Drain the chard stalks, add to the pan, and cook, stirring often, until the chard softens but does not brown, 4 to 5 minutes. Meanwhile, bring the chicken stock to a boil.

Add just enough chicken stock to cover the chard (keep the remaining broth hot), raise the heat to high, and simmer until the chard is very tender and the liquid has evaporated, leaving the chard lightly glazed. Transfer the chard to a platter, cover, and set aside.

Meanwhile, heat 1 tablespoon of the olive oil and the remaining 1 tablespoon butter in a medium skillet over medium heat. Add the zucchini strips and cook, stirring frequently, until the zucchini is slightly softened, 2 to 3 minutes. Add enough chicken broth to cover and cook until the zucchini is crisp-tender, 3 to 4 minutes. Drain, transfer to a platter, cover, and set aside.

Preheat the grill. Preheat the oven to 200°F.

TO FINISH THE SAUCE: Bring the fish broth to a simmer over medium heat. Stir in the butter and season to taste with salt and pepper. Add the remaining chiffonade of Swiss chard, the remaining ham, the almonds, tomato confit, spring onions, the thinly sliced fennel greens, the capers, the remaining lemon pulp, and the crushed chard-ham paste and stir well to combine. Keep warm over very low heat.

TO COOK THE FISH: Brush the grill lightly with olive oil. Grill the fillets until just cooked through, about 3 minutes on each side. Transfer the fish to a warm platter and keep warm in the oven while you garnish the serving plates.

Arrange the Swiss chard stalks and zucchini, alternating and overlapping them slightly, in a circular pattern in the centers of four warmed serving plates. (Keep each completed plate warm in the oven while you finish the others.) Place the sea bass fillets on top, drizzle each with 1 teaspoon extra-virgin olive oil, and sprinkle with a pinch of coarse salt. Spoon 4 or 5 small mounds of the sauce around each fillet. Serve immediately, with the remaining sauce in a sauceboat on the side.

SUGGESTED WINE

A DRY, SLIGHTLY "SMOKY" WHITE WINE WITH A FINE PEDIGREE,
SUCH AS A POUILLY FUMÉ "CUVÉE SILEX" 1995 D. DAGUENEAU, OR
A GAIA ET REY 1994 CHARDONNAY ANGELO GAJA, FROM ITALY

[*Saint-Pierre au Plat*]

ROASTED JOHN DORY NIÇOISE STYLE

Serves 4

JOHN DORY IS A DELICATELY FLAVORED LEAN WHITE-FLESHED fish that is at its best when prepared simply. Here, the fish is baked whole, surrounded by black olives, tomatoes, lemon, basil, and fennel. It's a delightful dish, with a simple, fragrant sauce. Niçoise olives added at the last minute bring out the fruity flavors of the oil. Quick and easy to prepare, this Mediterranean-style fish is best accompanied by an equally straightforward side dish, such as Fork-Mashed Potatoes with Olive Oil and Parsley (page 66).

2 John Dory (about 2 pounds each), cleaned and heads removed (see page 241)

1 medium tomato, quartered

1 lemon, sliced into thin rounds

4 branches fresh basil, 12 of the largest leaves removed and finely sliced

4 branches dried fennel or 1 teaspoon fennel seed

2 cups Chicken Stock (page 229) or water

1 teaspoon fine sea salt, or to taste

1/2 teaspoon freshly ground black pepper, or to taste

5 tablespoons olive oil

2 tablespoons unsalted butter

20 Niçoise olives, pitted by crushing the olives between two fingers and removing the pits

Preheat the oven to 450°F. Lightly oil an ovenproof skillet, preferably cast iron, or a flameproof baking dish just large enough to hold the fish.

Arrange the fish head-to-tail in the skillet and scatter on the tomato, lemon slices, basil branches, and fennel. Pour in the chicken stock and season with the salt and pepper. Set the pan over high heat and bring the stock to a boil. Transfer the pan to the oven and bake for about 8 minutes, basting often, until the fish is firm to the touch and just cooked through.

Transfer the fish, tomatoes, and lemons to a warmed serving platter. Discard the basil and fennel branches. Set the pan over medium-high heat, bring to a boil, and reduce the cooking juices by about two thirds; you should have about 1 cup. Strain the reduction into a small saucepan and return to medium-high heat. Stir in 1/4 cup of the olive oil and the butter, and cook, stirring constantly, just until the butter is melted; the sauce should not be emulsified, but just *tranché*, dotted with little drops of oil and butter. Add the olives, adjust the seasoning to taste, and pour the sauce over the fish. Drizzle the remaining 1 tablespoon olive oil and scatter the sliced basil leaves over the top.

To serve, fillet the fish, place one fillet on each serving plate, and spoon on the olives and sauce.

SUGGESTED WINE

A MODERATELY RICH CHARDONNAY, SUCH AS A BEAUNE BLANC 1994, DOMAINE JACQUES PRIEUR, OR AN ESTANCIA CHARDONNAY RESERVE 1993, FROM MONTEREY, CALIFORNIA

TURBOT STEAMED IN SEAWEED, WITH ASSORTED SHELLFISH

Serves 4

THIS UNUSUAL DISH FEATURES TURBOT wrapped in a quartet of dried salted Japanese seaweeds, steamed, and then served in a savory broth with an array of clams, cockles, and periwinkles. The seaweed— sold in Japanese markets and health food stores—keeps the turbot moist while adding a fragrant, toasty flavor of its own. If you can't find all the seaweeds called for, try to use at least two different varieties. (Pictured opposite, a salt farmer hand-harvesting fleur de sel. For more information about sea salt, see page 247.)

FOR THE SAUCE

2 cups Chicken Stock (page 229)

1 turbot head, eyes removed, split lengthwise in half, soaked in cold water for 5 minutes, drained, and patted dry

2 tablespoons cold unsalted butter

2 teaspoons fresh lemon juice

Freshly ground black pepper

FOR THE SHELLFISH (see page 242)

20 *palourdes*, scrubbed

16 *venus*, scrubbed

24 cockles, scrubbed

24 periwinkles, scrubbed

24 *clams*, scrubbed

16 *praires*, scrubbed

FOR THE TURBOT

4 dried wakame leaves, soaked in cold water for 2 to 3 hours

4 dried dulse leaves, soaked in cold water for 2 to 3 hours

4 dried lettuce-of-the-sea leaves, soaked in cold water for 2 to 3 hours

4 sheets kombu (kelp), soaked in cold water for 2 to 3 hours

Four 8-ounce turbot fillets with skin (see page 242)

6 tablespoons unsalted butter: 4 tablespoons softened 2 tablespoons, melted

Coarse sea salt, preferably fleur de sel

4 tablespoons very cold salted butter, sliced into shavings with a vegetable peeler and chilled

TO PREPARE THE FISH BOUILLON: In a large saucepan, combine the chicken stock and turbot head and bring to a boil over high heat. Reduce the heat to low, cover the pot with a sheet of kitchen parchment, and cook at a barely perceptible simmer for 1 hour.

Remove and discard the turbot head, raise the heat to medium-high, and boil, uncovered, until the bouillon reduces by one quarter. Strain through a fine strainer lined with cheesecloth into a bowl.

TO PREPARE THE SHELLFISH: Soak each of the different shellfish separately in a bowl under cold running water for about 1 minute; drain. Cook each variety separately in a pot with a tablespoon of water: Bring to a boil over medium-high heat, cover, and cook until the shells open, about 5 minutes, depending on the variety. Remove the shellfish as they are done, and strain the cooking juices; discard any shellfish that have not opened. Reserve the cooking juices from the littleneck clams in a small bowl. Shell all the shellfish except the littleneck clams and reserve each variety in its own juices.

TO PREPARE THE TURBOT: Preheat the oven to 200°F. Drain all the seaweed.

Brush the fillets all over with the softened butter and season on both sides with coarse salt. Wrap each fillet snugly in a combination of the different seaweeds. Fill the bottom of a steamer with water and bring to a boil. Place the fillets on a steamer rack, cover, and steam until the fish is just cooked through and the tip of a small sharp knife pierces the center of the fillet with no resistance, about 12 minutes.

Unwrap the fish, reserving the seaweed. Peel the white and black skins off the fillets. Make a bed of half the seaweed in the bottom of a medium casserole. Brush the fillets on both sides with the melted butter and lay them on the seaweed in the casserole. Reserve about 2 tablespoons of the remaining seaweed for the garnish and cover the fish with the rest of the seaweed. Put the turbot in the oven to keep warm. Chop the reserved 2 tablespoons seaweed and set aside.

In a large skillet, gently reheat the shellfish in their liquid.

MEANWHILE, FINISH THE SAUCE: Place ¼ cup of the turbot bouillon in a small saucepan (reserve the rest for another use), bring to a boil over medium heat, and reduce by half. Add the liquid from the littleneck clams, then whisk in the 2 tablespoons cold butter, the lemon juice, the reserved chopped seaweed, and a pinch of freshly ground pepper.

Remove the turbot fillets from the seaweed and place on four warmed soup plates. Using a slotted spoon to drain the juices, spoon the shellfish around the fillets, drizzle the sauce over the fish, and top with the butter shavings. Serve immediately.

> SUGGESTED WINE
>
> A DRY WHITE WINE, SUCH AS A SAVENNIÈRES 1990 CLOS DE LA
> COULÉE DE SERRANT, OR A PRESTON CELLARS 1994 CHARDONNAY,
> COLUMBIA VALLEY RESERVE, FROM WASHINGTON STATE

BROILED SWORDFISH RUBBED WITH DRIED ZESTS, WITH BROCHETTE OF ROOT VEGETABLES

Serves 4

ORANGE AND LEMON PEELS, oven-dried to concentrate their essence, are pulverized, then combined with a generous amount of coarsely ground black pepper and sea salt to make a spiced dry rub for meaty swordfish steaks. Brochettes of potatoes cooked in goose fat and carrots, celery root, onions, and artichoke hearts cooked in chicken stock go well with the swordfish steaks, or simply serve the fish with its garnish of warmed lemon and orange sections, which offer a soothing counterpoint to the citrus-pepper rub.

3 oranges

2 lemons

2 cups goose or duck fat

2 large all-purpose potatoes, peeled, quartered, and carved into 4 even cylindrical pieces to match the carrots

2 medium carrots, peeled, cut into 4 pieces, and carved into even cylindrical pieces

3 to 4 cups Chicken Stock (page 229) or water

4 small onions, peeled

Two ⅜-inch slices celery root, cut into triangles 1 inch across at the base and 2 inches high

3 tablespoons olive oil

4 small purple artichokes, trimmed (see page 248)

¼ cup coarsely ground black pepper

Coarse sea salt, preferably fleur de sel

Four 1-inch-thick swordfish steaks (about 8 ounces each)

Freshly ground black pepper

4 teaspoons fruity extra-virgin olive oil

EARLY IN THE DAY, OR THE DAY BEFORE SERVING, MAKE THE CITRUS PEEL POWDER: Preheat the oven to 200°F.

With a vegetable peeler, remove the zest from the oranges and lemons in wide strips; reserve. With a paring knife, cut away all the white pith from the citrus fruit. Working over a bowl, cut the segments free from the membranes, allowing the segments to drop into the bowl. Cover and refrigerate.

Spread the strips of orange and lemon zest on a baking sheet, place in the oven, and bake for about 3 hours, until thoroughly dried. Transfer to a blender or food processor and pulverize into a fine powder. Transfer to a small jar.

TO PREPARE THE VEGETABLES: Spoon the goose fat into a small saucepan and submerge the potatoes in it. Bring to a low simmer over medium-low heat (do not allow the fat to boil) and cook until the potatoes are just tender but still offer slight resistance when pierced with the tip of a small sharp knife, about 45 minutes. Remove the potatoes with a slotted spoon and set aside. Reserve the goose fat for another use.

Meanwhile, place the carrots in a saucepan, add stock just to cover, and bring to a boil over medium heat. Reduce the heat to medium-low and cook at a low boil until the carrots are just tender, about 20 minutes. Remove with a slotted spoon and set aside. Add the onions to the boiling stock; if necessary, add additional stock to just cover and bring to a boil. Reduce the heat and boil gently until tender, 10 to 12 minutes. Drain and set aside.

While the carrots and onions are cooking, cook the celery root in the same way until just barely tender; test for doneness after 15 minutes. Drain and set aside.

Heat 1 tablespoon of the olive oil in a small saucepan over medium heat. Add the artichokes, cover, and cook until just barely tender, 5 to 8 minutes. Transfer to a plate and set aside.

Thread the cooked vegetables onto four wooden skewers, placing one of each vegetable on each one. Grease a small baking sheet with olive oil, place the skewers on the sheet, drizzle with 1 tablespoon of the olive oil, and set aside.

TO PREPARE THE FISH: Combine the citrus powder with the coarsely ground pepper and 2 teaspoons coarse salt. Rub the mixture gently into both sides of the swordfish, coating well. Place on a broiling pan and set aside.

Preheat the broiler. Place the vegetable skewers under the broiler and cook, turning occasionally, until golden all over, 5 to 7 minutes. Remove and cover loosely with foil to keep warm.

Place the swordfish under the broiler and cook, turning once, until lightly browned and gently resistant to the touch, 2 to 4 minutes per side.

MEANWHILE, PREPARE THE CITRUS GARNISH: Heat the remaining 1 tablespoon olive oil in a medium skillet over medium heat. Place the orange and lemon segments in the pan and cook, without turning, just until the fruit softens and begins to release its juices, about 2 minutes. Sprinkle the fruit with a pinch or two of black pepper.

Arrange the slices of citrus fruit in the center of the four warmed serving plates. Place the swordfish steaks on top of the citrus and drizzle each with 1 teaspoon extra-virgin olive oil. Lay a vegetable skewer across the top of each plate and serve immediately.

SUGGESTED WINE

A DRY, FULL-FLAVORED, PERFUMED WHITE WINE,
SUCH AS A DOMAINE DE TREVALLON BLANC 1996,
FROM THE BOUCHES-DU-RHÔNE, OR A VIE DI
ROMANS 1996 SAUVIGNON DE FRIOUL, FROM ITALY

FILLET OF COD WITH WHITE BEAN PURÉE AND BABY SQUID

Serves 4

THIS RUSTIC DISH — IN SHADES OF WHITE, BEIGE, AND TAN — is made bright with the addition of olive oil, sherry vinegar, and lemon. Use pieces of cod cut from the center of the fillet if possible; the center is a more even thickness than the head or tail.

FOR THE BEANS

1 cup white beans, such as Great Northern, picked over, rinsed, soaked overnight in water to cover, and drained

1 medium carrot, peeled

1 medium onion

1 small celery stalk with leaves

2 garlic cloves, unpeeled

¼ cup extra-virgin olive oil

4 fresh sage leaves

1 branch fresh rosemary

Fine sea salt and freshly ground black pepper

3 tablespoons sherry vinegar

½ cup extra-virgin olive oil

Four 6- to 8-ounce cod fillets with skin

Fine sea salt and freshly ground black pepper

1¼ pounds baby squid, cleaned

Juice of 2 lemons

TO PREPARE THE BEANS: Place the beans, carrot, onion, celery, and garlic in a large saucepan and add cold water to cover. Bring to a boil over high heat, reduce the heat to medium, and cook until the beans are tender, about 1½ hours.

Drain the beans, reserving the cooking liquid, and return them to the pan. Add 2 tablespoons of the olive oil, ¼ cup of the reserved cooking liquid, the sage, rosemary, and salt and pepper to taste, mix well, and set aside for about 20 minutes to allow the flavors to blend.

Remove the carrot, onion, celery, garlic, and herbs from the beans and discard. Transfer ½ cup of the beans to a small bowl and set aside for the garnish. Put the remaining beans in the bowl of a food processor and process to a smooth purée, adding 1 to 2 tablespoons of the reserved cooking liquid if necessary. With the back of a spoon, press the purée through a fine strainer into a bowl and set aside. Reserve the cooking liquid.

TO COOK THE COD: Heat ¼ cup of the olive oil in a cast-iron or other heavy-bottomed skillet over medium heat. Place the cod fillets skin side down in the skillet, season with salt and pepper, and cook, turning once, until nicely browned on both sides, about 5 minutes on each side. Transfer to a warmed platter and cover loosely to keep warm.

TO COOK THE SQUID: Heat 2 tablespoons of the olive oil in a large cast-iron skillet over high heat. Add half the squid, stir to coat with oil, and cook, stirring, just until golden and cooked through, 1 to 1½ minutes. Transfer to a bowl and cover to keep warm. Heat the remaining 2 tablespoons oil, cook the remaining squid, and add to the bowl. Season with salt and pepper and stir in the lemon juice.

Meanwhile, reheat the bean purée in a small saucepan over medium-low heat. Stir in the remaining 2 tablespoons olive oil and the sherry vinegar and adjust the seasoning to taste. Reheat the reserved whole beans in a small skillet with 3 tablespoons of the reserved cooking liquid.

To serve, divide the bean purée among four deep dinner plates. Scatter the whole beans over the purée, then place the cod fillets in the center. Garnish with the baby squid and serve immediately.

"This recipe is a nostalgic one for me, with flavors reminiscent of the Basque country where I grew up. With only three main ingredients, fresh cod, white beans, and baby squid, the dish reflects the simplicity of regional home cooking."

SUGGESTED WINE

A SOMEWHAT RUSTIC WHITE WINE, SUCH AS A PACHERENC DU VIC BILH SEC,
"CUVÉE ERICKA" 1995 CHÂTEAU LAFFITTE TESTON, OR AN
ITALIAN TERRE DI FANCIACORTA 1996, CA' DEL BASCO, FROM LOMBARDY

SAUTÉED SEA BREAM WITH CLAMS, WHITE BEANS, AND GIROLLES

Serves 4

THE INTENSE, full-bodied reduction sauce served with this simply prepared fish marries fish fumet with sherry vinegar, Cognac, red wine, tomatoes, and veal stock. The complexity of the sauce is set off by a fresh "stew" of beans, clams, and girolles, brightened with lemon, tomato, and basil

FOR THE BEANS

½ cup shelled fresh white beans, or ½ cup dried beans, such as Great Northern, picked over, rinsed, soaked overnight in water to cover, and drained

1 medium carrot, peeled

1 medium onion

2 sprigs fresh parsley

1 medium stalk celery

1 branch fresh rosemary

1 fresh sage leaf

Fine sea salt

FOR THE RED WINE STOCK

1 tablespoon olive oil

1 sea bream head, eyes removed, split lengthwise in half, soaked in cold water for 5 minutes, drained, and patted dry (see page 242)

1 sea bream backbone, cut into 4-inch lengths, soaked in cold water for 5 minutes, drained, and patted dry (see page 242)

8 medium shallots, coarsely chopped

Coarse sea salt, preferably fleur de sel

2 tablespoons black peppercorns, coarsely ground

2 cups sherry vinegar

¼ cup Cognac

4 cups red wine

3 tablespoons tomato paste

FOR THE CLAMS

1 tablespoon olive oil

1 small shallot, finely chopped

1 medium garlic clove, chopped

40 littleneck clams, scrubbed, soaked for 1 minute in a bowl under cold running water, and drained

¼ cup dry white wine

FOR THE SAUCE

4 cups Veal Stock (see page 230)

1 tablespoon olive oil

4 medium ripe tomatoes, quartered

½ cup fresh basil leaves, chopped

20 small sprigs fresh dill

2 sprigs fresh parsley

4 tablespoons unsalted butter

FOR THE MUSHROOMS

2 tablespoons olive oil

1½ cups small girolle or other small wild mushrooms, trimmed and cleaned (see page 238)

Fine sea salt

3 medium ripe tomatoes, peeled, halved, seeded, and cut into 1-inch strips

1 lemon, skin and bitter white pith cut off, sectioned, and cut into small dice

1 tablespoon unsalted butter

10 fresh basil leaves

20 coriander seeds (about ¼ teaspoon)

2 to 3 tablespoons fresh lemon juice

Freshly ground black pepper

FOR THE FISH

Four 8-ounce sea bream fillets, skinned (see page 242)

2 tablespoons black peppercorns, coarsely ground

Coarse sea salt, preferably fleur de sel

¼ cup all-purpose flour

2 tablespoons unsalted butter

1 tablespoon grapeseed or canola oil

1 garlic clove, unpeeled, very lightly crushed

½ teaspoon sherry vinegar

TO PREPARE THE BEANS: In a large saucepan, combine the beans, carrot, onion, parsley, celery, rosemary, sage leaf, and cold water to cover. Bring to a boil over medium heat, cover, reduce the heat, and simmer until the beans are very tender, about 30 minutes for fresh beans, about 1½ hours for dried. Drain the beans. Season to taste with salt and set aside.

TO PREPARE THE RED WINE STOCK: Heat the olive oil in a large heavy-bottomed casserole over medium-high heat. Add the fish head and bones and cook, stirring, just until lightly browned, about 5 minutes. Reduce the heat to medium, add the shallots, season with salt, and cook until the shallots become translucent, 2 to 3 minutes. Add the pepper and vinegar and simmer until reduced by half. Add the Cognac, red wine, and tomato paste, stir to combine, reduce the heat to medium-low, and cook until reduced by half.

MEANWHILE, PREPARE THE CLAMS: Heat the olive oil in a large pot over medium heat. Add the shallot and garlic and cook for 2 minutes without coloring. Increase the heat to high, add the clams and white wine, cover, and cook until the shells open, 2 to 3 minutes. Transfer the clams to a bowl, discarding any that have not opened. Strain the cooking liquid through a sieve lined with cheesecloth into a bowl. Set 12 clams in their shells aside in a small bowl; shell the remaining clams and place them in a separate bowl. Cover the clams and clam juice and reserve in the refrigerator.

TO FINISH THE SAUCE: Add the veal stock to the reduced red wine stock and bring to a boil over high heat. Add the olive oil and cook until reduced by half, 50 to 60 minutes.

Reduce the heat to medium, add all but 2 tablespoons of the reserved clam cooking liquid, and stir to blend. Add the quartered tomatoes, the basil, dill, and parsley, reduce the heat to low, and simmer for 2 hours.

Strain the stock mixture through a fine sieve into a clean saucepan and return to medium heat. Add the butter and stir with a wooden spoon in a figure-8 motion until the butter is incorporated and the sauce glows with a satiny sheen. Keep warm over low heat, stirring from time to time.

TO PREPARE THE MUSHROOMS: Heat 1 tablespoon of the olive oil in a medium skillet over medium heat. Add the girolles and cook, stirring occasionally, just until the mushrooms begin to give off their moisture, about 2 minutes. Season with salt, add the tomato strips, and cook for 1 minute. Stir in the lemon dice.

Transfer the girolle mixture to a wide shallow pot and set over medium heat. Add the 2 tablespoons reserved clam juice, the shelled and unshelled clams, the butter, the remaining 1 tablespoon olive oil, the basil leaves, and coriander seeds and stir gently to combine well. Measure ½ cup of the white beans and add them to the mushroom mixture; reserve the remaining beans for another use. Add lemon juice to taste, then season to taste with salt and pepper. Keep warm over low heat.

TO PREPARE THE FISH: Sprinkle the fillets with the pepper and salt, then dredge in the flour, tapping the fish lightly to remove the excess. Heat the butter and oil with the garlic clove in a large skillet over medium heat. Add the fillets and cook until light golden brown, about 4 minutes per side. Add the sherry vinegar and shake the pan to blend with the butter and oil, then spoon over the fillets and immediately remove from the heat.

To serve, place the sea bream fillets in the center of four warmed soup plates. Arrange the clams and mushrooms around the fillets, then ladle some of the sauce over the clams and mushrooms. Serve immediately, with the remaining sauce in a sauceboat on the side.

SUGGESTED WINE

A DRY, AROMATIC WHITE WINE, SUCH AS CHÂTEAU
ST. BAILLON 1991 "CUVÉE OPPIDUM" CÔTES DE PROVENCE,
OR A DRY, NOT TOO TANNIC RED, SUCH AS AN ITALIAN
CHIANTI CLASSICO 1995 RISERVA, VIGNA DEL SORBO, FONTODI

CRISPY SAUTÉED SEA BREAM WITH ORANGE "BEEF DAUBE" SAUCE

Serves 4

THIS RECIPE combines two quintessentially Mediterranean elements—the *daurade,* or sea bream, and the *daube au boeuf,* a beef stew flavored with orange. The combination of seafood and meat is classic.

FOR THE SAUCE

¼ cup olive oil

1¼ pounds boneless beef top round, cut into small cubes

2 celery stalks with leaves, cut into 2-inch pieces

2 medium onions, minced

1 medium carrot, peeled and coarsely diced

1 medium shallot, minced

1 small garlic bulb, cut horizontally in half

4 medium tomatoes, quartered

1 bottle (750 ml) dry red wine

2 oranges

4 cups Veal Stock (page 230) or Chicken Stock (page 229)

1 sprig fresh thyme

1 bay leaf

Fine sea salt and freshly ground black pepper

FOR THE CANDIED ORANGE ZEST

2 oranges

1 sugar cube or 1 teaspoon sugar

2 tablespoons olive oil

Four 8-ounce sea bream fillets, skin left on (see page 242)

Coarse sea salt, preferably fleur de sel

TO PREPARE THE SAUCE: Heat 2 tablespoons of the olive oil in a cast-iron or other heavy-bottomed casserole over medium-high heat. Working in two or three batches, add the beef and brown on all sides, stirring frequently. Remove with a slotted spoon and set aside.

Heat the remaining 2 tablespoons olive oil in another casserole over medium-low heat. Add the celery, onions, carrot, shallot, garlic, and tomatoes. Cook, stirring often, until the vegetables soften but do not brown, about 5 minutes. Stir in the browned beef, pour in the red wine, and cook until it reduces by half.

Cut the oranges in half and add to the casserole along with the stock, thyme, and bay leaf. Reduce the heat to medium-low and simmer for 2½ hours.

Remove from the heat and season to taste with salt and pepper. Strain through a coarse sieve into a bowl, pressing gently on the solids to extract all the sauce. Cover the sauce with plastic wrap and set aside; if desired, save the beef and vegetables for another use.

TO PREPARE THE CANDIED ORANGE ZEST: With a sharp paring knife or a vegetable peeler, remove the zest from the oranges. Squeeze the juice from the oranges and set aside. Cut the orange zest into fine julienne.

Bring a medium saucepan of water to a boil. Put the zest into a strainer, lower the strainer into the boiling water, and blanch for 30 seconds. Remove and rinse under cold water. Repeat the process four times.

In a small saucepan, combine the blanched zest with the reserved orange juice and the sugar and simmer over medium heat until the liquid evaporates. Set the candied zest aside.

TO COOK THE FISH: Heat the olive oil in a large cast-iron or other heavy-bottomed skillet over medium-high heat. Place the bream fillets skin side down in the pan and cook, without turning, until the skin becomes crispy and begins to curl, 6 to 8 minutes. Transfer the fillets, skin side up, to a rack and let stand while you bring the sauce to a simmer; this allows the fish to cook through completely.

Meanwhile, bring the sauce to a simmer.

Spoon the sauce into the center of four warmed serving plates. Place one fillet in the center of each plate, skin side up. Garnish with the candied orange zest and a sprinkling of coarse salt, and serve immediately.

SUGGESTED WINE

A RICH, FULL-BODIED, HIGHLY PERFUMED WHITE WINE, SUCH AS A
TOKAY PINOT GRIS 1995 MUENCHBERG, A. OSTERTAG, OR AN
EILEEN HARDY CHARDONNAY 1995 BRL HARDY, FROM AUSTRALIA

SOLE WITH FRESH FIGS, BAKED IN FIG LEAVES

Serves 4

THE COMBINATION OF FRESH FIGS, LEMON, and a vanilla bean may seem more suited to dessert than a savory main dish, but it makes a wonderful complement to delicate sole fillets. Half the figs and lemon slices are slowly baked to a confit that garnishes the dish, the rest cooked with the fish. This recipe was inspired by a trip to the Amazon, where local cooks prepare fish by simply wrapping it in banana leaves and baking it. The fish comes out moist and delicately scented by the leaves. In this version, fig leaves (or grape leaves, if necessary) replace the banana leaves.

8 firm but ripe purple figs, cut lengthwise into quarters, leaving the quarters still attached at the stem end

8 thin lemon slices

2 sole (about 1½ pounds each), heads, tails, and black skin removed and cut crosswise in half

20 fresh fig leaves, washed and patted dry

2 teaspoons coarse sea salt, preferably fleur de sel

15 black peppercorns

½ vanilla bean, split

10 Indonesian long peppercorns (see page 247)

2 tablespoons olive oil

TO MAKE THE FIG AND LEMON CONFIT: Preheat the oven to 200°F. Generously oil a small baking pan.

Arrange 4 of the figs and 4 of the lemon slices in the baking pan. Bake for about 50 minutes, until the figs are slightly dried but still moist. Remove the pan and set aside. Increase the oven temperature to 350°F.

TO PREPARE THE FISH: Lightly moisten the bottom of a baking dish large enough to hold the fish in a single layer. Line it with a layer of fig leaves, completely covering the bottom of the pan. Arrange the pieces of sole side by side in the dish. Season with salt. Place the uncooked figs and lemon slices around the sole. Scrape the seeds from the vanilla bean and sprinkle over the fish. Scatter on the peppercorns and drizzle with the olive oil. Cover with the remaining fig leaves, tucking them in around the fish to seal.

Bake the fish for about 15 minutes, until just cooked through. Remove the fig leaves and transfer the fish and fruits to warmed serving plates. Garnish with the reserved fig and lemon confit and serve immediately.

SUGGESTED WINE

A DRY, NOT TOO COMPLEX WHITE WINE, SUCH AS A SANCERRE BLANC 1995 "CLOS DE LA NEORE," F. VATAN, OR A VINA CASABLANCA 1996, SAUVIGNON BLANC, FROM CHILE

[*La Ferme*]

POULTRY AND MEAT

"On Sundays, as a child, there would always be a chicken roasting in the fireplace when you entered a neighbor's house. It would have a beautiful golden color and smelled so good that everyone immediately sat down around the kitchen table, hands folded, as if waiting for a religious ceremony to start."

I REMEMBER THOSE CHICKENS SLOWLY GILDING

above the flames and the thick steaks of Chalosse beef sizzling on the grill. On other occasions, there would be glistening slices of duck foie gras sautéing in butter in a cast-iron pan. It is these products that I grew up with—the Landaise chickens, the Chalosse beef, the farm-produced foie gras—that I still love and feature today on my menus.

Two of my favorite ways of preparing meats and poultry are the oldest and most rustic—cooking *à la broche*, or spit-roasting, and cooking *à la ficelle* (literally, "by the string"), where a piece of meat, such as a leg of lamb, is suspended by string above the fire of a big, open hearth, the way we did it on the family farm. The food cooks purely and simply by the heat of the fire: The outside becomes seared, crisp, and delicious; the inside, juicy and tender.

Most of the recipes present the meat or poultry whole, to be cut or sliced only when serving. Keeping the primary ingredient whole retains its character and keeps the meat succulent. Alain Chapel always taught his chefs to exalt the ingredients of a dish. "The food alone," he often said, "is the star, not the cook."

You will encounter numerous contemporary elements in the recipes in this chapter, such as the "condiment sauces" (the cèpe "marmalade" on the facing page accompanies the Poached Chicken in the Pot). Yet my cooking is firmly grounded in the old traditions and classic techniques. It's the mingling of these two threads—the traditional elements of French cuisine and the contemporary— that excites me. Cuisine can never remain static. It is vital, luminous, always evolving, in touch with its time, but grounded in yesterday.

TRUFFLED FOIE GRAS RAVIOLI IN CHICKEN BROTH

Serves 4 as a first course

RAVIOLI STUFFED WITH FOIE GRAS and chopped truffles float in a clear amber-colored chicken broth, its color enriched by deeply browned onions. Paper-thin slices of truffle are used to garnish the broth just before serving. A pasta maker is essential for rolling out the ravioli dough to the required thinness.

FOR THE RAVIOLI DOUGH

1¼ cups all-purpose flour

1 large egg

1½ tablespoons olive oil

Pinch of fine sea salt

14 ounces foie gras confit or terrine, cut into 20 equal cubes

2 ounces black truffles, finely chopped and mashed with the back of a knife

Savory Chicken Broth (page 229)

1½ ounces black truffles, sliced paper-thin with a mandoline

TO MAKE THE RAVIOLI DOUGH: Combine all the ingredients in the bowl of a food processor and process until the dough is very smooth and forms a ball. Form the dough into a disk, wrap with plastic wrap, and refrigerate for at least 2 hours.

TO PREPARE THE RAVIOLI: Roll the foie gras cubes in the chopped truffles to coat them lightly, then refrigerate. Reserve any remaining chopped truffles for the garnish.

Using a pasta machine, roll out the dough to the thinnest setting. Cut the ravioli dough into twenty 2- by 4-inch rectangles. Arrange the rectangles in front of you with a short side facing you. Place a foie gras cube in the center of the upper half of each rectangle. Lightly moisten a ¼-inch border around the edge of the rectangle with water, then fold the bottom half of the rectangle over the top, aligning the edges. Press firmly all around the edges with your fingers to seal the dough.

Meanwhile, bring a large pot of salted water to a boil. In a large saucepan, bring the chicken broth to a simmer over medium-low heat.

Lower the ravioli into the boiling water and cook for 1 minute. With a slotted spoon, gently transfer the ravioli to a bowl containing about ½ cup of the hot chicken broth, to keep the ravioli from sticking to each other.

Divide the ravioli among four warmed soup plates. Ladle the chicken broth over the ravioli, sprinkle on any remaining chopped truffles, and garnish with the truffle slices.

CHICKEN FRICASSEE WITH MORELS

Serves 4

THE ARRIVAL IN EARLY SPRING of fragrant morels is celebrated in kitchens throughout France. In this recipe, an easy, rustic fricassee of chicken, browned in butter and then baked, turns elegant when paired with a creamy morel ragout.

FOR THE MUSHROOM RAGOUT

6 tablespoons unsalted butter

2 shallots, thinly sliced

2 pounds morel mushrooms, trimmed and thoroughly rinsed (see page 238)

Coarse sea salt

2½ cups heavy cream, ¼ cup whipped to soft peaks

Juice of ½ lemon

Fine sea salt and freshly ground black pepper

¼ cup olive oil

3 tablespoons unsalted butter

4 boneless chicken breasts with skin

Fine sea salt and freshly ground black pepper

4 boneless skinless chicken thighs

2 garlic cloves, unpeeled, lightly crushed

½ cup Chicken Stock (page 229)

1¾ cups Chicken Jus (page 230)

Preheat the oven to 375°F.

TO PREPARE THE RAGOUT: Melt 4 tablespoons of the butter in a large casserole over medium heat. Add the shallots and cook, stirring occasionally, until translucent, about 4 minutes. Add the mushrooms and the remaining 2 tablespoons butter, stir well, and season to taste with coarse salt. Cover and cook over medium-low heat for 20 minutes, stirring from time to time.

Using a slotted spoon, transfer the mushrooms to a plate and set aside. Raise the heat to medium and reduce the cooking liquid by half, to about 2 tablespoons. Add the 2¼ cups cream and continue to cook, stirring frequently, until the sauce is reduced and thick enough to coat the back of a wooden spoon, 12 to 14 minutes. Return the mushrooms to the skillet, stir in the lemon juice and whipped cream, and season to taste with salt and pepper. Remove from the heat and cover to keep warm.

MEANWHILE COOK THE CHICKEN: Heat 2 tablespoons of the olive oil in a large, deep ovenproof skillet over medium heat. Add the butter. Season the chicken breasts with salt and pepper and place skin side down in the skillet. Cook, turning once, until browned on both sides, 3 to 4 minutes each side. Transfer the chicken breasts to a plate. Season the chicken thighs, add to the skillet and cook, turning once, until browned on both sides, 3 to 4 minutes on each side. Return the breasts to the skillet and add the garlic and the remaining 2 tablespoons oil.

Place the skillet in the oven and cook until the juices run clear when the chicken is pierced with a skewer, about 10 minutes. Transfer the chicken to a wire rack set over a platter. Reduce the oven temperature to 250°F.

Pour off the fat from the skillet, set over medium-high heat, and deglaze with, the chicken stock, scraping up all the browned bits on the bottom of the pan. Add the chicken jus and bring to a boil, then reduce the heat to medium and cook until reduced by one quarter. Strain the sauce through a fine strainer into a medium skillet.

To serve, place the chicken on a baking sheet and return to the oven to heat through. Add the juices from the platter to the sauce and bring to a boil.

Bring the mushroom ragout to a boil and then spoon onto the top half of four warmed serving plates. Place a chicken breast and thigh on the bottom half of each plate and spoon sauce generously over the chicken. Serve immediately.

S U G G E S T E D   W I N E

AN ELEGANT, NOT TOO CONCENTRATED RED WINE, SUCH AS AN
ALOXE-CORTON 1990, FROM TOLLOT-BEAUT, OR A PESQUERA
CRIANZA 1991 RIBERA DEL DUERO, FROM SPAIN

[*Pâtes Mi-Séchées, Crémées et Truffé aux Ris de Veau, Crêtes et Rognons de Coq*]

HALF-DRIED PASTA TUBES WITH SWEETBREADS, COCKSCOMBS, AND KIDNEYS

Thinly rolled fresh pasta rounds are passed through the pasta machine a final time to give them an oval shape and make them even thinner. The ovals are laid over wooden sticks to dry (one third of the oval hangs down; the rest wraps around the stick to form a tube). When dry, the ovals are cooked in chicken stock, then finished in a béchamel sauce enriched with cream, mascarpone, grated Beaufort cheese, and truffle juice.

Meanwhile, cockscombs and cock's kidneys are blanched separately and then simmered in chicken stock. Lobster is boiled in water infused with coriander and peppercorns; the tails and claws are shelled and the tail meat is cut into medallions. Blanched sweetbreads are placed on a bed of diced vegetables, moistened with chicken stock, and braised in the oven, then cut into escalopes.

To finish, the sweetbreads, cockscombs, and kidneys are heated with butter, girolles, and fresh truffle to make a ragout. A veal jus is reduced and flavored with chopped truffle. The sauced pasta is arranged on plates and the ragout spooned over. The lobster is warmed in butter and placed on top of the ragout. The cream sauce is spooned over the ragout; the veal jus is spooned around the plate for contrasting color.

POACHED CHICKEN IN THE POT WITH WINTER VEGETABLES AND CÈPE "MARMALADE"

Serves 4

THIS OPULENT VERSION of *poule au pot*, made with the famous plump and buttery-flavored chickens from Bresse, has a stuffing studded with foie gras and cèpe mushrooms and lightly flavored with Cognac. Aromatic vegetables cooked in chicken broth and then drizzled with a buttery Barolo wine vinegar sauce accompany the chicken, along with a "marmalade" of cèpes, truffle, and truffle juice.

FOR THE STUFFING

1½ tablespoons olive oil

1 chicken heart (reserved from one of the chickens), cut into small dice

1 chicken liver (reserved from one of the chickens), cut into small dice

3 ounces boneless skinless chicken breast, cut into small dice

1 shallot, minced

3 ounces white sandwich bread (about 5 slices)

⅔ cup milk

2 ounces raw duck foie gras, cut into small dice

2 ounces cèpe (porcini) mushrooms (including the reserved stem from below), trimmed and wiped clean (see page 238), cut into small dice

1 tablespoon chopped fresh chervil

1 tablespoon chopped fresh parsley

2 tablespoons heavy cream

3 large egg yolks

2 tablespoons Cognac

¼ ounce black truffle, finely chopped (optional)

Fine sea salt and freshly ground black pepper

Two 3-pound free-range chickens, 1 heart and 1 liver reserved

Fine sea salt and freshly ground black pepper

1 onion

1 carrot, peeled

1 celery stalk, peeled

2 tablespoons coarse sea salt

FOR THE VEGETABLES

7 cups Chicken Stock (page 229)

2 celery stalks from the pale green heart, peeled and split lengthwise in half

4 large carrots, peeled

8 small leeks, trimmed and rinsed well

4 small turnips with green tops, greens trimmed to 2 inches, outer two layers peeled off

FOR THE SAUCE

1 tablespoon aged red wine vinegar, preferably Barolo wine vinegar

5 tablespoons unsalted butter, cut into pieces

FOR THE CÈPE "MARMALADE"

1 large cèpe (porcini) mushroom, stem removed and reserved for stuffing (above), cap wiped clean (see page 238) and very finely diced

1 small black truffle, chopped

¼ cup truffle juice

1 small shallot, chopped

2 tablespoons aged red wine vinegar, preferably Barolo wine vinegar

Fine sea salt and freshly ground black pepper

TO MAKE THE STUFFING: Heat 1½ teaspoons of the oil in a small nonstick skillet over medium heat. Add the chicken heart, liver, and breast meat and cook, stirring, until just cooked through, 1 to 2 minutes. Remove from the heat and let cool.

In a small skillet, heat the remaining 1 tablespoon oil over medium heat. Add the shallot and cook, stirring occasionally, until translucent, about 2 minutes. Remove from the heat.

In a small bowl, soak the bread in the milk.

In a medium bowl, combine the foie gras, cèpes, shallot, chervil, and parsley. Remove the bread from the milk, squeezing out the excess liquid with your hands, and add to the foie gras mixture. Stir in the cream. Stir in the egg yolks one at a time, mixing well. Stir in the Cognac and then the truffle, if using. Season to taste with salt and pepper.

TO COOK THE CHICKENS: Season the cavities of the chickens with salt and pepper. Stuff the cavities with the stuffing and truss the chickens.

In a large stockpot, combine 2½ quarts of water, the onion, carrot, celery, and salt and bring to a boil. Add the chickens. They should be completely covered by the water; if necessary, add water to cover by 1 inch. Bring back to a boil, lower the heat, and simmer until tender, 40 to 50 minutes. With tongs, transfer the chickens to a colander to drain.

MEANWHILE, COOK THE VEGETABLES: Bring the chicken stock to a boil in a wide pot. Add the vegetables, cover, and simmer, removing the vegetables as they are cooked. Using a slotted spoon, transfer the vegetables to a serving dish and cover to keep warm.

TO MAKE THE SAUCE: Transfer ¾ cup of the chicken stock to a small saucepan and bring to a boil. Add the vinegar and butter and stir until blended and smooth. Keep warm over very low heat.

TO MAKE THE MARMALADE: Combine the cèpe, chopped truffle, truffle juice, and shallot in a small saucepan. Add 1 cup of the chicken stock, bring to a boil over medium-high heat, and reduce by half. Reduce the heat to low, stir in the wine vinegar, and season to taste with salt and pepper. (Save the remaining chicken broth for another use.)

To serve, carve the chickens and arrange on a serving platter with the stuffing. Spoon a bit of the cèpe marmalade over the chicken and serve the rest in a small bowl on the side. Arrange the vegetables on a platter, drizzle on the sauce, and serve.

SUGGESTED WINE

A FINE AND FLAVORFUL RED WINE WITHOUT TOO MUCH TANNIN,
SUCH AS A MORGON 1993, A BEAUJOLAIS APPELLATION
FROM R. LAPIERRE, OR A PINOT NOIR 1995 FROM AU BON
CLIMAT, IN SANTA BARBARA

ROAST CHICKEN STUFFED WITH GIROLLES, NEW POTATOES, AND SPRING ONIONS

Serves 4

THIS CHICKEN, ROASTED on a spit (or in the oven), has a rich stuffing of fresh duck foie gras, bacon, and chicken liver, as well as a second stuffing, under the skin, of mixed herb butter. The herb butter permeates the meat while cooking, giving it a wonderful flavor and texture. A garnish of sautéed new potatoes, girolle mushrooms, and pearl onions is tossed in an aromatic brown chicken glaze just before serving.

Two 3-pound free-range chickens

FOR THE CHICKEN GLAZE

2 tablespoons chicken fat (reserved from the chickens)

2 small garlic cloves, peeled

1 small onion, chopped

1 sprig fresh thyme

About 2 cups Chicken Stock (page 229) or water

FOR THE HERB BUTTER

10 tablespoons (1¼ sticks) unsalted butter, softened

½ bunch *each*: fresh parsley, chervil, and tarragon, stems removed, leaves chopped

½ bunch fresh chives, chopped

Fine sea salt and freshly ground black pepper

FOR THE STUFFING

3½ ounces raw duck foie gras, cut into ½-inch cubes

Fine sea salt and freshly ground black pepper

2½ ounces slab bacon or pancetta, diced

1½ ounces chicken liver (reserved from the chickens), cut into ½-inch cubes

3½ ounces white sandwich bread (about 6 slices), crusts removed and cut into ½-inch cubes

Fine sea salt and freshly ground black pepper

FOR THE VEGETABLES

3 tablespoons olive oil or goose fat

1¼ pound small new potatoes, scrubbed

Coarse sea salt

1¼ pounds girolle mushrooms, trimmed and cleaned (see page 238)

4 tablespoons unsalted butter

1 small shallot, finely chopped

1 sprig fresh thyme

½ pound pearl onions, peeled

1 tablespoon sugar

Fine sea salt and freshly ground black pepper

Pull out and reserve the two pockets of fat from inside the body cavity of each chicken; reserve 2 tablespoons of the fat for the chicken glaze. Cut off the wing tips, coarsely chop with the neck, and set aside for the glaze.

TO PREPARE THE CHICKEN GLAZE: Coarsely chop the chicken fat. Place it in a small saucepan and heat over medium heat until it starts to melt. Add 1 garlic clove and the chopped wing tips and necks and cook, stirring often, until browned, about 10 minutes. Pour off any excess fat and stir in the onion, thyme, and the remaining garlic. Pour in enough chicken stock to barely cover. Bring to a boil, lower the heat, and simmer until syrupy and reduced to about ⅓ cup. Strain into a small saucepan, add a drop of water, and set aside.

MEANWHILE, MAKE THE HERB BUTTER: In a medium bowl, mix the softened butter and chopped herbs until well blended. Season to taste with salt and pepper. Place the herb butter on a piece of plastic wrap and spread it evenly about ¼ inch thick. Cover with another piece of plastic and, using a rolling pin, gently roll into an even sheet about ⅛ inch thick. Place in the freezer to chill until firm.

TO PREPARE THE STUFFING: Heat a medium nonstick skillet over medium-high heat. Add the foie gras cubes and sauté until lightly browned, about 30 seconds. Season with salt and pepper. Transfer the foie gras, with its fat, to a fine sieve set over a small bowl to drain; reserve the fat in the bowl. Add the bacon to the skillet and cook, stirring frequently, until it begins to render its fat. With the slotted spoon, transfer to a small bowl. Add the chicken livers to the fat remaining in the skillet and cook, stirring, until seared on all sides, about 1 minute. Season with salt and pepper. Remove with the spoon and add to the bacon. Pour off the fat from the pan. Add the foie gras to the bacon and add the reserved foie gras fat to the skillet. Heat over medium-high heat, add the bread cubes to the skillet, and cook, tossing and stirring often, until golden, about 4 minutes. Add to the bowl and gently mix all the ingredients together.

TO ROAST THE CHICKEN: Preheat the oven to 350°F. Cut the chilled herb butter into 2- to 3-inch-wide sheets. Oil your hands, and very gently work your hands between the skin and flesh of each chicken, starting at the neck end and loosening the skin over the breasts and thighs. Slide the herb butter sheets under the skin and then massage the skin with your hands so that the butter softens and moves over the chicken flesh.

Divide the stuffing between the cavities of the chickens, packing it gently, and truss the chickens. (If spit-roasting, oil the string before trussing to prevent it from burning during cooking.) Lightly season the chickens all over with salt and pepper and place in a roasting pan or on a spit. Roast, basting often, for about 1 hour and 10 minutes, until the skin is golden brown and the juices run clear when the thigh is pierced. Transfer the chickens to a wire rack set over a platter and let rest for 10 minutes. Just before serving, skim off any fat from the chicken juices and add the juices to the chicken glaze.

WHILE THE CHICKEN IS ROASTING, PREPARE THE VEGETABLES: Heat 2 tablespoons of the oil in a large skillet. Add the new potatoes, stir to coat with the oil, and season with coarse salt. Cover and cook over medium-low heat, shaking the pan often, until the potatoes are golden brown and tender, 30 to 35 minutes.

Meanwhile, in another large skillet, heat the remaining oil over high heat. Add the mushrooms and sauté, stirring often, until tender, about 10 minutes. Add 1 tablespoon of the butter and the shallot and cook for 1 minute. Add the girolles to the cooked potatoes, add the thyme, and toss to mix. Set aside.

In a small skillet, combine the pearl onions with 2 tablespoons of the butter and the sugar. Add enough water to just cover and season with a pinch of salt. Bring to a boil, then reduce the heat to low and simmer until the liquid has reduced to a golden brown, bubbling glaze and the onions are tender, 8 to 10 minutes. Gently roll the onions around in the pan to coat with the glaze, and add to the potatoes.

To serve, add the remaining 1 tablespoon butter and the reserved chicken glaze to the vegetables and reheat over low heat until the liquid is simmering. Remove the trussing strings and place the chickens on a large serving platter. Surround the chickens with the vegetables and serve.

SUGGESTED WINE

A MATURE, CONCENTRATED RED WINE, SUCH AS A CLOS
DE PAPES 1982 CHÂTEAUNEUF-DU-PAPE OR AN ITALIAN
BAROLO SPERSS 1990, FROM ANGELO GAJA

ROAST DUCK STUFFED WITH ORANGE LEAVES, WITH CARAMELIZED ORANGE SAUCE

Serves 4

ORANGE LEAVES STUFFED INTO THE BIRDS' cavities just before roasting add great fragrance and flavor to this uncomplicated roast duck. If you live in a sunny clime where orange trees flourish, you can pluck off a few leaves just before preparing dinner. Or, if you mail-order oranges from a Florida orange-grower, ask them to tuck in a handful of leaves—or several oranges with the leaves still attached—with your order. If you can't get orange leaves, however, you can substitute lemon leaves. Make sure the leaves have not been sprayed with pesticides or such. The sweet-and-sour orange sauce made from orange zest, juice, and sliced orange segments provides an intensely flavored, colorful accompaniment to the tender, crisp-skinned duck.

Two 4½-pound ducks

Fine sea salt and freshly ground
    black pepper

A handful of fresh orange leaves
    (unsprayed) (optional)

2 tablespoons olive oil

2 tablespoons unsalted butter

1 tablespoon water

3 tablespoons sherry vinegar

⅔ cup Veal Stock (page 230)
    or duck stock

2½ tablespoons unsalted butter

Juice of ½ lemon (optional)

FOR THE SAUCE AND GARNISH

4 large oranges

¼ cup sugar

TO ROAST THE DUCKS: Preheat the oven to 425°F.

Season the ducks inside and out with salt and pepper. Divide the orange leaves, if using, between the cavities of the ducks and truss them.

Heat the olive oil and butter over medium heat in a roasting pan large enough to hold the ducks. Add the ducks and brown on all sides. Place in the oven and roast, basting often with the pan juices, until the juices from the cavities run clear, about 1 hour.

Meanwhile, using a paring knife or a vegetable peeler, remove the zest from 1 of the oranges in long strips. Cut into julienne strips and set aside. With a sharp knife, peel 2 of the oranges, removing all the bitter white pith. Slice between the membranes to release the orange segments, and set aside on a plate. Squeeze the juice from the remaining 2 oranges.

TO PREPARE THE SAUCE: Place the julienned orange strips in a small saucepan, add cold water to cover, and bring to a boil. Drain the orange strips and return to the saucepan, cover with cold water again, and bring to a boil; drain and set aside.

In a small deep skillet, heat the sugar and 1 tablespoon water over medium heat, stirring frequently, until the sugar dissolves. Brush down the sides of the pan with a wet pastry brush and continue to cook, without stirring, until the syrup turns golden, swirling the pan so it caramelizes evenly. Add the sherry vinegar and orange juice, bring to a simmer, and simmer until slightly reduced. Add the stock and the reserved orange zest and cook until the sauce is reduced and syrupy, about 15 minutes.

While the sauce is reducing, remove the ducks from the oven and place on a wire rack set over a platter. Let rest for 15 minutes, then remove the trussing strings.

TO FINISH THE SAUCE: When the sauce has reached a syrupy consistency, bring to a boil. Add 2 tablespoons of the butter and, holding the pan at an angle to the hot burner, swirl the sauce until the butter has melted and the sauce takes on a glossy sheen. Add the lemon juice, if you wish.

Meanwhile, in a small skillet, gently warm the orange segments in the remaining 1½ teaspoons butter.

To serve, place the ducks on a serving platter and surround with the orange segments. Spoon a bit of the sauce over the ducks and pass the remaining sauce in a sauceboat.

SUGGESTED WINE

A RICH AND UNCTUOUS RED WINE, SUCH AS A VACQUEYRAS
1990, LE CLOS CAZEAU, OR A NEYERS ZINFANDEL
CONTRA, FROM CALIFORNIA'S COSTA COUNTY PATO VINEYARD

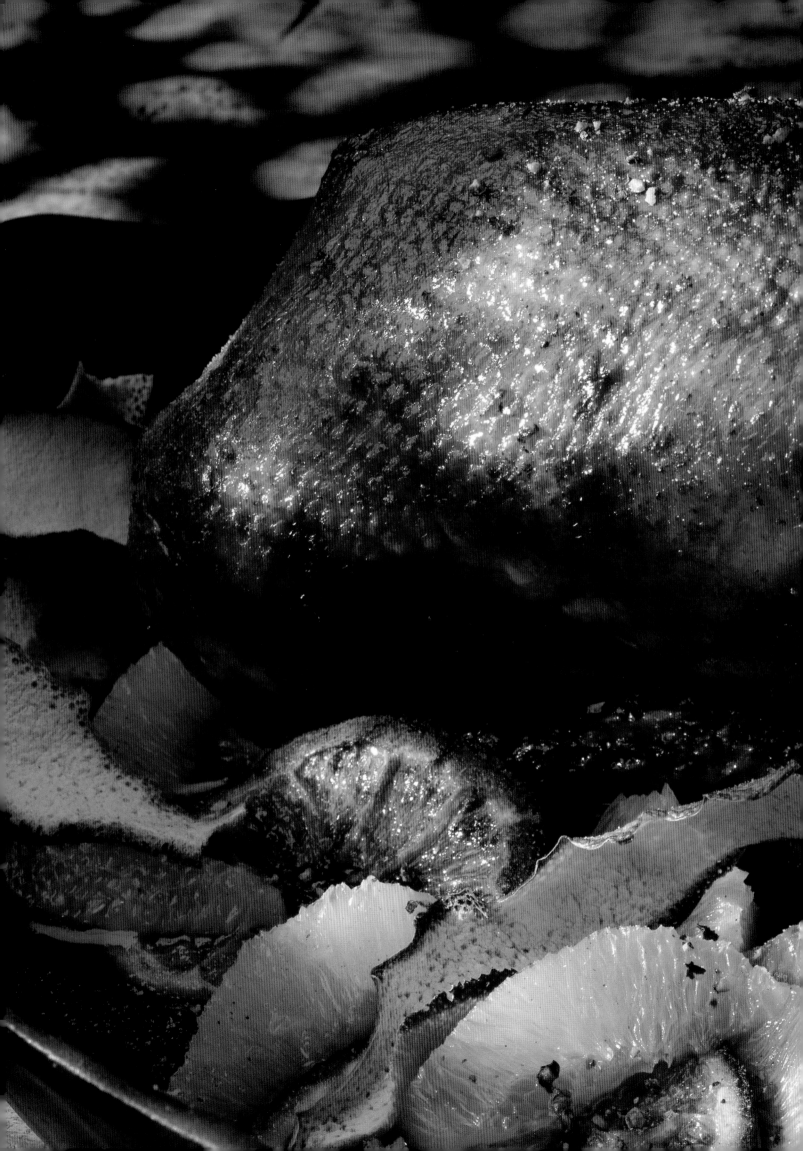

SAUTÉED FOIE GRAS WITH PORT WINE SAUCE AND SAUTÉED APPLES AND GRAPES

Serves 4

THE GRAPES, APPLES, AND PORT are reduced to an intensely flavored sauce for the opulently rich foie gras.

FOR THE SAUCE

¾ pound seedless green grapes

3 Granny Smith apples

Reserved foie gras trimmings (from below)

½ cup port

½ cup Duck Jus (page 231) or pan juices from a roast duck

Fine sea salt and freshly ground black pepper

6 tablespoons unsalted butter

3½ tablespoons sugar

1 large lobe fresh duck foie gras (about 1¼ pounds), cut into 4 escalopes, trimmings reserved for sauce

Coarse sea salt, preferably fleur de sel, and freshly ground black pepper

TO PREPARE THE SAUCE: Reserve 40 of the grapes for the garnish. Purée the remaining grapes in a blender or food processor, then strain the juice through a fine strainer into a bowl and reserve. Or press the grapes through a food mill or a juicer.

In a medium pot of boiling water, blanch the reserved 40 grapes for 10 seconds, then drain and immediately transfer to a bowl of ice-cold water to help loosen the skins. Drain and, using a small sharp knife, peel the grapes. Put them in a bowl and set aside.

Peel and core the apples. Coarsely chop 1 apple, and cut the remaining 2 into 6 wedges each.

Heat a medium skillet over medium heat. Add the foie gras trimmings and cook, stirring, until slightly browned. Stir in the chopped apple and cook until the apple is well browned. Deglaze the pan with the port, stirring to scrape up the browned bits stuck to the bottom and sides of the pan, then cook until reduced by half. Stir in the reserved grape juice and cook until the liquid has reduced by half. Stir in the duck jus and cook, stirring, until reduced by half and the sauce is smooth and syrupy. Season to taste with salt and pepper. Strain through a fine strainer into a bowl, pressing down firmly on the solids with the back of a spoon to squeeze all the liquid out, then set aside.

Melt 1 tablespoon of the butter in a medium skillet over medium heat. Add the sugar and cook until it begins to dissolve. Then add the apple sections and stir to coat. Cook, stirring frequently, until the apples are light golden brown but still firm. Add the peeled grapes and 4 tablespoons of the butter, stirring to coat the grapes with the butter, and cook, stirring often, until the apple sections are tender and golden brown, about 10 minutes. Remove from the heat and set the pan aside.

TO COOK THE FOIE GRAS: Season the escalopes with salt and pepper. Heat a medium skillet over medium heat. Place the escalopes in the pan and cook, turning once, until golden brown on both sides, 2 minutes on each side; take care that the livers do not burn, and lower the heat slightly if they brown too fast. Remove from the heat.

Meanwhile, reheat the sauce and stir in the remaining 1 tablespoon butter until melted.

To serve, divide the hot apple sections among four warmed serving plates. Place the foie gras on top of the apples, spoon the sauce over, and scatter 10 grapes around each plate. Season the foie gras with coarse salt and pepper and serve immediately.

"Foie gras is the king of ingredients found in my native region of the Landes. From the cradle I've eaten it and have never grown tired of it. With its smooth, delicate texture, it's extremely versatile, and you'll see it in salads, terrines, tourtes, raviolis, and stuffings. But I especially love it fresh, simply sautéed in butter and served hot with succulent sautéed fruit and a wine sauce. Every bite is voluptuous."

SUGGESTED WINE

A CABERNET SAUVIGNON OR MERLOT, SUCH AS A
CHÂTEAU TROTANOY POMEROL 1982 OR AN AUSTRALIAN
PENFOLDS BIN 707 1994 CABERNET SAUVIGNON

DUCK TOURTE

THIS RICH DUCK TOURTE encased in flaky puff pastry is made from duck, veal, chicken, chicken livers, pork, and foie gras. For the filling, chicken livers are first sautéed in olive oil with minced shallot. The pan is deglazed with Cognac and the livers seasoned; the mixture is finely chopped. Duck and chicken breasts, veal tenderloin, and pork loin and fat are ground together and stirred into the liver mixture. Finally, raw foie gras that has been pressed through a sieve to make a fine paste is stirred into the mixture along with crème fraîche, truffle juice, Madeira, more Cognac, and salt and pepper. Cubes of raw foie gras are gently folded in.

To assemble the tourte, a terrine mold is lined with puff pastry and filled with half of the filling mixture. Tender duck breast fillets that have been marinated in a mixture of Madeira and Cognac are arranged on top and the remaining filling mixture is carefully spread over. More pastry covers the tourte and the edges are crimped to seal. After the tourte has chilled, it is brushed with egg glaze and a hole is cut into the top to allow steam to escape during baking. Slices, crisp and golden, are served hot or warm, with a Rouennaise sauce made by reducing duck stock with red wine, and thickening it with pig's blood.

TRUFFLE AND FOIE GRAS TOURTE WITH A TRUFFLE REDUCTION SAUCE

Serves 4

A CLASSIC PITHIVIERS is a dessert made of two large disks of puff pastry filled with almond cream. It originated in the town of Pithiviers, south of Paris. Unlike the traditional version, these individual pithiviers are savory instead of sweet, filled with foie gras and truffles. An intense reduction sauce of veal jus, truffles, and truffle juice is served with the pithiviers, and a bit is poured into a hole in the center of the top crust to permeate the filling just before serving.

FOR THE PITHIVIERS

4 ounces black truffles

2 tablespoons unsalted butter

Fine sea salt

2 tablespoons dry Madeira

3 tablespoons Veal Jus (page 231)

1¼ pounds puff pastry

8 ounces duck or goose foie gras confit or terrine, cut into four ½-inch-thick slices

Coarse sea salt and freshly ground black pepper

2 medium egg yolks, beaten, for glaze

FOR THE SAUCE

2½ cups Veal Jus (page 231)

¾ cup truffle juice

4 ounces black truffles, finely chopped

Freshly ground black pepper

TO PREPARE THE PITHIVIERS: Using a mandoline or a very sharp knife, cut the truffles into ⅛-inch slices. You will need 24 slices; finely chop any extra truffle and reserve for the sauce.

Melt the butter in a skillet over medium heat until foaming. Add the truffle slices and cook, turning once, until they change color, about 1 minute. Season with salt, add the Madeira, and bring to a boil. Add the veal jus and cook until almost all of the liquid has evaporated and the truffles are nicely glazed, about 1 minute. Transfer the truffles to a plate and let cool to room temperature.

On a lightly floured surface, roll out the puff pastry ⅛ inch thick. Using plain round cutters, cut out four 4¼-inch circles and four 3¼-inch circles from the dough.

Arrange the smaller puff pastry circles on a large baking sheet. Carefully place 6 truffle slices on each circle, overlapping them if necessary and leaving a ½-inch border around the sides. Lay a slice of foie gras over the truffles on each circle, trimming to fit if necessary. Season to taste with coarse salt and pepper.

Using a pastry brush, moisten the border of each pastry circle with the egg glaze. Cover with the larger pastry circles, pressing the pastry gently around the filling and pressing firmly to make sure the edges are well sealed. Using the tip of a paring knife, gently notch the edges of the pastry, creating a scalloped edge. With the knife, score a pinwheel design on top of each pithiviers, without piercing the dough. Cut a small hole in the center of each pithiviers to allow steam to escape. Brush the tops with the remaining egg glaze and refrigerate until the dough is firm, at least 1 hour.

TO BAKE THE PITHIVIERS: Preheat the oven to 350°F.

Bake the pithiviers until golden brown, about 20 minutes. Immediately transfer the pies to a wire rack to cool slightly.

MEANWHILE, MAKE THE SAUCE: In a small saucepan, bring the veal jus to a boil. Boil until reduced to 1¼ cups. Add the truffle juice and truffles (including any reserved from the pithiviers), reduce the heat to medium, and boil gently until the sauce has reduced to a syrupy consistency; you should have about ¾ cup. Remove from the heat.

To serve, place the pithiviers on four warmed serving plates and pour about 1 tablespoon of the warm sauce through the hole in the center of each one. Spoon a bit of the sauce around the plates and serve the rest in a sauceboat on the side.

SUGGESTED WINE

A RICH AND UNCTUOUS RED WINE, SUCH AS A CHÂTEAU TERTRE RÔTEBOEUF 1989 ST. EMILION GRAND CRU OR A CAYMUS VINEYARD RESERVE 1995, FROM THE NAPA VALLEY

RABBIT "TOURNEDOS," RIBS, AND CONFIT, WITH BLACK RADISH AND WHITE TURNIP

BONED RABBIT THIGHS are rolled and wrapped in bacon. Then they're halved crosswise and tied to make small "tournedos"; shoulders are roasted with onion rounds, rosemary, garlic, and olive oil in a slow oven until the meat is tender and the onions golden. The meat is shredded and set aside with the onions. The "racks" are split down the backbone. Cylinders of black radish are briefly sautéed in olive oil, then cooked until tender in chicken stock.

To finish the dish, the tournedos are sautéed along with the racks in olive oil and basted with rabbit jus. When the rabbit is cooked, the pan is deglazed with vinegar. The deglaze and more rabbit jus are stirred into the roasted shoulder and onion mixture, along with small black Niçoise olives. The mixture is cooked until the jus has been absorbed by the meat to make a moist confit.

To serve, slices of the tournedos and ribs are placed on the dinner plates. The cooked cylinders of black radish are added to the plate, along with paper-thin rounds of raw young white turnip that have been tossed in olive oil. The confit is spread on toasted country bread and served alongside.

ROAST VEAL WITH VEGETABLES IN GARLIC-SHALLOT BUTTER

Serves 4

SIMILAR IN SPIRIT to the recipe on page 165, the veal is simply browned in olive oil and then roasted. It is accompanied by onions, carrots, and potatoes tossed in a garlic-and-shallot butter with ground almonds and diced prosciutto. At the restaurant, additional escargot butter is served on the side to accompany the sliced veal.

FOR THE VEAL

One 1¾-pound boneless veal rump roast

Fine sea salt

2 tablespoons olive oil

⅓ pound meaty veal scraps (from the butcher)

2 tablespoons unsalted butter

¼ cup Chicken Stock (page 229)

FOR THE VEGETABLES

3 tablespoons olive oil

6 pearl onions, outer layer peeled off

10 to 12 small new potatoes (about 10 ounces), scrubbed and cut in half

4 medium carrots, peeled and cut on the diagonal into ¼-inch slices

8 very slim young leeks, trimmed, rinsed well, and cut into 1½-inch pieces

2 tablespoons Garlic-Shallot Butter (page 233)

Fine sea salt

TO ROAST THE VEAL: Preheat the oven to 400°F.

Season the roast on all sides with salt. Heat the olive oil in a heavy medium casserole over medium heat. Add the veal and brown on all sides, about 8 minutes. Stir in the veal scraps and butter and place the casserole in the oven. Roast for about 40 minutes, basting often with the pan juices, until an instant-read thermometer inserted in the thickest part of the roast registers 140°F.

MEANWHILE, PREPARE THE VEGETABLES: Heat the olive oil in a medium pot over medium heat. Add the onions and potatoes and cook, stirring often, until lightly browned, about 8 minutes. Add the carrots, reduce the heat to low, and cook, stirring frequently, for 5 minutes. Add the leeks and cook, stirring often, until all the vegetables are tender when pierced with the tip of a small sharp knife, about 10 minutes longer. Remove from the heat and cover to keep warm.

Remove the veal from the oven and transfer to a wire rack set over a platter. Cover loosely with aluminum foil and let rest for 15 minutes.

WHILE THE VEAL RESTS, FINISH THE VEAL JUS: Set the casserole over medium heat and heat until the juices begin to bubble. Add 2 tablespoons of the chicken stock to the pot and stir and scrape up the browned bits stuck to the bottom and sides of the pot, then repeat with the remaining 2 tablespoons stock. Strain through a fine strainer into a bowl and set aside.

TO FINISH THE VEGETABLES: Return the pot to low heat, add the garlic-shallot butter and half of the veal jus to the vegetables, and toss to melt the butter and coat them well. (Save remaining jus for another use.) Season the vegetables with salt to taste. Arrange the vegetables on a warmed serving platter and place the veal roast on top. Serve immediately, slicing the veal and serving it with the vegetables.

SAUTÉED VEAL WITH BLANQUETTE OF VEGETABLES

Serves 4

THIS DISH PAYS HOMAGE to the classic *blanquette de veau*, in which chunks of stewing veal are cooked in a milk or cream sauce with carrots, onions, mushrooms, and turnips. In this interpretation, thick veal chops are pan-roasted and accompanied by vegetables that are cooked separately in a veal bouillon for flavor. They are combined before serving in a rich blanquette sauce with just a hint of lemon.

FOR THE VEAL BOUILLON

2¼ pounds veal tail or shoulder, cut into 2- to 3-inch pieces

About 6 cups Chicken Stock (page 229)

Reserved carrot, onion, mushroom, and spinach trimmings (from below)

FOR THE VEGETABLE BLANQUETTE

About 4 cups Chicken Stock (page 229) or water

4 large carrots, peeled and cut on the diagonal into thirds, trimmings reserved

8 medium spring onions (white part only), outer layer peeled off, trimmings reserved

4 medium turnips with green tops, greens trimmed to 3 inches, two outer layers peeled off, and cut in half

2 zucchini, preferably round, quartered and seedy center portions sliced off

2 small purple artichokes, trimmed (see page 248)

½ pound medium white mushrooms, trimmed and wiped clean, stems removed and reserved, caps cut on an angle into large irregular chunks

½ pound chanterelle mushrooms or other small wild mushrooms, trimmed and wiped clean, trimmings reserved

6 tablespoons unsalted butter

1 cup heavy cream

Coarse sea salt, preferably fleur de sel

¼ teaspoon fresh lemon juice, or to taste

¼ pound spinach, washed, tough stems removed and reserved, leaves torn into large pieces

FOR THE VEAL CHOPS

2 large rib veal chops (about 1 pound each), trimmed, boned, and lightly flattened (trimmings reserved for Veal Jus, page 231, if you wish)

¼ cup grapeseed oil

Coarse sea salt, preferably fleur de sel, and freshly ground black pepper

1 teaspoon unsalted butter

TO PREPARE THE VEAL BOUILLON: Combine the veal tail and cold water to cover in a medium pot and bring to a boil over high heat. Reduce the heat to low and simmer for 10 minutes; drain. Rinse out the pot, return the veal to the pot, and add enough chicken stock to cover. Add the reserved carrot, onion, chanterelle mushroom, and spinach trimmings and the white mushroom stems and bring to a simmer. Cook, partially covered, over low heat, frequently skimming off the scum that rises to the surface, for 3 hours. Strain the bouillon through a strainer lined with cheesecloth. Transfer ¾ cup to a medium saucepan and set aside; refrigerate or freeze the rest for another use.

MEANWHILE, PREPARE THE VEGETABLE BLANQUETTE: In a medium saucepan or deep skillet, bring 3 cups chicken stock to a simmer over medium-low heat. Add the carrots, return the chicken broth to a simmer, and cook until the carrots are tender when pierced with the tip of a small sharp knife, about 10 minutes. Using a slotted spoon, transfer the carrots to a large shallow pot. Cook the onions, turnips, zucchini, and artichokes separately in the same stock until tender, adding more stock to the pan as necessary: about 12 minutes for the onions, 8 minutes for the turnips, 6 minutes for the zucchini, and 12 minutes for the artichokes; add the vegetables to the pot with the carrots as each is cooked.

While the other vegetables are simmering, cook the mushrooms: in a medium skillet, combine the chanterelles and white mushrooms and pour in enough of the remaining stock to barely cover them. Add 2 tablespoons of the butter, bring to a simmer over medium heat, and simmer until the mushrooms are almost tender, about 10 minutes. Increase the heat to high and boil until the liquid is reduced by half and lightly thickened, about 8 minutes. Remove from the heat and set the pan aside.

TO COOK THE VEAL: Wipe any fat around the edges clean, then score lightly with a sharp knife to cut the cartilage that shrinks during cooking and would cause the meat to buckle. Heat the grapeseed oil in a large skillet over medium heat. Season the chops on both sides with salt and pepper and cook, turning once and basting frequently with the pan juices, until golden brown and gently resistant to the touch, about 8 minutes on each side; after the chops have cooked for about 4 minutes, add the butter to the pan to enrich the basting juices. Transfer the chops to a wire rack set over a platter to rest for about 10 minutes.

MEANWHILE, FINISH THE BLANQUETTE: Bring the reserved ¾ cup veal bouillon to a boil over medium-high heat and boil until reduced to about 3 tablespoons. Reduce the heat to medium, add the cream, and simmer, stirring often, until the sauce is reduced and thick enough to coat the back of a spoon. Whisk in the remaining 4 tablespoons butter. Add salt to taste and stir in the lemon juice.

Strain the sauce through a fine strainer and transfer to a blender. Blend the sauce to a satiny-smooth consistency. Add the sauce to the reserved vegetables in the pot and warm over medium heat, stirring frequently, until the vegetables are heated through; do not let the sauce boil. Keep warm over very low heat.

To serve, heat the mushrooms to a simmer over low heat. Place the spinach leaves on top (the heat from the mushrooms will wilt the spinach).

Slice the chops in half and place one half in the center of each of four warmed serving plates. Spoon the vegetable blanquette and the mushroom and spinach mixture around the veal and serve immediately.

SUGGESTED WINE

AN ELEGANT PINOT NOIR, SUCH AS A CLOS DE TART 1986,
BOURGOGNE GRAND CRU MOMMESSIN, OR A PINOT NOIR
RESERVE FROM THE TE KAIRANGA VINEYARD IN NEW ZEALAND.
FOR THE RECIPE ON PAGE 162, A RICH, VELVETY WHITE
WINE, SUCH AS A HERMITAGE BLANC 1982 "VELOURS" FROM
CHAPOUTIER OR A GERMAN DORSHEIMER PITTERMANNCHEN
REISLING SPÄTLESE 1991, FROM SCHLOSSGUT DIEL.

SWEETBREADS BRAISED TWO WAYS

Serves 4

THESE SWEETBREADS ARE A DELICIOUS example of the juxtaposition of opposites in one dish. Those sweetbreads that are "white-braised" taste faintly of the white wine and chicken stock they're cooked in, while the "brown-braised" sweetbreads are very different, tasting of caramelized meat juices and vegetables. The spring vegetables are sweet and flavored with olive oil.

FOR THE SWEETBREADS

8 veal sweetbread "hearts" (3 to 4 ounces each), soaked overnight in cold water to cover

All-purpose flour for dredging

1 tablespoon olive oil

Fine sea salt and freshly ground black pepper

6 tablespoons unsalted butter

2½ cups Chicken Stock (page 229)

1 cup Veal Jus (page 231)

1 cup dry white wine

FOR THE MIREPOIX

1 medium carrot, peeled and cut into small dice

1 medium onion, cut into small dice

1 medium leek (white and light green parts only), split lengthwise in half, rinsed well, and thinly sliced

1 medium celery stalk, peeled and sliced

FOR THE SPRING VEGETABLES

3 tablespoons olive oil

8 small carrots with green tops, tops trimmed to ¾ inch, peeled, and cut lengthwise in half

8 small purple artichokes, trimmed (see page 248) and quartered

8 asparagus spears, trimmed to 4-inch tips and peeled

8 small spring onions (white part only), outer layer peeled off

Fine sea salt

½ cup Chicken Stock (page 329)

1 ounce black truffle, chopped

1 tablespoon Veal Jus (page 231)

In a large pot of boiling salted water, blanch the sweetbreads for 10 minutes. Refresh under cold water, then pat dry.

Preheat the oven to 375°F.

Combine all of the mirepoix vegetables in a bowl; set aside.

TO PREPARE THE BROWN-BRAISED SWEETBREADS: Lightly dredge 4 of the sweetbreads in flour, and pat off the excess flour. Heat the olive oil in a deep medium ovenproof skillet over medium heat. Add the floured sweetbreads and cook for 1 minute. Sprinkle with salt and pepper, add 1 tablespoon of the butter, and continue cooking, basting with the butter and turning once, until lightly browned on both sides, 4 to 5 more minutes. Add half of the mirepoix and cook until the vegetables are golden brown, 4 to 5 more minutes. Add

1¼ cups of the chicken stock and the veal jus. Bring to a boil, reduce the heat, and simmer for 10 minutes, turning the sweetbreads several times. Cover the pan and set aside.

TO PREPARE THE WHITE-BRAISED SWEETBREADS: Melt 2 tablespoons of the butter in another deep medium ovenproof skillet over medium heat. Add the remaining mirepoix and cook, without coloring, for 2 minutes. Sprinkle the remaining 4 sweetbreads with salt and pepper and set them on top of the vegetables; cook for 2 minutes. Add the wine and boil until reduced by half. Add 1 more tablespoon butter and the remaining 1¼ cups chicken stock and bring to a boil. Cover and remove from the heat.

Put both pans of sweetbreads in the oven and bake for 10 minutes.

MEANWHILE, PREPARE THE VEGETABLES: Heat 1 tablespoon of the olive oil in a large deep skillet over medium heat. Add the vegetables, season with salt, and cook for 2 minutes. Add the remaining 2 tablespoons olive oil, cover, and cook until the asparagus and onions are tender when pierced with a small knife, about 2 minutes. Remove the asparagus and onions, add the chicken stock, and continue to cook, covered, until the carrots and artichokes are tender, about 4 more minutes. Return all of the vegetables to the pan, add the truffles and the remaining veal jus, and simmer until the stock has reduced around the vegetables, 2 to 3 minutes. Cover and set aside.

TO FINISH THE DISH: When the sweetbreads are cooked, transfer them to two separate plates; cover to keep warm. Boil the braising liquids in each pan until slightly thickened and intensified in flavor, then whisk 1 tablespoon of the remaining butter into each. Strain each sauce over the appropriate sweetbreads.

To serve, arrange the vegetables on a large serving platter. Alternate the browned and white sweetbreads on top of the vegetables. Serve each person a light and a dark sweetbread and some vegetables. Serve the two sauces on the side in sauceboats.

SUGGESTED WINE

A SOFT, PERFUMED RED WINE, SUCH AS A PINOT NOIR
D'ALSACE 1993, FROM ZIND HUMBRECHT, OR AN ITALIAN
ORNELLAJA 1992, FROM TENUTA DELL'ORNELLAIA

SPIT-ROASTED LAMB WITH CHUNKY VEGETABLES AND DRIED-FRUIT CRUMB TOPPING

Serves 4

THE LAMB OF BORDEAUX'S PAUILLAC is not as world renowned as the commune's famous wines—such as Château Latour and Château Mouton-Rothschild—but the breed is prized for its moist, tender, and very pale, almost white, meat. The topping of dried apricots and raisins is Moroccan inspired.

FOR THE LAMB

2 tablespoons Lamb Jus (page 231) or pan juices from a roast lamb or beef

2 tablespoons fresh orange juice

1 strip orange zest, removed with a vegetable peeler

4 pieces loin of lamb (about 6 ounces each)

2 tablespoons olive oil

Fine sea salt and freshly ground black pepper

FOR THE VEGETABLES

¼ cup olive oil

2 medium artichokes, trimmed to hearts (see page 248) and quartered

About 4 cups Chicken Stock (page 229)

2 medium turnips with green tops, greens trimmed to 3 inches, two outer layers peeled off, and cut in half

2 small fennel bulbs, trimmed, outer layer peeled off, cored, and quartered

2 small heads red leaf lettuce, outer leaves removed (reserve for another use) and cut in half

1 tablespoon unsalted butter

4 small cèpe (porcini) mushrooms, stems removed and wiped clean (see page 238), cut in half

1 garlic clove, crushed

Coarse sea salt, preferably fleur de sel, and freshly ground black pepper

2 tablespoons Lamb Jus (page 231) or pan juices from roast lamb or beef

¼ pound slab bacon or pancetta, blanched in boiling water for 2 minutes, drained, and thinly sliced

4 tablespoons Garlic-Shallot Butter (page 233)

FOR THE TOPPING

3 tablespoons unsalted butter

4 garlic cloves, quartered

1 teaspoon sugar

½ teaspoon olive oil

2 slices white bread, crusts removed and cut into small dice

8 fresh almonds, shelled, skinned, and finely chopped, or ¼ cup slivered almonds, finely chopped

10 golden raisins, soaked in ¼ cup water until plump, drained, and patted dry

2 dried apricots, sliced into thin strips

2 tablespoons Lamb Jus (page 231) or pan drippings from roast lamb or beef

1 tablespoon sherry vinegar

2 tablespoons dried bread crumbs

2 anchovy fillets, packed in oil, lightly mashed

1 branch rosemary, stem removed, leaves chopped

Freshly ground black pepper

TO PREPARE THE LAMB: Combine the lamb jus, orange juice, and orange zest in a small saucepan and bring to a boil over medium heat. Boil until reduced to a generous tablespoon. Remove from the heat and let cool.

Brush the orange glaze over the lamb. Place on a platter, cover, and refrigerate.

TO PREPARE THE VEGETABLES: Heat 1 tablespoon of the olive oil in a small skillet over medium-high heat. Add the artichokes and cook, stirring constantly, until lightly colored, about 1 minute. Add enough chicken stock to cover the artichokes and cook, stirring occasionally, until the artichokes are tender when pierced with the tip of a small sharp knife, about 15 minutes. Drain the artichokes and transfer to a large heavy saucepan (save the chicken stock for another use). Cook the turnips and then the fennel in the same way, cooking the turnips for about 8 minutes and the fennel for about 10 minutes; add to the artichokes.

Heat the remaining olive oil in a medium skillet, add the lettuce and cook for 30 seconds on each side, then cover and cook until tender, about 5 minutes. Transfer to the saucepan of vegetables.

Melt the butter in a small skillet over medium-high heat. Add the mushrooms and garlic and cook, stirring constantly, for 1 minute. Season with salt and pepper and add the mushrooms to the other vegetables, discarding the garlic clove. Cover and set aside.

Preheat the spit.

TO PREPARE THE TOPPING: Melt 1 tablespoon butter in a small skillet over medium heat. Add the garlic cloves and cook until lightly browned, about 4 minutes. Reduce the heat to low, add the sugar, and cook, shaking the pan constantly, until the garlic is golden brown and glazed, about 2 minutes. Transfer the garlic to a plate.

In another small skillet, heat 1 tablespoon of the butter with the olive oil over medium heat until the butter is foaming. Add the bread and cook, stirring frequently, until golden on all sides, 3 to 5 minutes. Transfer the croutons to paper towels to drain.

In a medium skillet, heat the remaining 1 tablespoon butter over medium heat until foaming. Add the almonds and raisins and cook, stirring frequently, until the almonds are light golden brown, about 4 minutes. Add the croutons, apricots, lamb jus, and vinegar and stir to combine. Cook, stirring frequently, until the mixture is dry and beginning to caramelize, about 2 minutes. Add the bread crumbs, anchovies, rosemary, and pepper to taste and stir well to combine. Transfer to a small serving bowl and set aside.

TO COOK THE LAMB: Brush the lamb lightly on both sides with the olive oil, then season with salt and pepper. Roast the lamb on the spit for about 15 minutes, until well browned and slightly resistant to the touch. Transfer the lamb to a wire rack set over a platter to rest for 5 minutes.

MEANWHILE, FINISH THE VEGETABLES: Add the lamb jus, bacon, garlic-shallot butter, and salt and pepper to taste to the vegetables and stir well to combine. Bring to a simmer over medium heat, then reduce the heat and simmer gently, stirring and shaking the pan occasionally, until the vegetables are heated through.

To serve, place one piece of lamb in the center of each of four warmed serving plates. Spoon the vegetables around and sprinkle some of the dried fruit topping over the meat. Serve immediately, with the remaining topping on the side.

SUGGESTED WINE

A SPICY RED WINE, SUCH AS A CHÂTEAU RAYAS 1989
CHÂTEAUNEUF-DU-PAPE OR A MOUNT VEEDER
CABERNET SAUVIGNON 1995, FROM RUTHERFORD
VINEYARDS IN THE NAPA VALLEY

SPIT-ROASTED LAMB WITH BRAISED BABY LETTUCE AND RICOTTA GNOCCHI

Serves 4

THE ITALIAN INFLUENCE IS EVIDENT in this rustic specialty from southeastern France. The spit-roasted lamb is paired with tender, buttery, braised lettuce and ricotta gnocchi. Made with ricotta cheese, not potato, and just enough flour to make a batter that can be shaped into quenelles, the gnocchi are exceptionally tender and light. The lettuces and the gnocchi complement the flavor of the baby lamb without overwhelming it.

FOR THE BRAISED LETTUCE

- 8 heads young Boston lettuce (about 3 ounces each), left whole, or 2 large heads Boston lettuce, cut into quarters, outer leaves removed
- 1 tablespoon olive oil
- 1½ tablespoons unsalted butter
- 1 carrot, peeled and cut into small dice
- 1 onion, cut into small dice
- 1 celery stalk, peeled and cut into small dice
- 2 garlic cloves, finely chopped
- Fine sea salt and freshly ground black pepper
- 1½ cups Chicken Stock (page 229) or water

FOR THE GNOCCHI

- 9 ounces ricotta cheese
- 7 tablespoons all-purpose flour, sifted
- 1 large egg
- 2 tablespoons olive oil
- ½ teaspoon fine sea salt
- 1 cup Chicken Stock (page 229)
- 1 tablespoon unsalted butter
- ½ cup freshly grated Parmigiano-Reggiano cheese
- 1 leg baby lamb (about 3 pounds), trimmed of fat, boned, and tied
- 2 racks baby lamb (about 2 pounds each)
- 2 tablespoons olive oil
- Fine sea salt and freshly ground black pepper

TO PREPARE THE BRAISED LETTUCE: Preheat the oven to 350°F.

Bring a large pot of salted water to a boil over high heat. Add the lettuce, cover, and cook just until the water returns to a boil. Drain and plunge the lettuce into ice-cold water. Drain well, pat dry, and set aside.

Heat the olive oil and 1½ teaspoons of the butter over medium heat in a medium ovenproof skillet just large enough to hold the lettuce in a single layer. Add the carrot, onion, celery, and garlic, cover, and cook until translucent, about 10 minutes. Place the blanched lettuce on top of the vegetables, season with salt and pepper, and pour over the chicken stock to cover. Add the remaining 1 tablespoon butter and bring to a boil. Cover, place in the oven, and cook for about 35 minutes, until the lettuce is tender. Remove from the oven and set aside.

MEANWHILE, PREHEAT THE SPIT AND PREPARE THE GNOCCHI: Place the ricotta, flour, egg, olive oil, and salt in the bowl of a food processor and process until the ingredients come together to form a smooth dough. Transfer the dough to a bowl.

Bring a large pot of salted water to a boil. Using two teaspoons, shape the dough into oval quenelles, dropping them one by one into the boiling water. When all of the dough has been used, return the water to a boil and boil for 1 more minute. Remove the gnocchi to a bowl with a slotted spoon.

TO COOK THE LAMB: Brush the leg and racks with the olive oil and season with salt and pepper. Place the leg on the spit and roast for 18 to 25 minutes. After the first 5 minutes, add the racks to the spit and roast for 12 to 15 minutes, until pink. Remove the lamb to a wire rack set over a platter and let rest for 10 minutes.

MEANWHILE, FINISH THE LETTUCE: Remove the lettuces from the pan and place on a cutting board; set the pan aside. Trim the stem ends of each lettuce or lettuce quarter and then fold the tips underneath (folding the lettuce approximately in half) to make a square packet from each piece. Boil the braising liquid until reduced and thickened, then return the lettuce packets to the pan and spoon the reduced liquid over to glaze. Cover and set aside.

TO FINISH THE GNOCCHI: Heat the chicken stock until almost boiling. Melt the butter in a medium skillet. Add the gnocchi and chicken stock and cook until the gnocchi are heated through, 1 to 2 minutes. With a slotted spoon, transfer the gnocchi to a warmed serving bowl, sprinkle with the Parmesan cheese, and toss to coat. Keep the chicken stock remaining in the pan warm over very low heat.

To serve, slice the leg of lamb and the racks and divide among four warmed serving plates, placing the lamb on the lower half of the plates. Reheat the lettuce over low heat, then lift the lettuce out of the liquid with a slotted spoon, leaving the braising vegetables in the pan. Arrange two lettuce packets at the top of each plate. Spoon a little of the warm chicken stock over the gnocchi and serve immediately.

SUGGESTED WINE

A SUBTLE AND SMOOTH PINOT NOIR, SUCH AS A
CHAMBOLLE-MUSIGNY CLOS DU VILLAGE 1988 FROM A. GUYON
OR A BUENA VISTA PINOT NOIR GRANDE RESERVE 1994,
FROM CALIFORNIA'S CARNEROS REGION

PAN-SEARED STEAK WITH A SWEET-AND-SOUR "CONDIMENT SAUCE"

Serves 4

THIS RECIPE PAIRS A SAUTÉED, butter-basted steak with an intensely flavored sauce created from a reduced sour cherry purée combined with a slow-cooked beef-flavored red-wine sauce. Serve this with a simple garnish, such as roasted new potatoes. (This recipe makes more than enough sauce for four people. Refrigerate the remainder to serve with other meats.)

FOR THE RED WINE SAUCE

1 tablespoon olive oil

2½ pounds beef shank, boned and cut into large cubes

2 onions, cut into large cubes

3 carrots, peeled and cut into large cubes

2 garlic cloves, unpeeled

3 tomatoes, cored and quartered

2 bottles (750 ml each) red wine

1 branch dried fennel or ½ teaspoon fennel seeds

1 cup Veal Stock (page 230)

Coarse sea salt

Generous ¼ teaspoon Szechuan pepper, finely ground in a spice grinder

FOR THE SOUR CHERRY SAUCE

1¾ cups cherry vinegar

14 ounces fresh sour cherries, pitted

1½ cups sour cherry nectar

1 tablespoon olive oil

1 onion, finely chopped

1 celery stalk, peeled and finely chopped

2 small shallots, finely chopped

One 1½-pound shoulder or sirloin steak, 1½ inches thick

Coarse sea salt

6 tablespoons unsalted butter

TO PREPARE THE RED WINE SAUCE: Heat the oil in a large heavy-bottomed saucepan over medium-high heat. Add the beef shank and cook, stirring occasionally, until browned, 5 to 7 minutes. Stir in the onions, carrots, and garlic and cook, without coloring, stirring occasionally, until the onions are translucent, 3 to 4 minutes. Stir in the tomatoes and cook until softened, 2 to 3 minutes. Add the wine and fennel, bring to a boil, and reduce by half. Add the veal stock, salt to taste, and the pepper, bring to a simmer, reduce the heat, and simmer gently for 1½ hours.

Strain the sauce through a fine sieve into a medium saucepan. Return to a simmer and cook until the sauce is thick and syrupy; you should have about 1¼ cups. Set aside.

TO PREPARE THE SOUR CHERRY SAUCE: Combine the vinegar, cherries, and sour cherry nectar in a blender and blend to a coarse purée, 30 seconds.

Heat the olive oil in a medium saucepan over medium heat. Add the onion, celery, and shallots and cook, without coloring, stirring occasionally, until translucent, 3 to 4 minutes. Add the sour cherry purée, remove from the heat, and let stand for 1 hour to infuse.

Bring the sour cherry sauce to a boil and reduce until very thick; you should have about 1¼ cups. Stir the sour cherry sauce into the red wine sauce and set aside.

TO COOK THE STEAK: Heat a large cast-iron or other heavy-bottomed skillet over medium heat until very hot. Season the steak with salt. Melt 2 tablespoons of the butter in the pan, add the steak, and cook for 6 minutes. Add the remaining 4 tablespoons butter to the pan, turn the steak over, and cook, basting often with the butter, until the steak is rare, about 6 more minutes. Transfer the steak to a wire rack set over a platter and let rest for 10 minutes.

Pour off the fat from the pan and add 2 tablespoons water to the pan to deglaze, scraping up the browned bits from the bottom. Strain the pan juices into the sauce and reheat the sauce over medium heat. Pour into a sauceboat.

To serve, thinly slice the steak against the grain. Arrange on four warmed plates and serve with the sauce on the side.

SUGGESTED WINE

A RED WINE WITH A TOUCH OF RUSTICITY, SUCH AS A DOMAINE DE LA COURTADE 1993, FROM THE ÎLE DE PORQUEROLLES, OR A VALBUENA 1993 RIBERA DE DUERO, FROM SPAIN

PEPPER-CRUSTED RIB ROAST OF BEEF WITH FRIED POTATOES AND HEARTS OF ROMAINE

Serves 4

A SMALL RIB ROAST IS ENCRUSTED with a combination of coarsely ground and crushed peppers; at the restaurant, up to four different kinds of peppercorns are used. Fried potatoes tossed with parsley and butter accompany the beef. They are cooked in goose fat here, but they are also excellent cooked in olive oil. A simple salad of hearts of romaine lettuce cuts the richness—and the spice heat—of the dish.

FOR THE SALAD

2 tablespoons red wine vinegar

5 tablespoons extra-virgin olive oil

Fine sea salt and freshly ground black pepper

2 hearts romaine lettuce, torn into small pieces

FOR THE BEEF

¼ cup coarsely ground black pepper

¼ cup crushed Szechuan peppercorns

One 2-pound rib roast on the bone, trimmed of excess fat, trimmings reserved

¼ cup olive oil

2 tablespoons unsalted butter

Fine sea salt

FOR THE POTATOES

Goose fat or olive oil for deep-frying

4 pounds large all-purpose potatoes

Coarse sea salt

6 tablespoons unsalted butter

1 bunch fresh flat-leaf parsley, stems removed, leaves coarsely chopped

FOR THE SAUCE

3 shallots, finely chopped

½ cup Cognac

2 cups Beef Jus (page 231)

¼ cup heavy cream, or more as needed

1½ teaspoons Dijon mustard

2 tablespoons unsalted butter, cut into small pieces

Fine sea salt and freshly ground black pepper

TO MAKE THE VINAIGRETTE: Whisk the vinegar with the olive oil in a small bowl. Season with salt and pepper; set aside.

TO PREPARE THE BEEF: Spread the black and Szechuan peppers on a plate. Coat the beef generously with 2 tablespoons of the olive oil, then turn it in the pepper mixture to coat, pressing the pepper into the meat with your fingers.

TO PREPARE THE POTATOES: Peel the potatoes and trim each one into a neat rectangle about 3 inches long. Cut each potato lengthwise into ½-inch-thick slices, then cut each slice into ½-inch-thick strips.

TO FRY THE POTATOES: Melt the goose fat in a large deep heavy skillet over medium heat (you should have 2 to 3 inches of fat) and heat until very hot. Thoroughly pat-dry the potatoes. Fry, in batches, turning occasionally, until golden brown, 7 to 10 minutes. Drain on paper towels and sprinkle with salt.

MEANWHILE, COOK THE BEEF: Heat 1 tablespoon of the butter and the remaining 2 tablespoons oil in a large cast-iron or other heavy-bottomed skillet over medium heat. Season the beef with salt, add to the pan, and cook, turning to brown on all sides. Add the remaining 1 tablespoon butter and the reserved beef trimming and cook, basting often with the pan juices, until medium rare, 12 to 14 minutes in all. Place on a wire rack over a plate, cover loosely with foil, and let rest for about 10 minutes.

TO MAKE THE SAUCE: Drain all the fat except 2 tablespoons from the skillet. Add the shallots and cook over medium heat, stirring frequently, until translucent, about 2 minutes. Add the Cognac, scraping up the browned bits in the bottom of the pan, and simmer until most of the liquid has evaporated. Add the beef jus and simmer until slightly reduced, about 3 minutes. Stir in the cream and simmer until the sauce has reduced and thickened enough to coat the back of a spoon, 3 to 5 minutes more.

Strain the sauce through a fine sieve and return to the pan. Reduce the heat to medium-low and gradually whisk in the mustard and butter. Season with salt and pepper and thin, if necessary, with a bit of cream; keep warm over very low heat.

TO FINISH THE POTATOES: Melt the butter in a large deep skillet over medium heat. Add the potatoes and heat through, tossing frequently. Add the parsley, season with coarse salt, and remove from the heat.

To serve, place the lettuce in a salad bowl and toss with the vinaigrette. Place the beef on a serving platter and arrange the potatoes around the beef. Pour the sauce into a sauceboat and serve the sauce and salad on the side.

SUGGESTED WINE

A YOUNG RED WINE, STRONG YET TENDER, SUCH AS A
CHÂTEAU DU TERTRE RÔTEBOEUF ST. EMILION GRAND
CRU 1992 OR A QUINTESSA 1995 FROM RUTHERFORD
VINEYARDS, IN THE NAPA VALLEY

[*Rôtie d'Épinard au Jus de Viande Corsé*]

COUNTRY BREAD WITH SPINACH AND REDUCED BEEF JUS

Serves 4 as an accompaniment

THESE OPEN-FACED SPINACH TOASTS (often referred to as *rôties*) make an attractive accompaniment to roast meats. The fresh spinach is quickly sautéed with browned butter, taking on a light, nutty taste, then combined with cream and a splash of pan juices from the roast, giving it a rich, velvety coating. The toasts, which are assembled just before serving and glazed quickly under the broiler, both add color and texture to the main course, and provide a way to soak up all the delicious meat juices. Choose young fresh spinach with full shapely leaves and a rich green color.

4 teaspoons unsalted butter

2 pounds fresh spinach, stems trimmed and carefully washed

1 large garlic clove, peeled

1 cup heavy cream

$^1/_2$ cup pan juices from roast beef

Fine sea salt and freshly ground black pepper

Eight $^1/_2$-inch-thick slices French baguette (or long, thin loaf Italian bread)

Melt the butter in a large skillet over medium heat and cook so that the butter foams up and subsides twice; at this point it should be a light, fragrant, nut-brown. Add the spinach. Stick a dinner fork through the garlic clove so that the tines protrude about $^1/_2$ inch and stir the spinach in the butter with the fork. Stirring gently, pour in the cream little by little. Simmer until the cream has reduced by half, then add the pan drippings little by little. Add salt and pepper to taste. Reduce the heat to low and simmer while you toast the bread.

Preheat the broiler. Toast the bread slices to deep golden brown and place on a baking sheet.

Divide the spinach among the toasts. Set under the broiler for about 30 seconds, until the sauce begins to bubble and turn light brown. Serve immediately, two toasts per serving, on the same plate as the slices of your roast.

[*La Gourmandises*]

DESSERTS

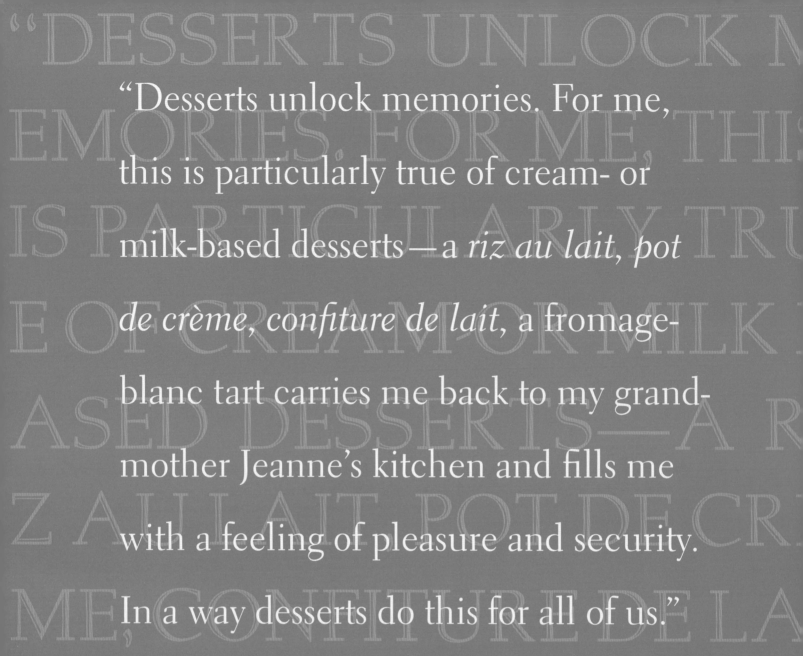

"Desserts unlock memories. For me, this is particularly true of cream- or milk-based desserts—a *riz au lait, pot de crème, confiture de lait*, a fromage-blanc tart carries me back to my grandmother Jeanne's kitchen and fills me with a feeling of pleasure and security. In a way desserts do this for all of us."

THE MAGIC OF SWEETS IS THAT THEY HELP US
recapture—sometimes several times a day—the taste of childhood.

I love to eat and I don't want to pass up anything, especially dessert! I adore sweets both humble and grand, from a rustic *pain perdu*, French toast with sautéed fruits, to a beautiful *baba au rhum* with a generous dose of rum and a big spoonful of vanilla-flecked whipped cream. This chapter is full of desserts that I love. The more rustic ones are from Moustiers; the more refined from Paris and Monte Carlo. All take their inspiration from the season: pears and apples in the fall; citrus and chocolate in the winter; berries of all kinds come spring and summer. Some are very easy, such as jasmine tea–flavored custards and the chocolate tart; others, such as the

calissons—modeled after the small diamond-shaped glazed marzipan candies from Aix-en-Provence—are more complex. Many offer contrasts: To a soft, sensuous dessert like rice pudding, I add crackly orange crisps. To a hot gratin of wild strawberries, I add the chill of honey ice cream. Others highlight one ingredient prepared several ways, as in the Tart of Pears, Caramelized and Raw.

As I see it, meals should be imbued with a feeling of abundance and generosity, and this is especially important to me at the conclusion of the meal. So at the end, after our guests have finished their desserts, we bring them one more small treat—a thin slice of tart, several small cakes, a little basket of madeleines.

It's a gesture that always brings a smile.

A NOTE ON WINES AND DESSERTS

—ᴍ—

For fruit desserts, try a sweet, mellow, liqueurlike late-harvest white wine from the following regions:

[*Alsace*] *Vendange tardive* ("late-harvest") bottlings of the following varietals:
Riesling, Gewürztraminer, Tokay, Pinot Gris

[*Loire*] Vouvray, Coteaux du Layon, Quarts de Chaume

[*Southwest*] Sauternes, Jurançon, Pacherenc du Vic Bilh

Or, choose a sparkling wine such as a semisweet Clairette de Die from the Rhône or a dry Blanquette de Limoux from the Midi.

—ᴍ—

For coffee, chocolate, and cream desserts, try a naturally sweet red wine, which you can enjoy either young or quite old, from the following two regions:

[*Languedoc-Roussillon*] Rivesaltes, Maury, Banyuls, Carthagène

[*Rhône Valley*] Rasteau

BRIOCHE FRENCH TOAST WITH SAUTÉED SEASONAL FRUITS

Serves 4

IN THIS VERSION of the simple *pain perdu*, the bread is heavily sugared, so when it is sautéed, it gets encased in a thin shell of buttery caramel. The sweetness of the bread is offset by a mixture of sautéed fruits sauced with reduced rum and orange and lemon juice. Here the choice of fruits is autumnal. In the summer, you can add or substitute a couple of fresh fig halves, a half cup of whole strawberries, or a quartered peach.

FOR THE FRUIT

¼ cup currants

1½ tablespoons dark rum

5 tablespoons unsalted butter

¼ cup granulated sugar

2 Reinette apples, peeled, cored, and quartered (see page 237)

1 Bartlett (Bartlett-Williams) pear, peeled, quartered, and cored

½ small pineapple, peeled, cored, and cut into ½-inch-thick rings

½ quince, peeled, cored and quartered

1 pomegranate, peeled and seeds scooped out

Juice of ½ orange

Juice of ½ lemon

FOR THE FRENCH TOAST

2 large eggs

1 large egg yolk

¾ cup granulated sugar

½ vanilla bean, split, or ½ teaspoon vanilla extract

1 cup milk

Four ¾-inch-thick slices brioche loaf

⅓ to ½ cup confectioners' sugar

4 to 6 tablespoons unsalted butter

1 to 1½ pints rich vanilla ice cream (optional)

TO PREPARE THE FRUIT: In a small bowl, soak the currants in the rum to soften. Melt the butter in a large skillet over medium heat. Stir in the sugar and cook, stirring, until it begins to dissolve, 1 to 2 minutes. Add the apples, pear, pineapple, quince, and pomegranate seeds, stir with a wooden spatula to coat with butter and sugar, and cook until softened, 7 to 10 minutes. Stir in the currants with the rum and the orange and lemon juices and simmer until the liquid is reduced by half. Remove from the heat and set aside.

TO PREPARE THE FRENCH TOAST: Beat together the eggs, egg yolk, and sugar. With a sharp knife, scrape the seeds from the vanilla bean into the bowl; or add the extract. Add the milk and stir until blended. Soak each slice of bread thoroughly in the egg mixture (about 2 minutes). Then remove with a slotted spatula and place on a platter. Using a fine strainer, sift confectioners' sugar over the top of each slice of bread to cover evenly.

Melt 4 tablespoons of the butter in a large skillet over medium heat. Add the brioche slices, sugared side down, and cook until lightly browned on the bottom, about 5 minutes. Sift confectioners' sugar over the tops, turn and brown on the other side, adding a tablespoon or two more butter if necessary. Remove from the heat and place each slice in a shallow serving bowl.

Spoon the fruit over the French toast and top, if you wish, with the vanilla ice cream. Serve immediately.

ROAST PINEAPPLE WITH "SCALES"

Serves 4

TART, SENSUOUS, AND SOPHISTICATED, this dessert combines a puff-pastry base with a filling of rum-flavored cream and a crown of alternating "scales" of caramelized pineapple and little puff-pastry circles. A pineapple-rum sauce surrounds the confection. The puff-pastry disks and the rum cream can be made several hours ahead; the pineapple and rum sauce should be prepared just before serving.

FOR THE PASTRY

⅔ cup confectioners' sugar

¼ pound puff pastry

FOR THE RUM CREAM

1 tablespoon dark rum

Sweetened Whipped Cream (page 235)

Basic Pastry Cream (page 235)

FOR THE PINEAPPLE

½ ripe pineapple (from a pineapple halved lengthwise), peeled

6 tablespoons unsalted butter

½ cup granulated sugar

FOR THE SAUCE

¼ cup dark rum

1 cup pineapple juice

4 sprigs fresh mint

TO MAKE THE PASTRY ROUNDS: Preheat the oven to 400°F.

Dust a work surface with the confectioners' sugar. Place the puff pastry on the sugar and roll out to a rectangle about 9 by 13 inches; the pastry should be paper-thin. Transfer the pastry to a nonstick baking sheet, prick all over with a fork, and bake for 10 to 12 minutes, until golden. Using a 3- to 4-inch round cutter, cut out four circles. Using a 1-inch round cutter, cut out 20 circles. Set aside.

TO MAKE THE RUM CREAM: In a large bowl, combine the rum and whipped cream. Fold in the pastry cream. Cover and refrigerate.

TO PREPARE THE PINEAPPLE: Cut the half pineapple lengthwise into three wedges and slice off the core. Cut the wedges crosswise into ½-inch slices; you will need 20 slices (reserve extra pineapple for another use).

Melt the butter in a large skillet over medium heat. Add the sugar and cook, stirring occasionally, until the sugar begins to caramelize, about 5 minutes. Add the pineapple and cook until well coated and infused with the caramel mixture, about 2 minutes per side. With tongs, remove the pineapple from the skillet and place in a single layer on a large deep platter.

TO MAKE THE SAUCE: Carefully add the rum to the skillet. Ignite the rum with a long match and cook until the flames die. Add the pineapple juice and simmer until thickened, about 5 minutes. Pour the sauce over the pineapple and cover with foil to keep warm.

TO ASSEMBLE THE DESSERT: Place a large pastry circle in the center of each of four dessert plates. Transfer the rum cream to a pastry bag fitted with a large plain tip. Pipe a spiral of cream onto each large pastry circle, covering it completely. Form the "scales" by alternating and overlapping the warm pineapple and the small pastry rounds on top of the rum cream. Spoon the rum sauce around and garnish with the mint.

[*Clafoutis à l'Ancienne aux Griottes*]

OLD-FASHIONED SOUR CHERRY CLAFOUTIS

FIRST, A CHERRY *GRANITÉ* is made from puréed ripe sour cherries sweetened with sugar syrup. The mixture is frozen for 5 hours, during which time it is raked with a fork every 30 minutes to form cherry-flavored ice crystals.

For the clafoutis, a batter is made from a buttery almond cream mixed with pastry cream. The batter is poured over pitted black sour cherries lining the bottom of individual earthenware clafoutis molds, then baked until set and slightly puffed. The clafoutis are served warm or cold, dusted with confectioners' sugar, and each is presented with a small cupful of icy *granité*.

STRAWBERRY TART WITH ALMOND CREAM

Serves 6

LATE SPRING AND EARLY SUMMER, when the flourishing strawberry plants in the Bastide's *potager* greet every morning with a new crop of just-ripened berries, there is no better dessert than this tart flavored with almonds plucked from the almond trees that also grow in the garden. The crust with its almond cream filling can be baked several hours ahead, and the strawberries arranged on top about an hour before serving.

FOR THE ALMOND CREAM

8 tablespoons (1 stick) unsalted butter, softened

½ cup slivered almonds, finely ground

⅓ cup sugar

¼ cup all-purpose flour

1 large egg

One 9½-inch tart shell made with Rich Sugar Pastry (page 234), unbaked

TO FINISH THE TART

½ cup strawberry jam

1 pound small strawberries (about 4 cups) rinsed, hulled, and cut lengthwise in half

2 tablespoons confectioners' sugar

Preheat the oven to 350°F.

TO MAKE THE ALMOND CREAM: Combine the butter, ground almonds, sugar, flour, and egg in a large bowl and beat until smooth.

TO BAKE THE TART: Prick the bottom of the tart shell all over with a fork. Using a pastry bag fitted with a large plain tip, pipe the almond cream in a spiral over the bottom of the chilled tart shell, starting in the center and covering it completely. Or use a spatula to spread the almond cream evenly over the bottom of the tart shell. Place the tart pan on a baking sheet and bake for about 30 minutes, until the crust is golden and the filling is lightly browned. Transfer the tart to a wire rack and cool for 10 minutes. Carefully remove the sides of the pan, then let cool completely on the wire rack.

To serve, spread a thin layer of strawberry jam over the almond cream. Working from the edges of the tart inward, arrange the strawberries, cut sides down and points toward the center, in concentric circles over the jam. Sprinkle the tart with the confectioners' sugar and serve.

[Tian d'Orange, Fine Crème Parfumée Légèrement Amère]

ORANGE TARTS WITH BITTER ORANGE CREAM

A DAY IN ADVANCE, a caramel-orange syrup is made by adding fresh orange juice to a golden-colored caramel and reducing the mixture to a syrup. When the syrup has cooled, orange segments are added and left overnight to macerate. The next day, sweet tart pastry is very thinly rolled out and cut into 3-inch rounds, which are weighted with beans and baked until crisp and golden. Next, a bitter orange marmalade is gently folded into softly whipped cream to make an airy bitter orange cream.

    To assemble, 3-inch metal pastry rings are set on a baking sheet. The macerated orange sections are arranged in an overlapping, circular fashion in the bottom of each and orange cream is piped over the orange sections, coming up three quarters of the way to the top. Then the crisp pastry rounds, spread with bitter orange marmalade, are set, marmalade side down, on top of the cream. The assembled tians are chilled for 2 hours, then carefully inverted onto serving plates. The metal rings are lifted off and the remaining orange-caramel syrup, cut with additional orange marmalade, is poured around the tians as a sauce.

TART OF PEARS, CARAMELIZED AND RAW

Serves 4

THE PEARS IN THIS PERFECT AUTUMN DESSERT are prepared two ways. Some are left raw, then grated; others are sliced, then sautéed with butter and sugar until caramelized. The grated pears are spread over a rich sugar pastry crust and topped by the sliced pears. Assemble the tart about 2 hours before serving so that the grated pears can slightly soften the crisp pastry crust. A scoop of pear sorbet served with each slice would offer pears in a third incarnation.

Rich Sugar Pastry dough (page 234), made with the optional baking powder

FOR THE FILLING

3 ripe Bartlett or Comice pears

Juice of ½ lemon

4 tablespoons unsalted butter

¼ cup sugar

1 pint pear sorbet or pistachio ice cream (optional)

TO MAKE THE TART CRUST: Let the chilled pastry stand until soft enough to roll. Line a baking sheet with kitchen parchment.

On a floured work surface, with a floured rolling pin, roll out the dough to a rough 12½- by 4½-inch rectangle, about ¼ inch thick. Using a small sharp knife, trim the dough into a neat 8- by 3¼-inch rectangle. Transfer to the baking sheet, prick all over with a fork, and refrigerate for 20 minutes.

Preheat the oven to 375°F. Place a second sheet of parchment over the dough and cover with rice, dried beans, or baking weights to keep the dough flat and prevent it from shrinking while baking. Bake in the center of the oven for 20 to 25 minutes, until golden brown. Transfer the baking sheet to a wire rack to cool.

TO PREPARE THE FILLING: Peel 1 of the pears and halve, core, and grate it. In a small bowl, toss with a little of the lemon juice; set aside. If desired, peel the remaining 2 pears. Halve the pears lengthwise, core, and cut lengthwise into ¼-inch slices. Toss with the remaining lemon juice.

Melt the butter in a large nonstick skillet over medium-low heat until foamy. Stir in the sugar and cook, stirring, until the sugar begins to dissolve, 1 to 2 minutes. Stir in the pear slices and cook, basting often with the butter and sugar and turning them once or twice, until golden brown and caramelized, 5 to 7 minutes. With a slotted spatula, carefully transfer the pears to a wire rack set over a baking sheet to drain and cool. Reserve the remaining caramel in the skillet.

TO ASSEMBLE THE TART: Spread the grated raw pear evenly over the cooled pastry crust. Arrange the pear slices, overlapping them slightly, in a row down the length of the tart.

Add 1 teaspoon of water to the skillet and reheat the reserved caramel, stirring until smooth. Brush the caramel over the top of the pear slices. Serve within 2 hours (don't refrigerate before serving), accompanied, if you wish, by scoops of pear sorbet.

RUSTIC CARAMELIZED AUTUMN FRUIT TARTS

Serves 4

FLAKY, SUGAR-GLAZED CRUSTS formed into shallow bowls or nests hold a mélange of sautéed and caramelized fruits. The pastry nests can be prepared several hours ahead, but the fruit must be cooked just before serving.

FOR THE PASTRY NESTS

²/₃ cup confectioners' sugar

10½ ounces puff pastry

FOR THE SAUCE

½ pound strawberries (about 2 cups), rinsed and hulled

1½ tablespoons granulated sugar

Juice of 1 lemon

FOR THE FRUIT

5 tablespoons unsalted butter

½ vanilla bean, split

¼ cup granulated sugar

1 Red or Golden Delicious apple, peeled, cored, and cut into eighths

1 Anjou pear, peeled, halved, cored, and cut into eighths

1 red plum, halved, pitted, and quartered

½ pound seedless green grapes

½ pound seedless red grapes

1 small banana, sliced on the diagonal

1 kiwi, peeled and sliced ¼ inch thick

12 strawberries, rinsed, hulled, and halved lengthwise

TO PREPARE THE PASTRY NESTS: Sprinkle a work surface with the confectioners' sugar. Roll the pastry out on the sugar about ¼ inch thick. Using a 3-inch round cutter, cut out four circles. Place the pastry circles sugar side up on a nonstick baking sheet and chill in the refrigerator for at least 1 hour.

Preheat the oven to 400°F.

Cover the pastry circles with an upside-down wire rack (this prevents the pastry from rising). Bake for about 8 minutes, until the pastry is golden. Immediately mold the pastry rounds into nests by fitting them over the bottoms of small bowls and pressing gently to shape. When the pastry nests are cool, unmold and set aside on a wire rack.

TO MAKE THE SAUCE: Purée the strawberries in a blender or food processor, strain through a fine sieve, and place in a small saucepan. Add the sugar and simmer over medium heat, stirring occasionally, until reduced by one third. Stir in the lemon juice, remove from the heat, and cover to keep warm.

TO COOK THE FRUIT: Melt 3 tablespoons of the butter in a medium skillet over medium heat. Using a small sharp knife, scrape the seeds from the vanilla bean into the butter. Add the sugar and stir until it dissolves, then add the apple and pear. Cook, turning occasionally, for 2 minutes. Add the plum, grapes, banana, kiwi, strawberries, and the remaining 2 tablespoons butter and cook, gently shaking the pan occasionally, until the fruit is tender and golden, 2 to 3 minutes, depending on the type of fruit. Using a slotted spoon, remove the fruit as it is done and transfer to a large plate.

When all the fruit is cooked, add 2 tablespoons of water to the skillet and cook the caramel, stirring, until smooth and well blended, about 30 seconds. Pour the caramel over the fruit.

To serve, place the pastry nests on four dessert plates. Fill each nest with warm fruit and drizzle with the strawberry sauce.

[*Gratin Tiède de Fraises des Bois, Glace au Miel*]

WARM WILD STRAWBERRY GRATINS
WITH HONEY ICE CREAM

FIRST, A HONEY-FLAVORED CRÈME ANGLAISE is frozen to make rich honey ice cream. Then, for the gratins, gelatin is stirred into warm lemon-flavored pastry cream. The cream is lightened with an Italian meringue and cooled.

To assemble the gratins, 4-inch metal pastry rings are placed on a baking sheet. Tiny wild strawberries are arranged inside the rings, then covered with the chilled cream. The top is smoothed and sprinkled with sugar, and the gratins are chilled.

At the last moment, the gratins are browned under the salamander, then carefully transferred to dessert plates and each one garnished with a scoop of honey ice cream. A pool of crème anglaise infused with fresh thyme is poured around the gratins, and roasted pine nuts, tossed in sugar, are sprinkled over all.

[*Tarte au Chocolat*]

DARK CHOCOLATE TART

Serves 6 to 8

EASY TO MAKE and intensely delicious, this is a dream of a chocolate tart. There are only four ingredients in the filling, all the more reason it's essential to use a very high quality chocolate. The tart can be baked up to a day ahead. At the restaurant, it is garnished with gold leaf as well as the shavings of chocolate.

FOR THE FILLING

7 ounces bittersweet chocolate, finely chopped

½ cup milk

1 large egg yolk

1 cup crème fraîche

One 9½-inch tart shell made with Rich Sugar Pastry (page 234), partially baked

One 3-ounce piece bittersweet chocolate, cut into thin shavings with a vegetable peeler or grater

TO PREPARE THE FILLING: Place the chocolate in a medium bowl. Bring the milk to a boil, pour over the chocolate, and stir gently until the chocolate is melted and smooth, being careful to avoid creating air bubbles.

In a small bowl, lightly beat the egg yolk with the crème fraîche. Add the crème fraîche mixture to the chocolate mixture and stir to blend. Set aside to cool completely.

TO BAKE THE TART: Preheat the oven to 325°F.

Pour the chocolate filling into the tart shell. Bake in the center of the oven for 18 to 25 minutes, until the filling is just set; it will still be somewhat soft, but it will firm up as it cools. Transfer to a wire rack to cool to room temperature.

To serve, slice the tart and place on individual serving plates. Sprinkle the chocolate shavings over and around each slice.

LEMON TARTLETS WITH ORANGE CHIPS

Serves 8

MONACO'S NEIGHBOR, the old French resort town of Menton, is famous for its lemons, its annual lemon festival, and its lemon tarts. This interpretation of the tart has a sweet-and-sour filling that gets topped by thin-sliced, sugared orange "chips" that have been caramelized and dried in the oven. A garnish of orange, clementine, grapefruit, and lime sections carries the citrus theme further. If you're feeling less than ambitious, however, the basic lemon tart is delicious all by itself.

FOR THE ORANGE CHIPS

2 cups granulated sugar

1 seedless orange (peel and white pith removed), sliced paper-thin

Eight 3-inch tartlet shells made with Rich Sugar Pastry (page 234), partially baked

FOR THE FILLING

½ cup fresh lemon juice, strained

3½ tablespoons unsalted butter, melted

¾ cup confectioners' sugar

2 large eggs, lightly beaten

FOR THE GARNISH

1 seedless orange

1 lime

1 clementine

1 grapefruit

TO MAKE THE ORANGE CHIPS: Preheat the oven to 325°F. Line a large baking sheet with parchment paper.

Combine the sugar and 4 cups of water in a medium saucepan and bring to a boil over medium-high heat, stirring occasionally. Then boil, without stirring, until reduced by half, about 10 minutes.

Remove the syrup from the heat. Add the orange slices and set aside for about 5 minutes.

Using a slotted spoon, remove the orange slices from the syrup (reserve it for another use, if desired) and arrange in a single layer on the baking sheet. Bake the orange slices for about 20 minutes, until they begin to caramelize. Turn off the oven. Let the orange chips dry in the warm oven for about 1 hour, until crisp. Set aside, on the baking sheet, in a dry place.

MEANWHILE, MAKE THE FILLING: In a medium bowl, combine the lemon juice, butter, and confectioners' sugar and mix thoroughly. Beat in the eggs with a wooden spoon. Set aside.

TO BAKE THE TARTS: Preheat the oven to 300°F.

Divide the lemon filling among the tartlet shells. Bake for about 17 minutes, until the filling is set in the center and the crust is nicely browned.

MEANWHILE, PREPARE THE GARNISH: With a sharp knife, peel all the citrus fruits, removing the bitter white pith. Then slice between the membranes to remove the segments of fruit. Remove any seeds, and set the segments aside on a plate.

To serve, place a warm tartlet in the center of each dessert plate. Spoon the citrus fruit over and around the tartlets and garnish with the orange chips.

FROMAGE BLANC AND WILD STRAWBERRY TARTLETS

Serves 6

FRENCH-STYLE FROMAGE BLANC IS A YOUNG, fresh, barely fermented cheese with a delicate taste, and a creamy, smooth texture, despite its low fat content. A versatile ingredient, it's used to make a classic Alsatian cheesecake and here it appears in a delicious light and tangy cheese tartlet topped with the tiny highly perfumed wild strawberries that appear in the late spring. (Use a combination of strawberries and raspberries if wild strawberries are not available.)

FOR THE FILLING

2 cups fromage blanc

2 large eggs

1 large egg yolk

Grated zest of 1 lemon

½ cup granulated sugar

Six 4-inch tartlet shells made with Rich Sugar Pastry (page 234), partially baked

FOR THE TOPPING

½ cup heavy cream

2 tablespoons confectioners' sugar

½ vanilla bean, split, or ½ teaspoon pure vanilla extract

FOR THE COULIS

1 pint wild strawberries

2 tablespoons granulated sugar

Juice of 1 lemon

FOR THE GARNISH

1 pint wild strawberries, stemmed, or raspberries

Preheat the oven to 350°F.

TO MAKE THE FILLING: Combine the fromage blanc, eggs, egg yolk, lemon zest, and sugar in a large bowl. Whisk together until well blended.

Fill the tartlet shells with the mixture. Place the tartlets on a baking sheet and bake in the center of the oven for 5 to 8 minutes, until the filling is just set.

MEANWHILE, MAKE THE TOPPING: In a small bowl, combine the heavy cream and confectioners' sugar. Using a small sharp knife, scrape the seeds from the vanilla bean into the cream, or add the vanilla extract.

Spoon the cream mixture on top of the tartlets and return to the oven for 2 minutes, until the topping is lightly browned. Transfer to a wire rack and let cool for 5 minutes. Remove the tartlets from their molds and let cool on the rack.

TO MAKE THE COULIS: Process the berries in a blender or food processor to a purée. Strain through a fine strainer into a small saucepan and set over medium-low heat. Bring to a simmer and simmer until reduced by one third. Stir in the lemon juice.

To serve, place one tartlet in the center of each of six individual serving plates and top with the wild strawberries. Spoon the warm coulis around the tartlets.

[*Vacherin Glacé Vanille, Fraise*]

MERINGUES WITH VANILLA ICE CREAM AND STRAWBERRY SORBET

THE CLASSIC *VACHERIN* —a large round dessert made of layered rings of meringue—is here recast into individual meringues filled with vanilla ice cream and strawberry sorbet.

To begin, 2-inch-long meringue strips are baked until crisp and dry. Sliced strawberries are dipped in a sugar syrup and dried in a low oven. Vanilla crème anglaise is frozen to make vanilla ice cream, and puréed strawberries are frozen to make sorbet. Strawberry juices are strained, sweetened, and reduced to make strawberry jus. Finally, 2-inch-high metal pastry rings are set on a baking sheet and filled halfway with the strawberry sorbet, and then vanilla ice cream. The rings are lifted off and the meringue strips are spaced evenly around the sides. Vanilla ice cream is then piped in between each strip of meringue, the desserts are topped with the dried strawberry slices and fresh strawberries, and the jus is spooned around the base.

[Calisson aux Fruits Confits et Amandes]

CALISSONS OF CANDIED FRUIT AND ALMOND

THE CALISSON, of Aix-en-Provence, a small diamond-shaped marzipan candy glazed with shiny royal icing, has been re-envisioned as an oval orange-cream-filled pastry finished with a puff pastry crust glazed with royal icing. To start, plain white royal icing is spread over a sheet of thinly rolled chilled puff pastry dough. Three-inch calisson-shaped ovals are cut out with a cookie cutter, and the iced ovals are left to dry for 2 hours. Then the ovals are baked at a low temperature to cook without coloring the icing. Pastry cream flavored with fresh orange juice and whipped cream into which chopped candied fruits have been folded makes the filling. A thin layer of almond sponge cake, flavored with citrus zests, is cut into ovals the size of the iced pastries.

To assemble the calissons, the oval cookie cutters are placed on a baking sheet. The sponge-cake ovals are set into the cookie cutters, the cookie cutters are filled three quarters full with cream, the cream is smoothed, and the calissons are chilled for 2 hours. Just before serving, the frosted pastry ovals are placed on top of the cream in the molds. The calissons are set in the center of dessert plates, the molds are lifted off, and mandarin orange segments are arranged around the dessert.

[*Cake aux Poires et au Miel*]

PEAR AND HONEY LOAF CAKE

Serves 6 to 8

THIS SIMPLE CAKE of honey-coated pears is lovely at breakfast with a *café au lait*. The pears, cooked in butter, honey, and eau-de-vie, are also delicious by themselves, served over vanilla ice cream. For this recipe, use fragrant, ripe but still firm pears and a floral-perfumed honey, ideally a *toutes-fleurs*, or mixed-flower blend, from Provence, if you can find it; a lavender or acacia honey will also work well.

FOR THE CAKE BATTER

10 tablespoons (1¼ sticks) unsalted butter, softened

1¾ cups confectioners' sugar

1 tablespoon baking powder

Pinch of fine sea salt

4 large eggs, lightly beaten

1¾ cups all-purpose flour, sifted

FOR THE PEARS

3 tablespoons unsalted butter

2¼ pounds Bartlett or Comice pears, peeled, quartered, and cored

2 tablespoons *toutes-fleur* or other flower-scented honey

¼ cup pear eau-de-vie

TO PREPARE THE CAKE BATTER: In a large bowl, combine the butter and confectioners' sugar and beat until smooth. Beat in the baking powder and salt. Add the eggs one at a time, mixing well after each addition. Add the flour and mix thoroughly, until smooth. Cover the bowl with plastic wrap and set aside at room temperature for 1 hour.

Preheat the oven to 400°F. Generously butter and flour a 9- by 5-inch loaf pan.

TO PREPARE THE PEARS: Melt 1½ tablespoons of the butter in a large skillet over medium heat. Add half the pears and cook, turning occasionally, until golden, about 5 minutes. Add 1 tablespoon of the honey and stir gently, then add 2 tablespoons of the eau-de-vie and continue cooking for another 1 to 2 minutes to allow the flavors to blend. Using a slotted spoon, transfer the pears to a large bowl to cool. Repeat with the remaining pears.

TO BAKE THE CAKE: When the pears are cool, gently fold them into the batter. Spoon the batter into the loaf pan and bake in the center of the oven until a crust forms on the surface of the cake, about 10 minutes. Using a sharp knife, make a slash down the center of the cake. Reduce the oven temperature to 325°F and continue baking until a toothpick inserted in the center of the cake is clean and dry when removed, about 1 hour.

Allow the cake to cool in the pan on a wire rack for about 10 minutes, then remove it from the pan and let cool completely on the wire rack before serving.

[*Petits Pots de Thé au Jasmin*]

JASMINE CUSTARDS

Serves 4

THIS VARIATION OF A POT DE CRÈME, the classic custard, is infused with the fragrance and flavor of jasmine tea and has a crackly topping of caramelized brown sugar, like a crème brûlée. The recipe was created by the late chef Alain Chapel.

1¼ cups heavy cream

3 tablespoons milk

2 tablespoons jasmine tea leaves

½ cup granulated sugar

4 large egg yolks

⅓ cup light brown sugar, sifted

TO PREPARE THE CUSTARDS: Combine the cream and milk in a small saucepan and bring to a boil. Add the tea and remove from the heat. Cover and let infuse for 15 minutes.

Preheat the oven to 300°F. Set four pot de crème cups or four 3½- by 1½-inch-deep ramekins in a medium roasting pan or baking dish.

In a medium bowl, whisk the granulated sugar and egg yolks together until thick and pale yellow. Strain the cream through a fine sieve. Whisking constantly, gradually add the cream to the egg mixture. Pour the custard into the cups, filling them about three-quarters full.

Place the roasting pan in the oven and pour enough water into the pan to come about halfway up the sides of the pot de crème cups. Bake for 40 to 45 minutes, until the custards are just set. Remove from the water bath and allow to cool completely.

To serve, preheat the broiler. Sprinkle the cool custards evenly with the brown sugar and place under the broiler until the sugar melts and caramelizes, about 2 minutes. Let cool for 1 minute, then serve.

RICE PUDDING WITH MARINATED STRAWBERRIES AND ORANGE CRISPS

Serves 4

RICE PUDDING, A BELOVED "NURSERY FOOD" in France, evokes warm memories for most everyone. In this recipe, it is dressed up and given new texture, color, and crackle. For the pudding itself, Arborio rice is slow-cooked with milk, sugar, and the seeds of a vanilla bean for flavor. It is served capped by a thin, brittle orange crisp, more like a candy than a cookie, and surrounded by strawberries marinated in sugar. You must lift the orange crisps off the baking sheet at exactly the right moment, after they're firm enough to lift but before they're so firm they adhere to the sheet. If they do break, don't despair: Crumble them into chunky bits and sprinkle them on as a crackly topping.

FOR THE STRAWBERRIES

1 pint strawberries, rinsed, hulled, and sliced

1½ tablespoons sugar

Juice of ½ lemon

FOR THE PUDDING

⅓ cup Arborio rice

2 cups milk

¼ cup sugar

½ vanilla bean, split

1 large egg yolk, beaten

FOR THE SABAYON

1 large egg yolk

2 tablespoons sugar

2 tablespoons water

¼ cup Banyuls wine

¼ cup heavy cream, whipped to soft peaks

TO PREPARE THE STRAWBERRIES: Place the berries in a shallow bowl and toss with the sugar and lemon juice. Cover with plastic wrap and let marinate in the refrigerator for at least 2 hours.

TO MAKE THE PUDDING: Bring a large heavy saucepan of water to a boil. Add the rice and boil for 1 minute, then drain and rinse with cold running water.

Add the milk and sugar to the pot and, using a small sharp knife, scrape the seeds from the vanilla bean into the pot. Bring to a boil, add the rice, reduce the heat to low, cover, and cook, stirring occasionally, until the rice is tender and has absorbed three quarters of the milk, about 15 minutes; it will still be somewhat soupy. Remove from the heat and let cool, uncovered, for about 10 minutes.

Whisk the egg yolk into the pudding, cover, and refrigerate until serving.

TO MAKE THE SABAYON: Combine the egg yolk, sugar, and water in a heatproof bowl or the top of a double boiler set over barely simmering water. Using a whisk, beat until pale, light, and thick, 3 to 5 minutes. Remove from the heat and whisk until completely cool. Fold in the wine and whipped cream.

To serve, place a 2¾- to 3-inch metal pastry ring on the center of each serving plate Spoon the pudding into the molds and smooth the tops. Spoon the strawberries and their juices around the puddings. Lift off the rings and top each pudding with an orange crisp. Serve the Sabayon in a sauceboat on the side.

Variation: Rice puddings may also be served with fresh strawberry coulis: Combine ½ pint rinsed and hulled strawberries with 1 tablespoon sugar in a blender. Purée and then strain through a fine sieve. Serve chilled.

[*Croquant à l'Orange*]

ORANGE CRISPS

Makes 6 crisps

2 tablespoons unsalted butter, softened	5 tablespoons all-purpose flour
½ cup sugar	2 tablespoons fresh orange juice

In a medium bowl, combine the butter, sugar, flour, and orange juice. Using a wooden spoon, beat until smooth. Cover with plastic wrap and refrigerate for at least 2 hours.

Preheat the oven to 350°F. Butter two large nonstick baking sheets.

Spoon the batter, a tablespoonful at a time, onto the baking sheets, placing 3 cookies on each sheet and allowing ample room between them. Using the back of the spoon, spread the batter into 2-inch rounds. Bake for about 5 minutes, until golden. Transfer the baking sheet to a wire rack to cool for just 45 seconds.

With a spatula, carefully remove the crisps from the baking sheet and let cool completely on the wire rack. (If the crisps stick to the baking sheet, return it briefly to the oven.)

MASCARPONE MACAROONS

Makes about 18 sandwiches

THESE LIGHTER-THAN-AIR LITTLE CAKES, delicately crunchy on the outside, soft on the inside, may be made in many colors and flavors—raspberry, chocolate, pistachio, coffee—though these are flavored just with ground almonds and sugar, then sandwiched with a rich, sweet mascarpone cream filling. Make these when the weather is cool and dry; macaroons, with their fragile egg-white composition, hate humidity and will lose their crispness if they are prepared in damp weather. The macaroons are cooked on doubled baking sheets; if you have only two baking sheets, bake the macaroons in two batches, but bring the oven temperature back up to 450°F before baking the second batch.

FOR THE MACAROONS	FOR THE FILLING
½ cup sliced blanched almonds	½ cup mascarpone
2 cups confectioners' sugar	½ cup heavy cream
4 large egg whites, at room temperature	¼ cup granulated sugar

TO MAKE THE MACAROONS: Preheat the oven to 450°F. Line two large baking sheets with kitchen parchment and set each on top of a second baking sheet; this will prevent burning.

Put the almonds in a food processor and grind to a powder. Add 1¾ cups of the confectioners' sugar and pulse until well blended. Sift onto a sheet of waxed paper or kitchen parchment and set aside. In a large bowl, beat the egg whites until frothy. While beating, gradually add the remaining ¼ cup confectioners' sugar. Continue to beat until the egg whites are stiff but not dry. Sprinkle ⅓ cup of the sugar-almond mixture over the egg whites and, using a large rubber spatula, gently fold in. Working gently so that the egg whites do not deflate, gradually fold in the remaining sugar-almond mixture.

Transfer the mixture to a pastry bag equipped with a plain ⅓- to ½-inch tip (you can also work without a tip, using a pastry bag with a ½-inch opening). Pipe 1½-inch rounds, about ⅔ inch high, onto the parchment-lined baking sheets, leaving about 1 inch between them. Lower the oven temperature to 300°F, place the baking sheets in the center of the oven, and bake for 9 to 10 minutes, until the macaroons are dry and crisp; watch very carefully, and lower the oven temperature if the macaroons begin to color too much. The ideal is for them to remain as white as possible, delicately crispy on the outside, soft on the inside. Remove each pan to a wire rack. Gently lift one corner of the parchment and pour a tablespoonful of room-temperature water between each pan and the parchment, then tip the pan so that the water flows over the bottom. Wait for about 30 seconds, until the steam and the moisture have permeated the paper, then, using a metal spatula, very carefully transfer the macaroons to a wire rack to cool. (The macaroons can be made 1 to 2 days ahead and stored in a cool dry place until ready to serve. Once filled, they must be served within 1 hour because the cream softens the crisp cookie.)

TO MAKE THE FILLING: Combine the mascarpone, cream, and sugar in a large mixing bowl. Beat just until the mixture holds soft peaks. Cover and refrigerate.

TO ASSEMBLE THE "SANDWICHES": When the macaroons are cool, spread ⅓ inch of filling on the flat side of one macaroon and very gently press a second macaroon on top. Repeat with the remaining macaroons and filling. Keep in a cool dry place (not the refrigerator) until ready to serve, and serve within 1 hour.

COFFEE AND CHOCOLATE PARFAIT WITH DARK CHOCOLATE SAUCE

Serves 4

IMPRESSIVE TO SERVE and not terribly difficult to assemble, the coupe is composed of three parts: a parfait of chocolate sorbet, coffee *granité*, and coffee ice cream, topped with a milk-shake froth and chocolate shavings; a slice of toasted brioche; and a small individual pitcher of chocolate sauce to dip your brioche or your ice cream into. The ideal bite would include a little bit of each element.

FOR THE COFFEE GRANITÉ

4 cups hot, strong espresso

¾ cup sugar

FOR THE CHOCOLATE SAUCE

2 cups milk

¼ cup heavy cream

½ cup unsweetened cocoa powder

3 ounces bittersweet chocolate, chopped

FOR THE MILK SHAKE

1 cup milk

1 cup light cream

1 cup crushed ice

FOR THE PARFAIT

1 pint chocolate sorbet

1 pint coffee ice cream

TO FINISH THE DESSERT

3 tablespoons unsweetened cocoa powder

One ¼-pound chunk bittersweet chocolate, cut into thin shavings with a vegetable peeler or grater

Four ½-inch-thick slices plain or chocolate chip brioche, lightly toasted

TO MAKE THE COFFEE GRANITÉ: Combine the coffee and sugar in a baking dish and stir until the sugar dissolves. Let cool, then transfer to the freezer. Freeze for 20 to 30 minutes, or until ice begins to form around the edges of the dish. Break the ice into small crystals by raking it with two forks, then return to the freezer. Continue freezing and raking every 30 minutes or so until the mixture is entirely frozen, about 5 hours (the finished ice should be slightly chunkier than sorbet).

TO MAKE THE CHOCOLATE SAUCE: Place the milk, cream, cocoa powder, and chocolate in a small heavy-bottomed saucepan and heat over low heat, stirring frequently, until the cocoa dissolves and the chocolate melts. Strain the sauce through a fine sieve into a clean saucepan and set aside.

JUST BEFORE SERVING, MAKE THE MILK SHAKE: Combine the milk, cream, and crushed ice in a blender and blend until thick and frothy, about 3 minutes.

To serve, spoon the chocolate sorbet into four glass coupes. Using the back of a spoon, press the sorbet into an even layer over the bottom and halfway up the sides of each coupe. Fill the centers with the coffee *granité*. Cover with the coffee ice cream. Spoon just the froth from the milk shake over the ice cream to cover. Sift the cocoa powder through a fine strainer over the froth. Top with the chocolate shavings. Serve with a slice of brioche and warm chocolate sauce.

[*Baba au Rhum*]

BABA GLAZED WITH APRICOT-RUM SAUCE

YEASTED BABA CAKES are baked in individual baba molds, then poached in a sugar syrup lightly flavored with lemon. After poaching, the babas are set aside to cool and drain until they are just moist (not soggy). Before serving, the babas are brushed with a warm apricot glaze and cut lengthwise in two. Aged rum is poured over the cakes, which are then served with dollops of vanilla-scented whipped cream.

THE OLD BACHELOR'S FRUIT PRESERVES

Makes ¹/₂ gallon

THESE PRESERVES are not really preserves in the traditional sense, but rather a mélange of sun-drenched fruit soaked in alcohol. The heady confiture is not served at breakfast or teatime, but with coffee, after the evening meal. Fruit and alcohol are served together in a glass or cup or, more informally, in a still-hot coffee cup. These are a traditional treat in Provence at the end of Christmas or New Year's Eve dinner.

No matter the quantity, you always use the same weight of sugar as fruit, so if you would like to make a little more, for example, with 5 pounds of fruit, use 5 pounds of sugar. Increase the brandy proportionately as well. Choose four to six of the following fruits, depending on market availability; you don't necessarily need equal amounts of each fruit. Once the confiture is begun, you can continue replenishing it, adding more sugar, fruit, and alcohol. Be sure to cover the fruit with the alcohol or it will spoil.

3 pounds granulated sugar

3 cups marc de Provence, pear or raspberry eau-de-vie, Armagnac, or kirsch

FOR THE FRUIT
Enough of 4 to 6 different kinds to equal 3 pounds:

Medium strawberries, rinsed, hulled, and halved

Blackberries, rinsed and patted dry

Raspberries

Blueberries, rinsed

Peaches, peeled, pitted, and sliced into eighths

Ripe but firm pears, peeled, halved, cored, and cut into ¹/₂-inch slices

Combine the sugar and marc de Provence in a large saucepan and heat over medium-low heat, stirring occasionally, until the sugar completely dissolves, about 5 minutes. Remove from the heat and set aside to cool.

Layer the fruits in a wide-mouth ¹/₂-gallon canning jar or a ¹/₂-gallon ceramic pot with a tight-sealing lid. Arrange the fruits in the following order: strawberries, blackberries, raspberries, blueberries, peaches, and pears. Pour in enough of the sugar mixture to cover the fruit and almost fill the jar; leave about 1 inch empty to allow for the slight expansion of the mixture as it ferments. (If you have any marc de Provence left over, save it for another use, such as poaching fruit.) Seal the jar and set in a cool dark place. Let macerate for at least 2 months, turning the jar upside down every week or two, so that any sugar settled on the bottom will permeate the fruits.

Serve in small stemmed glasses, generously dispensing the liquid in the jar along with the fruit.

[*Confiture de Lait*]

MILK JAM

Makes 2 pints

THIS LIGHT-GOLDEN SWEET MILK CONFIT has the consistency of thick honey and the taste of caramelized milk. Serve it at breakfast, to spread on large slices of toasted country bread instead of jam, or as an accompaniment to brioche or scones with afternoon tea.

2 quarts whole milk

3 cups sugar

Scant ⅛ teaspoon bicarbonate of soda

In a large heavy, preferably copper, saucepan, bring the milk to a boil over medium-high heat. Add the sugar and bicarbonate of soda and stir well with a wooden spoon to combine. Reduce the heat to medium-low so that the mixture remains at a very gentle simmer. Cook, stirring often at first and then constantly as the mixture thickens, until the mixture turns golden brown and thickens to the consistency of taffy, 45 minutes to 1 hour. (Take care that the milk at the bottom of the pot doesn't burn; if it starts to get too brown, remove from the heat for a few seconds and reduce the heat slightly.)

Remove from the heat and scrape into two 1-pint canning jars. Let cool, then seal the jars and refrigerate. Unopened, the confiture will keep for at least 1 month in the refrigerator.

BASIC RECIPES

STOCKS

PURE, INTENSELY FLAVORED STOCKS are essential for the recipes in this book. Unless you make these stocks from scratch, rather than using commercially produced stocks or broths, you cannot truly appreciate the dishes of which they are a critical part. None of the basic stocks call for the traditional bouquet garni of herbs, so they taste pure, essential, and neutral—not fussy. The recipes for the stocks produce large quantities, which can be frozen and used over several months in many different recipes; freeze the stock in small containers for convenience.

Fond Blanc de Volaille

CHICKEN STOCK

Makes about 2 quarts

THIS STOCK HAS A DELICATE, neutral chicken flavor. Use chicken backs and legs to make up the 6 pounds; an inexpensive stewing chicken will give good flavor as well.

> 6½ pounds raw chicken carcasses and/or parts
>
> 2 medium onions, quartered
>
> 1 large leek (green parts only), rinsed well and cut into 2-inch pieces
>
> 3 medium carrots, peeled and cut in half
>
> 2 celery stalks, cut into 2-inch pieces
>
> 1 medium tomato, quartered
>
> 6 parsley stems
>
> 1 tablespoon coarse sea salt
>
> 1 teaspoon black peppercorns

Place the chicken in a large stockpot. Cover with cold water and bring to a boil over high heat. Boil for 5 minutes, skimming the surface frequently. Drain the chicken and rinse under cold water. Rinse out

the stockpot to remove the scum, return the chicken to the pot, and cover with cold water. Add the vegetables, parsley stems, salt, and peppercorns and bring to a boil over high heat. Reduce the heat and cook, uncovered, at a bare simmer for 2 hours, without stirring or skimming. Remove from the heat and let cool briefly.

Strain the stock through a strainer or colander lined with cheesecloth into a large bowl. Let the stock cool completely, then store, covered, in the refrigerator for no more than 24 hours; or freeze in small containers. Before using, scrape off and discard the fat on the surface.

Bouillon de Poule

SAVORY CHICKEN BROTH

Makes about 1 quart

THIS IS A BEAUTIFUL, AMBER-COLORED broth used as a base for a soup with foie gras ravioli (page 142), and it could be served with many other additions, such as noodles, rice, or tortellini. All alone, it is nice instead of tea at the end of the day. Its rich color comes from deeply browned onions.

> One 4- to 5-pound chicken or fowl
>
> 2 medium carrots, peeled
>
> 2 leeks, trimmed, split lengthwise in half, and rinsed well
>
> 2 celery stalks
>
> 2 garlic cloves, unpeeled
>
> 1 branch fresh thyme
>
> 1 bay leaf
>
> 1 teaspoon fine sea salt
>
> 2 medium onions, cut in half

Place the chicken in a large stockpot. Cover with cold water and bring to a boil over high heat. Boil for 5 minutes, skimming the surface frequently. Drain the chicken and rinse under cold water. Rinse out the pot to remove the scum and return the chicken to the pot. Add the carrots, leeks, celery, garlic, herbs, salt, and cold water to cover by at least 2 inches. Bring to a boil over high heat.

Meanwhile, to char the onions, cover an electric stove-top burner with heavy-duty aluminum foil and heat on medium heat, or heat a cast-iron pan on a gas stove-top burner over medium heat. When the burner is hot, place the onions cut side down on the foil or in the pan and cook until the cut sides are dark brown; do not let them turn black.

Add the onions to the stockpot, reduce the heat to medium-low, and simmer gently for 3 hours.

Remove the chicken from the broth and save for another use, if desired. Strain the broth through a strainer lined with cheesecloth into a bowl or other storage container. Let cool, then cover and refrigerate for no more than 24 hours; or freeze in several small containers. Before using, scrape off and discard the fat on the surface.

Jus de Volaille
CHICKEN JUS

Makes 2 cups

UNLIKE THE CHICKEN STOCK and Savory Chicken Broth, this jus is made with very little water. Accordingly, it need not be reduced to use in a sauce. It's critical to the flavor and color of the jus that the bones be very well browned before the water is added.

    1 tablespoon olive oil
    2¼ pounds chicken carcasses
    6 garlic cloves, crushed
    8 tablespoons (1 stick) unsalted butter
    ½ teaspoon salt

In a large saucepan or a small pot, heat the oil over high heat. Add the chicken and cook, stirring occasionally, until golden brown, 10 to 15 minutes.

Reduce the heat to medium and add the butter and garlic; cook, stirring occasionally, until the chicken and garlic are well browned all over, 8 to 10 minutes longer.

Add ½ cup water and bring to a boil; boil until reduced to a glaze. Repeat with another ½ cup water and reduce by three quarters. Then add water to come just to the tops of the bones (about 4 cups) and the salt and bring to a boil. Reduce the heat and simmer very gently for 20 minutes.

Strain the jus through a fine strainer into a clean saucepan. Return to a simmer and skim to remove the fat. Continue simmering if necessary to reduce to 2 cups. Pour into a bowl or other storage container and let cool. Refrigerate for up to 3 days; or transfer to two smaller containers and freeze.

Fond de Veau
VEAL STOCK

Makes 1 quart

RICH AND SAVORY, this veal stock has a wonderfully smooth, almost gelatinous texture. The flavor is full, warm, and satisfying, yet it's neutral enough to provide background and body without overpowering other flavors. You'll need a very large stockpot for this recipe. It's important that your baking sheets or roasting pans be large enough to hold the veal bones without crowding; well-browned bones will give the stock its full flavor and rich color. Pay careful attention during the cooking so that the bones caramelize to a golden brown but don't burn.

    11½ pounds meaty veal bones and veal
       trimmings, rinsed and patted dry
    ½ cup vegetable oil
    8 white mushrooms, trimmed, wiped clean, and
       quartered
    1 medium onion, minced
    3 medium tomatoes, quartered

5 medium carrots, peeled and cut into 1½-inch
   pieces

1 medium celery stalk, cut into 1½-inch pieces

1 garlic bulb, cut in half through the equator,
   one half reserved for another use

3 tablespoons tomato paste

1 tablespoon coarse sea salt

1 tablespoon black peppercorns

Preheat the oven to 400°F.

Spread the veal bones and trimmings over the bottoms of two large roasting pans or baking sheets. Drizzle with 6 tablespoons of the oil and roast for about 30 minutes, until they start to brown, turning the bones after 15 minutes.

Meanwhile, heat 1 tablespoon of the oil in a medium skillet over medium-high heat. Add the mushrooms and sauté until they just start to brown and give off their liquid, 4 to 5 minutes. Transfer to a large bowl and set aside. Add the remaining 1 tablespoon oil to the skillet, add the onion, and sauté until golden brown, about 5 minutes. Remove to the bowl. Add the tomatoes, carrots, celery, and garlic to the mushrooms and onions and stir to coat with the cooking juices.

Spread the vegetables over the veal bones and roast until everything is a rich golden brown, 45 minutes to 1 hour. Watch the cooking carefully and check every 15 minutes after the first half hour to make sure the vegetables don't burn; anything burned will ruin the flavor of the stock.

With a slotted spoon, transfer the veal bones and trimmings and the vegetables to a large strainer set over a bowl to drain off the fat, then transfer to a large stockpot. Pour in enough water to cover by at least 3 inches (6 to 7 quarts). Add the tomato paste, salt, and peppercorns and bring to a boil over medium-low heat. Skim, then reduce the heat and cook, uncovered, at a bare simmer for 6 hours, skimming from time to time as necessary.

With a slotted spoon, remove the bones and vegetables and discard. Strain the stock through a strainer lined with cheesecloth into a large pot.

Bring to a boil over high heat, reduce the heat to medium, and boil gently, skimming carefully, until the stock has reduced to 1 quart. Remove from the heat and cool completely.

Transfer the stock to a bowl or other container and store, covered, in the refrigerator for no longer than 24 hours; or freeze in several small containers. Before using, scrape off and discard the fat on the surface.

Jus de Veau (ou d'Autres Viandes)

VEAL (OR OTHER MEAT) JUS

Makes about 5 cups

THIS INTENSE AND SAVORY highly reduced stock has a distinctive caramelized flavor that is more comparable to the rich pan drippings from a roast than it is to a classic stock; in fact, this jus is virtually a sauce, the essence of veal, smothered with butter. It can be made equally well with duck, beef, lamb, pigeon, or rabbit substituting for the veal. A cast-iron pot is used at the restaurant for this stock; foods cooked in cast-iron brown well, and browning is essential to making a good rich jus.

This jus has a very different flavor from that of the Veal Stock (page 230) because it's made without tomato. It also has a different texture; because it's made without bones, it's not gelatinous. As with all these stocks, there are no herbs, so the jus tastes simply of the veal. The butter will harden on top of the jus when chilled and acts as a seal, keeping air out; remove the butter before using the jus.

3 tablespoons nonfruity olive oil (not extra-virgin)

½ pound (2 sticks plus 2 tablespoons)
   unsalted butter

4½ pounds meaty veal scraps and trimmings,
   rinsed and patted dry, or inexpensive veal cut,
   such as stew meat, cut into 1-inch cubes

(continued)

3 medium carrots, peeled and cut into
½-inch slices

6 parsley stems

1 garlic head, cut in half through the equator

1 celery stalk, trimmed and cut into 3-inch pieces

1 tablespoon fine sea salt

½ teaspoon freshly ground black pepper

Heat the oil in a large stockpot over medium-high heat. Add 10 tablespoons of the butter and let melt. Add the veal and stir with a wooden spoon to coat with oil and butter mixture, then add the carrots, parsley, garlic, salt, and pepper. Cook, stirring frequently, until the meat is well browned on all sides. When the meat is golden, remove the meat and vegetables from the stockpot with a slotted spoon and set aside.

Add 1 cup of water to the stockpot and scrape up the browned bits from the bottom. Let the water evaporate (for a heartier jus, add another cup of water to the pan and let it evaporate again).

Return the meat and vegetables to the stockpot and add enough water to cover by at least 2 inches. Bring to a boil over high heat, reduce the heat to medium, and simmer for 3 hours, stirring from time to time.

Add the remaining butter to the stock and stir until melted. With a slotted spoon, remove the meat and vegetables and discard. Strain the stock through a strainer lined with cheesecloth into a large clean pot.

Bring the stock to a boil, reduce the heat to medium-high so that it boils gently, and cook until it reduces by half, or about 5 cups, about 20 minutes.

Pour into a bowl or other storage container and let cool. Store in the refrigerator for up to 3 days; or transfer to several small containers and freeze. Before using, scrape off and discard the fat on the surface.

SAVORY BASICS

Here are a few preparations called for periodically in the recipes in this book. The tomato confit is very useful and good to prepare in quantity to have on hand.

Tomate Confite
TOMATO CONFIT

Makes about 1½ cups

These versatile slow-baked tomatoes are used in many recipes, from tarts and salads to vegetable side dishes. After baking in a low oven for three or four hours, the tomatoes' flesh becomes more dense, the flavor intensified; the olive oil renders the tomato pieces satiny in texture. (The tomatoes may take less or more time depending on how your oven is calibrated.)

4½ pounds large plum tomatoes, peeled, quartered lengthwise, and seeds and membranes removed

6 medium garlic cloves, unpeeled

8 branches fresh thyme

¼ cup olive oil

2 teaspoons coarse sea salt

Preheat the oven to the lowest setting. Grease a large baking sheet with olive oil.

Arrange the tomatoes on the baking sheet. Scatter the garlic and thyme over the tomatoes. Drizzle the olive oil over the tomatoes and sprinkle with the coarse salt. Bake for 2 to 3 hours, turning the tomatoes over once halfway through the cooking process; the tomatoes will shrink and dry slightly, but they should still be quite plump and moist. Remove from the oven and set aside to cool.

These can be prepared several hours or a day ahead: Transfer the tomatoes, along with the garlic and thyme, to a plate, cover with plastic wrap, and refrigerate. For longer storage, place the tomatoes, garlic, and thyme in a jar, cover with olive oil, seal the jar, and refrigerate for up to 3 days.

Dentelles de Parmesan

LACY PARMESAN CRISPS

Makes 10 to 12 crisps

AS DELICATE AS LACE and as fragile as a butterfly's wing, these lovely cheese crisps are a tangy and attractive accompaniment to pastas (see page 56) and other dishes. You can also serve them alone with apéritifs. It's best to make these at the very last minute, especially if the weather is humid.

> 1 tablespoon all-purpose flour
>
> 3½ ounces Parmigiano-Reggiano cheese, finely grated (about 1 cup)
>
> About 1 teaspoon unsalted butter, softened

In a medium bowl, combine the flour and Parmesan and mix together by gently rubbing the flour and cheese between your fingertips.

Heat a 5- or 6-inch nonstick frying pan over medium heat, then very lightly brush a little butter over the bottom of the pan. Sprinkle a heaping tablespoon of the cheese mixture into the pan in a circle, using just enough to lightly cover the bottom of the pan. Heat for about 15 seconds, then, when the cheese has started to bubble all over, remove the pan from the heat, tilt it, and slide a spatula under the crisp to remove it. Immediately place the crisp over a rolling pin, or over a small bottle on its side, to give it a curved shape. Wait a few seconds until it sets, then transfer to a wire rack to cool. Repeat with the remaining cheese mixture, carefully wiping the spatula clean after each crisp.

Beurre d'Escargot

GARLIC-SHALLOT BUTTER

Makes about 2 cups

THIS CLASSIC BUTTER MIXTURE, in which escargot are prepared and served, is used to glaze vegetable side dishes and accompany roasted meats.

> 18 tablespoons (2¼ sticks) unsalted butter, softened
>
> ¼ cup slivered almonds, finely ground
>
> 2 slices prosciutto di Parma or other cured ham (about 2 ounces), cut into very small dice
>
> 1 garlic clove, finely chopped
>
> 1 medium shallot, finely chopped
>
> ½ cup fresh flat-leaf parsley leaves, finely chopped
>
> Fine sea salt and freshly ground black pepper

In a small bowl, combine the butter, ground almonds, prosciutto, garlic, shallot, and parsley. Season with salt and pepper and mix well to blend. Shape into a log, wrap in plastic wrap, and refrigerate or freeze.

Rôties à l'Ail

GARLIC TOASTS

Makes about 40 toasts

IN MOUSTIERS, these garlic toasts are served in a basket lined with a napkin, accompanied by an assortment of savory condiments and spreads, such as tapenade (page 62), Fennel "Marmalade" (page 20), eggplant caviar (page 31), and/or a dish of tiny red radishes.

> 1 baguette, sliced into ¼-inch rounds
>
> About ¼ cup olive oil
>
> ½ garlic clove

Preheat the oven to 375°F.

Arrange the baguette slices on a baking sheet. Using a pastry brush, lightly brush the top of each slice with olive oil. Toast in the oven until the slices are golden brown. Remove from the oven and cool for several minutes, then lightly rub the cut side of the garlic clove once or twice across the top of each slice. (They can be prepared an hour or two before serving.)

SWEET BASICS

THE MANY DESSERT TARTS IN THIS BOOK can be made successfully with the Rich Sugar Pastry and recommended fillings or toppings. However, at the restaurant, the Fromage Blanc and Wild Strawberry Tartlets (page 206) is made with *pâte sablée.*

Pâte Sucrée

RICH SUGAR PASTRY

Makes enough dough for one 9¹⁄₂- to 11-inch tart, six 4-inch tarts, or eight 3-inch tarts

> 1¹⁄₂ cups all-purpose flour, or more as needed
>
> ¹⁄₄ cup confectioners' sugar
>
> ¹⁄₂ teaspoon baking powder (optional)
>
> 1 large egg, lightly beaten
>
> 8 tablespoons (1 stick) cold unsalted butter, cut into pieces and softened

TO MAKE THE DOUGH BY HAND: In a medium bowl, combine the flour, confectioners' sugar, and baking powder, if using. Mix well. Add the soft butter and mix well with a wooden spoon. Add the egg and mix until the dough forms a smooth ball.

TO MAKE THE DOUGH USING A FOOD PROCESSOR: Combine the butter, confectioners' sugar, egg, and baking powder, if using, and the salt in the bowl of the processor and process until well blended, 5 to 7 seconds. Add the flour, ¹⁄₂ cup at a time, and process until the dough just holds together. It should be soft and pliable but not sticky; if it seems sticky, add up to 2 more tablespoons of flour and process for a few seconds until blended.

Gather the dough into a ball. Press into a disk, wrap in plastic, and refrigerate until well chilled, at least 2 hours. The dough can be refrigerated for up to 3 days or frozen for up to 1 month.

TO MAKE ONE LARGE TART SHELL: On a lightly floured surface, roll out the dough to a circle about ¹⁄₈ inch thick. Fit the dough into a fluted tart pan with a removable bottom and trim off the excess. Refrigerate for at least 30 minutes before baking.

TO MAKE INDIVIDUAL TART SHELLS: For 3-inch tart shells, divide the dough into eight pieces; for 4-inch tart shells, divide the dough into six pieces. On a lightly floured surface, roll out each piece to a circle about ¹⁄₈ inch thick. Fit the dough into eight 3-inch or six 4-inch fluted tart pans and trim off the excess. Refrigerate for at least 30 minutes before baking.

TO PREBAKE THE TART SHELL(S): Preheat the oven to 350°F.

Line the tart shell(s) with parchment paper or aluminum foil and fill with dried beans, rice, or pastry weights. *To partially bake the tart shell(s),* bake for 15 minutes. Remove the foil and weights and transfer to a wire rack to cool. *To fully prebake the tart shell(s):* After removing the foil and weights, return the tart pan(s) to the oven and bake for 10 to 15 minutes longer, until the crust is golden brown. Transfer to a wire rack to cool.

Crème Pâtissière

BASIC PASTRY CREAM

Makes 1 1/4 cups

1 cup milk
3 large egg yolks
3 tablespoons sugar
3 tablespoons cornstarch

Put the milk in a medium saucepan and bring to a boil over medium-high heat, stirring occasionally. Meanwhile, combine the egg yolks, sugar, and cornstarch in a medium bowl and whisk until pale yellow.

Whisking constantly, add a little of the simmering milk mixture to the eggs, then whisk the egg mixture into the milk in the saucepan. Bring to a boil, whisking constantly, and cook just until thickened, about 15 seconds longer. Transfer to a small bowl, cover with plastic wrap, placing it directly on the surface of the pastry cream to prevent a skin from forming, and let cool. Refrigerate until chilled, at least 1 hour.

Crème Chantilly Vanillée

SWEETENED WHIPPED CREAM

Makes 2 cups

1 cup heavy cream
2 tablespoons superfine sugar
1/2 vanilla bean, split

In a medium bowl, whip the cream with the sugar until soft peaks form. Scrape the seeds from the vanilla bean into the cream and continue to whip until the cream is stiff; do not overbeat. Whipped cream can be made up to 2 hours ahead; cover with plastic wrap and refrigerate until ready to use. Whisk briefly before using if necessary.

APPENDIX

EDITORS' NOTE

Alain Ducasse finds the inspiration and direction for his cooking in the raw products he builds his recipes around. He is a fierce supporter of small-scale artisanal food producers and particularly of those products raised in his home region. Like that of many of his compatriot chefs, his food is intensely and passionately connected to the land on which it grows.

As we worked to shape this book, we realized that if we didn't explicitly acknowledge and respect the differences between his ingredients and ours, we lost something of the essence and meaning of his work. In order to accord his specific choice of ingredient the same respect that we accord his cooking technique, we offer this part of the book as a collection of annotations to his recipes, taking his work a necessary step farther for the North American home cook. We give you information about his ingredients where they differ from ours, as well as providing some ways of making his recipes with products more readily available to us.

As a general rule, we recommend using products that are local, and thus fresh, rather than attempting to buy imports from Europe. Many of us have access to farmers' markets that sell ingredients that, although different from those that Ducasse uses, are of equally excellent quality. Fresh produce and fish of whatever variety will always taste better than an imported product not at its prime.

Ducasse's food honors evolution: of seasons, of learning, of pleasure. The way to join in the spirit of Ducasse's cooking is not to adopt his products but rather to adopt his orientation toward them. By using that which is freshest and most perfect even when different from his, you not only will enjoy the essence of his food, but will participate in the same evolution that inspired it.

INGREDIENTS

FRUITS AND VEGETABLES

The produce used in Ducasse's restaurants is of superior quality and fruits and vegetables are used seasonally. Therefore, these recipes use both spring (called *primeurs* in France) and large vegetables, depending on the season for which the dish was created: Sweetbreads Braised Two Ways, for example, is a spring dish, and so it's garnished with a variety of small, young vegetables. Poached Chicken in the Pot, on the other hand, is garnished with large, mature, winter vegetables instead because it is a winter dish.

As a rule, the vegetables called for in these recipes are smaller—sometimes by as much as half—than the vegetables we buy in our supermarkets. If you grow your own vegetables or have access to a vegetable garden, use them for these recipes. Or, shop at a farmers' market if you can.

Except in a few instances, the vegetables that are used in these recipes are not what we think of as "baby" vegetables. Since (with the exception of baby artichokes) commercial baby vegetables, while pretty to look at, mostly lack the flavor of the mature vegetable, it makes sense to buy small but mature vegetables.

A mandoline is used in Ducasse's restaurants to thinly slice vegetables. We recommend the Japanese mandoline slicer sold in gourmet shops and Asian markets under the name of Benriner; it does a good job of slicing without tearing.

[*Apples, Reinette*] A variety of apple available in France, *pommes reinettes* are smallish apples with crisp, juicy, firm flesh with some acidity. They are an all-purpose apple, which means that they hold their shape during cooking. Golden Delicious apples can be used in any recipe that calls for Reinettes.

[*Artichokes*] There are several different varieties of artichokes available in France, including the large *camus breton* from Brittany and the smaller *poivrade*-type artichokes, including *poivrades* (sometimes called *barigoules*), *violets*—native to Provence—and *épineux*, artichokes grown in Italy, the leaves of which are tipped with spines. The *poivrade*-type artichokes have a more refined and yet more bitter flavor than the *camus*. The various varieties are used as they come into season.

For cooking purposes, the difference between the *camus* and the *poivrade*-type artichokes is in their preparation. Much more of the *poivrade* is edible. It needs simply to be trimmed of outer leaves and choke; even the stem is tender enough to eat. Once trimmed, the hearts are cut in halves or quartered to be used as a vegetable garnish or on their own as the main ingredient (as in Provençal-Style Artichokes on page 72). They may also be eaten raw; they have a somewhat astringent taste. Only the bottoms of the larger *camus* artichokes are tender—the leaves and chokes are removed and the fibrous stem is broken off at the base to remove, along with it, any fibers in the bottoms. The bottoms are pared down to a disc and puréed in sauces or quartered for a vegetable garnish. (The tough stems may be peeled, long-cooked until tender, and used in a gratin.)

When buying, choose artichokes that are very firm, with crisp leaves that show no black, and tight heads. In France, the artichokes are sold on the stem; if you find them with long stems, they can be stored like flowers in a container of water in the refrigerator.

Poivrades are sometimes imported here (particularly for French restaurants). Otherwise, you can substitute baby artichokes. Aside from a difference in size (the *poivrades* being larger), the main difference between the two is that the immature choke of the baby artichokes is edible and so needn't be removed.

[*Cardoons*] Cardoons are very popular in the Mediterranean. They look something like celery with their fleshy, ribbed stalks that grow in bunches. Cardoons are larger and flatter than celery, however, and their stalks are silver-gray rather than green. They taste a bit like artichokes (an interesting mixture of sweet and bitter) and a bit like celery. Like some celeries, cardoons are "blanched"—that is, covered in black plastic sheets so that they aren't exposed to sunlight, to keep them white. The outer stalks are tough and bitter and should be discarded in favor of the inner, more tender, lighter-colored heart.

Celery can be substituted in recipes that call for cardoons.

[*Cherries, Sour*] Sour cherries, or pie cherries, are in season here from June through July. Montmorency is the variety you're most likely to come across. If you can't find fresh sour cherries for the Pan-Seared Steak (page 175), jarred cherries can be substituted (see Sources, page 251).

[*Fava Beans*] *Fevettes*, or baby fava beans, are used in several of the recipes. When small and young, these baby favas can be eaten raw. The beans need to be shelled and then popped out of their individual jackets; use a fingernail to rip the skin and then just peel it off.

Fresh baby lima beans can be substituted for fava beans. Or mature fava beans may be substituted: Skin them and blanch for 30 seconds before using.

[*Fennel*] Both mature and young spring, or mini, fennel are used in these recipes. The larger fennel is trimmed of its tough outer layer and is used cut into pieces. The small fennel is so tender that it need not be trimmed at all, and is used whole. (Sizewise, spring fennel is to mature fennel as spring onions are to large mature onions.)

The fronds of the young fennel are dried and used to flavor fish broths and sauces.

Our larger fennel can be fibrous and tough; the outer layers should always be removed.

[*Mesclun*] Mesclun is a mixture of several salad greens planted as a bed, not as separate heads, and picked when young and tender. In theory, mesclun is picked by the chef, depending on the mixture desired.

[*Mushrooms*] Several different varieties of wild mushrooms are used in these recipes. They are chosen for each dish on the basis of season and to add a specific flavor. If you cannot get wild mushrooms, use whatever fresh cultivated mushrooms are available to you. All wild mushrooms (with the exception of truffles) should be stored wrapped in a damp towel in the refrigerator.

By far the most prevalent mushrooms in Ducasse's recipes are **girolles** (also called golden chanterelles), a very small mushroom with a distinctive yellow-orange color and a peppery flavor that some say is reminiscent of apricots. **Chanterelles** are also used; they can be distinguished from girolles by their dark heads that cap orange feet. Chanterelles and girolles find their way into many of these recipes because their subtle flavor marries easily with a variety of ingredients. (Their flavors being more aggressive, cèpes and morels, below, must be used more cautiously.) Because of their small size, chanterelles and girolles are often used whole in stews.

European chanterelles are available from the end of April through the summer. The season here starts in June and runs through November.

To clean girolles, scrape the foot of the stem, then quickly rinse them and immediately towel-dry

them. Chanterelles are very clean and needn't be rinsed; trim the bottoms of the stems and wipe clean if neccessary.

Morilles, or *morels*, grow in central France. They have short stems, hollow, cone-shaped, honeycombed caps, and a slightly spongy texture. French *morilles* are lighter colored than our dark brown morels, but they taste the same. The largest American producers of morels are in the Northwest, Montana, and Idaho. Morels are expensive, both in France and America. They are in season here from mid-April to mid-June. (They are often paired with asparagus, which has the same season.) The best-tasting morels are from areas where there have been forest fires; morels that have pushed up through ash are black, not gray, with a woodsy, smoky flavor.

Morels are more difficult to clean than other wild mushrooms because they collect dirt and other debris in their honeycombs. To clean, trim the bottoms of the stems (reserve them to flavor stocks). Then dunk the mushrooms into a bowl of water and then quickly remove them, repeating this four or five times, changing the water each time. Immediately drain and towel-dry them.

Cèpes (usually called *porcini* in America) are fleshy, meaty mushrooms with reddish caps and thick stems. French tradition demands that they not be cut into little pieces, so they are often cut into thick slices that include both head and stem. Where a small mushroom is required, as in the Fall Vegetables, *cèpes buchons* are used whole—small cèpes with caps that look like champagne corks.

Although cèpes are grown both in the Bordeaux and Auvergne regions of France, they are most associated with Bordeaux. Their European season is May through November or December, and our season is about the same. The cèpe season here starts in the Northwest—Washington, Oregon, and Montana—and then works its way south toward Mexico.

Cèpes are rarely available here retail; most of those sold go to restaurants. If you do manage to get some, clean them by peeling the stems with a small sharp knife and wiping the caps with a damp towel.

Ducasse may be the largest buyer of **truffes** (truffles) in the world, using hundreds of pounds of black and white truffles a year.

Black truffles are traditionally associated with Périgord but are grown in Provence as well. They are in season from November through March. About 30 percent of the European crop is now grown on "plantations," in which saplings have been inoculated with truffle spores and planted. (A plantation takes ten years to begin producing.) Three plantations have been started in the United States but are not yet producing truffles. *White truffles* are grown in the Piedmont and Umbrian regions of Italy. Their season runs from October to December or January, depending on the year.

Truffles should be cleaned with a toothbrush and stored in the refrigerator, wrapped in tissues. They will last up to a week (assuming, of course, that they are fresh when they arrive), but they do lose flavor as they sit.

The best canned or jarred black truffles are called "first cooking truffles" (available at specialty stores and from mail-order sources; see page 251). For these, fresh truffles are put in the can or jar with a little salt and a little water, sealed, and sterilized. The truffle cooks in the tin and has a strong perfume and flavor. Use these up as soon as possible after opening.

[*Onions*] In addition to the standard yellow onion, Ducasse works with *oignons nouveaux* (spring onions) and with *cébettes*. *Cébettes* are a variety of spring onion that grows in Provence. They look like scallions and taste mildly of garlic. Scallions can be substituted for both varieties of spring onion.

[*Potatoes*] When determining which type of potato to use in a recipe, what makes the most sense is to consider texture and starch content, not name or variety. Potatoes can be divided into three groups, depending on starch content: high-, medium-, and low-starch. High-starch potatoes have a dry, mealy texture and fall apart when cooked—our russet, or baking potato, is a good example. Medium-starch potatoes

are sold as all-purpose; they are finer textured, not as dry as a russet, and hold their shape better in cooking. Yellow-fleshed Yukon Gold potatoes are medium-starch. Red-skinned and new potatoes are low-starch potatoes, with a very moist, firm, waxy texture. Different potatoes will give a different result in recipes.

Tiny new waxy potatoes are used in recipes for vegetable stews in which the potato is served in the skin. An all-purpose potato such as the Yukon Gold works well for *gnocchi* and the Potato and Leek Gratin. If you like, experiment with other types of potatoes in the gratin to see which result you prefer: Russets will fall apart and the starch will thicken the broth; Yukon Gold potatoes will be brittle but creamy; while red potatoes will stay firm and hold their texture.

[*Pumpkin*] The pumpkin used in France is a different variety from those sold in supermarkets here. Try pie pumpkin or butternut squash in recipes that call for pumpkin.

[*Radish, Black*] A variety of winter radish (which takes longer to mature than spring radishes) with black skin, some black radishes are shaped like a turnip and some are long and cylindrical, like daikon. The flesh is white and compact-textured. The taste is something like that of a turnip, with the bitterness and bite of a radish.

[*Strawberries, Wild and Cultivated*] There are recipes here for both tiny wild strawberries, *fraises des bois*, and cultivated strawberries, *fraises*. The two strawberries are not, surprisingly, interchangeable because their flavors and perfumes are so different from each other. Wild strawberries are often combined with fromage blanc, but vanilla ice cream and wild strawberries is a favorite combination.

Raspberries are a better substitute for wild strawberries than are cultivated strawberries.

[*Zucchini*] In several recipes that use zucchini, a variety of small, round zucchini is called for. These zucchini are grown in the South of France and are easier to stuff than long, slender zucchini. Standard zucchini can be used in place of the round; cut it into sections.

FISH

You're unlikely to find here many of the fish Ducasse works with in Paris and Monaco, as they're harvested from European waters and rarely land on these shores. Though a knowledgeable fish retailer can special-order such fish if you want to taste the recipes as created, it is more practical to substitute other more available fish for the species that Ducasse uses. The object of such substitution is not so much to duplicate flavor—a difficult goal, as different species of fish taste as different as say, lamb and beef—but to find an alternate fish that cooks similarly enough to the original choice to work in the preparation. A fish with a similar texture and fat content is usually a safe choice. A recipe for a mild white-fleshed fish such as European sea bass is usually better served by the substitution of another mild, delicate, white-fleshed fish, such as snapper, than by an oily, strong-flavored species, such as bluefish. When substituting fish, remember that different shapes and sizes of fish fillets and steaks cook differently. For example, an 8-ounce snapper fillet from a smallish fish will be thin and flat, whereas an 8-ounce halibut fillet cut from a large halibut will be narrow and thick. *Adjustments will need to be made accordingly in cooking times and instructions.*

Ducasse prefers to work with larger fish that produce thicker fillets. The decision to skin or not to skin a fish depends on the cooking technique: If the fish is to be sautéed, the skin is left on because it will become crisp. If the fish is baked or poached, the skin is removed because it's unappealing.

The following entries provide suggestions for substitutions: Feel free to experiment with other fish. The freshness of the fish and your own sense of taste are ultimately what are important.

[*Cod*] Cod is harvested from both the North American and the European sides of the Atlantic, and you shouldn't have much trouble finding it. If you can find cod with skin, buy it: The skin helps to hold the flaky flesh together. In the recipe for Fillet of Cod with White Bean Purée and Baby Squid, the cod is cooked skin-on for its crispy texture.

Stockfish and *salt cod* are two different preserved cod preparations used in the South of France. The difference is that *morue*, or salt cod, is cod that is salted and then, usually, dried for a certain period, while *stockfisch*, or stockfish, is not salted but is air-dried until its texture is almost rock hard. Although we tend to think of prepared salt cod as very dry and hard, too, it does in fact come in different degrees of dryness. The *morue* that Ducasse uses, for example, is moist enough that it is supple even before soaking. Stockfish was traditionally dried on racks of sticks (thus the German name *stock* for stick and *fisch* for fish) and must be soaked for a longer time than salt cod.

Rather confusingly, *stockfisch* is also the name of a traditional French dish, a specialty of the area around Nice and Monaco, originally made with dried and salted haddock or cod cooked with tomatoes, red peppers, onions, and olives. (Throughout the Mediterranean, the dish is made with cod rather than haddock because haddock isn't available.) In Ducasse's recipe, the stockfish has been replaced by *tripettes* (the dried and salted strip found behind the innards and beneath the backbone of the cod), which are stewed, as the stockfish is traditionally cooked, and a fat piece of salt cod is added. *Tripettes* are an extremely local product, available only in the region around Nice (as are the Perugina sausages [page 246] served with Ducasse's recipe); you won't even find them in Paris.

What is generally sold as salt cod here is more akin to stockfish than the salt cod Ducasse uses because it is salted and thoroughly dried. When buying salt cod, look for the fattest, whitest pieces you can find.

[*Dover Sole*] Known in France simply as *sole*, true Dover sole tastes unlike any other flatfish—including those that borrow its name. Its flesh is pure white and its thin fillets are surprisingly meaty.

It is harvested in the European Atlantic. Only the black skin of sole need be removed before cooking; the white skin melts into nothing.

Dover sole is the only true sole marketed in North America; other American flatfish or flounder, such as Pacific Coast "Dover sole," are much softer textured than true sole. One way of telling the difference between a flounder and a true sole is shape. Sole is a narrow fish, while flounders have rounder fillets. (The other way to tell is price.)

You may be able to find imported Dover sole in specialty markets. Or you can substitute other flatfish, such as lemon sole, flounder, or fluke. If you do, be aware that the texture will be different, as noted above. American flatfish also doesn't skin as easily as true sole. You'll need either to cut off the skin carefully with a knife, or skin it after cooking. If you cook it with the skin on, scale it first.

[*European Sea Bass*] This is the species the French call either *loup de mer* or *bar*, depending on the body of water from which it's harvested: Taken from the Atlantic Ocean, it's sold as *bar*; captured in the Mediterranean, it's called *loup de mer*, or "sea wolf." This excellent silver-skinned fish has firm, relatively lean white flesh. Its texture lies somewhere between the delicate flesh of a black sea bass or snapper and that of the firmer-textured wild striped bass. For all of Ducasse's recipes that call for European sea bass you can substitute wild striped bass or other white-fleshed fish such as snapper, black sea bass, Chilean sea bass, blackfish, or farm-raised striped bass. (Note that farm-raised striped bass—a hybrid cross of wild striped bass and freshwater white bass—is a smaller fish than the wild. They are marketed at about 1½ to 2 pounds and have a less meaty texture—and less wonderful flavor—than the wild fish.)

Generally, these recipes call for a whole fish; head and bones may be used for stock. It may be difficult to find whole fish of the size (3 to 4 pounds) used in the recipes. Black sea bass and snapper are usually marketed as smaller fish and there are currently various commercial size limits (depending on the state) on wild striped bass that preclude finding a fish that weighs less than about 6 to 8 pounds (and they often weigh much more). In that case, buy 6- to 8-ounce fillets, and ask for the bones and heads from a white-fleshed fish such as striped bass, snapper, blackfish, or black sea bass for the stock.

When grilling delicate snapper, sea bass, and blackfish fillets, use a grill basket to keep the fish from sticking to the grill grate; if they stick, these fragile fillets will fall apart when you try to flip them.

There are two recipes that call for grilled European sea bass. A 1-inch-thick wild striped bass fillet (6 to 8 ounces) will take 3 to 4 minutes per side. An 8-ounce snapper or black sea bass fillet (about ½ inch thick) will take about 3 minutes per side.

The recipe for Bass Fillets Baked in Parchment with Fennel-Truffle Sauce calls for a 3-inch-square fillet of European sea bass. A 3-inch-square wild striped bass fillet (about 1 inch thick) will need 12 minutes in the oven. A 3-inch-square snapper fillet (about ¾ inch thick) will take about 8 minutes in the oven.

The recipe for Sautéed Bass "Tournedos" with Crisp Potato Ravioli may be easier to make (if you're alone in the kitchen) if you brown the tournedos top and bottom, and on the sides, and then finish baking in the oven. This will give you time to cook the ravioli, with the fish kept warm in the oven.

[*John Dory*] European John Dory is a firm, fine-textured white-fleshed fish with thin, meaty fillets, found predominantly in the eastern Atlantic. It's an odd-looking fish with a huge head and a dark "thumbprint" mark on its side. There is an American species of dory on this side of the Atlantic that tastes similar to the European and, though not fished commercially, is sporadically available on the East Coast of the United States. American dory is differentiated from the European species because it isn't marked with the thumbprint. Another species of dory is imported from New Zealand; it will have been frozen.

Surprisingly, the two fish that make the best substitutes for John Dory are very different from each other: Dover sole and pompano, both of which have thin fillets with firm, tight flesh. Pompano is oilier than dory but has a remarkably similar texture and is milder tasting than other oily fish. Permit, a larger pompanolike fish, also makes a good substitution: Choose fish under 4 pounds because the flavor is less desirable above that weight.

Roasted John Dory Niçoise Style tastes good made with other whole white-fleshed fish such as snapper and black sea bass, or even with a monkfish tail. Two 2- to 2½-pound snappers (each about 2 inches thick at the widest point) will take 25 to 30 minutes to cook. Boned monkfish tail weighing 1½ pounds (4 to 6 small fillets) will take 20 to 30 minutes to cook.

[*Rockfish*] European rockfish, or *poisson de mer*, is not a particular variety of fish but rather any number of small bony fish that live in and around rocks in the Mediterranean and are used to flavor regional soups and stews. (Larger specimens of these fish are cooked in bouillabaisse.)

To substitute for the rockfish used in Ducasse's fish stocks, you'll need to buy whatever inexpensive white fish is available. Unfortunately, fish has gotten so expensive in America that there really isn't much of what we used to call "trash fish" around. Porgies, wolffish, American rockfish (which encompasses a large variety of West Coast species, some of which, when filleted, look something like—and are often erroneously sold as—snappers, for much more money than they should be) and milkfish are some still relatively inexpensive types of white fish.

[*Sea Bream, Gilt-Head Bream*] *Daurade royale*, or gilt-head bream, swims in the Mediterranean and is one of the best-tasting fish in the family of sea breams. Gilt-head bream is a pretty fish, distinguishable from other breams by the large gold strip that runs like the bridge of a pair of glasses between its eyes. Its flesh is firm and white with few bones.

You won't find bream here, although you will find porgies, other members of the bream family

that swim in the Atlantic. Porgies are typically a much smaller fish than Ducasse's *daurade*, however, so they are unsuitable for the recipes in this book. Snapper, grouper, and black sea bass, all of which are roughly the same shape as a bream, make excellent substitutions. Snapper and sea bass are both softer-fleshed than *daurade*. Grouper has relatively firm flesh. If you live on the West Coast, you might try American rockfish, though the flesh is substantially softer than *daurade*.

In Crispy Sautéed Sea Bream with Orange "Beef Daube" Sauce, the fillets are sautéed skin-on because the skin becomes deliciously crisp. Snapper and sea bass fillets give similar results when sautéed with the skin. If you use grouper, however, skin the fillets; the skin is unpleasantly tough.

In Sautéed Sea Bream with Clams, White Beans, and Girolles, the fish is skinned so that the crushed peppercorns will adhere.

[*Turbot*] Turbot is a large, European flatfish with thick, firm, white flesh. You won't find wild European turbot in these waters, but you may see it farmed, from Greenland; it won't have the flavor of the wild but it's a serviceable substitute. (Note that the farmed is only slightly less expensive than the European, which is very expensive.) Otherwise, either East or West Coast species of halibut, or even salmon, make a good substitute for turbot in Turbot Steamed in Seaweed, with Assorted Shellfish. If you're buying halibut for this recipe, make sure to buy a fillet, not a steak—halibut is more often sold in steak form.

SHELLFISH AND OTHER SEA CREATURES

With a few exceptions, you will be able to find most of the shellfish and other sea creatures used in Ducasse's recipes. Where the shellfish isn't available (European clams are very different than ours, for instance) you will find excellent substitutions available here.

[*Clams, Oysters, and Periwinkles*] A variety of different clams is used in these recipes. Some, like the long, narrow razor clam, are available here. Others, such as the *venus*, *praires*, and *palourdes*, are not. Since there are so many types of excellent clams available here, we think it's wise not to get lost in the particulars but to follow Ducasse's intent instead by substituting a number of different varieties of Atlantic and Pacific clams.

So, for example, in the recipe for Turbot Steamed in Seaweed, with Assorted Shellfish, five different types of clams are listed: *venus*, *praires*, *palourdes*, *clams*, and *coques*. *French clams* are small American clams; that is, littleneck or cherrystone clams. *Coques* are cockles, tiny, ridged, green-and-white-shelled clams that are sold here imported from New Zealand. The other three clams are not available here. Choose three different varieties available in your area, such as soft-shell clams, Manilla clams, butter clams, or pismo clams.

Periwinkles, or *bigorneaux*, that grow along the Atlantic Coast, may be available at some ethnic markets.

Belon oysters are a variety of flat oyster cultivated near the mouth of the Loire River in France. Belons are also cultivated here on the East and West coasts. They have an unmistakable, slightly metallic flavor.

[*Eels*] Two different types of eels are used in French cooking: *congre*, or saltwater eel, and *anguille*, or freshwater eel. *Congre* is traditionally used in soups and chowders in the Mediterranean, Brittany, and Gascony because its gelatinous but somewhat tasteless flesh gives body to broths. You can buy saltwater eel in Asian markets, and it's sometimes sold frozen in supermarkets. If you can't find eel, substitute a fishhead to provide the gelatin.

[*Langoustines, Langoustes, and Homards*] These three crustaceans are grouped together because they all look something like one another (*langoustines* look like mini-lobsters, while *langoustes*, or spiny lobsters, have large tails and no claws; *homards* are clawed lobsters) and they resemble each other in flavor. Of the three, langoustines have

the most refined flavor, followed by spiny lobsters and then clawed lobsters.

Langoustines are sold here as scampi, Dublin Bay prawns, and sometimes prawns (confusingly, since large shrimp are also sold here as prawns). If you live in a major international food community, you can probably find langoustines from New Zealand, but they'll be very expensive. An average whole langoustine weighs about 4 ounces; the cleaned tail weighs about 1 ounce. You can substitute shrimp in Ducasse's recipes that call for langoustines. Buy medium-to-large shrimp graded as 16/20s or U-15s in the industry—16/20 means sixteen to twenty shrimp per pound (each shrimp weighs slightly less than 1 ounce), while U-15 means that there are fewer than fifteen shrimp per pound (each shrimp weighing slightly more than 1 ounce).

Clawed lobsters are harvested in both American and European waters. Spiny lobsters are harvested in the Mediterranean and eastern Atlantic, off the coasts of Florida and California, in the Caribbean, and in South Africa, New Zealand, Australia, and Brazil. If you live where spiny lobsters are fished, you can buy them fresh. Otherwise, you'll see them frozen in the shell (sold as "lobster tails"). Note that varieties of spiny lobster that grow in cold waters (from New Zealand, Australia, South Africa, and Brazil) are said to be of a better quality than those from the warm waters of Florida, California, and the Caribbean.

If you can't get spiny lobster, substitute clawed lobster in Ducasse's recipes.

[*Sea Scallops*] The difference between European sea scallops and those found in North America is largely one of processing. Here, sea scallops are almost always sold shucked (they are processed on the boat and delivered to shore in bags), while they're sold live, in their shells, in France. Since the processors traditionally remove the roe from the scallop during shucking, we are actually buying only the white adductor muscle; European scallops are served with the bright orange roe attached. You may be able to find live scallops in their shells in Asian markets.

When buying sea scallops, it's important to be aware that many scallops sold here are soaked for a short time in a phosphate-and-water mixture to increase their weight and prolong their shelf life. This processing not only ruins the sweet taste of the scallop but also causes it to absorb water. This means that when you sauté the scallops, they will throw off the water in the pan and steam instead of brown. Wholesalers are required to identify scallops as either "wet" (processed) or "dry" (unprocessed) but there is no regulation at the retail level so the cook is on his own. You can spot a soaked scallop by its unnaturally bright white color. "Dry" scallops range in color from ivory to pinkish beige to tan. Processed scallops are also usually sitting in liquid since, just as they absorb the chemical dip, they also give it up as they stand. "Dry" scallops are sticky and flabby and smell faintly of the sea. "Wet" scallops are taut and swollen with liquid, and slippery to the touch; they smell like nothing at all, or mildly chemical.

If you can buy scallops live in their shells, do so for the recipe for Scallops Steamed in Their Shells. If not, you'll need to buy scallop shells separately at a kitchenware store. Unfortunately, the shells you buy will be from different scallops (i.e., not matching pairs), so they won't fit together easily; you'll need to fit them together as well as possible and use the pastry dough to fill in the gaps. An easier solution is to buy only twelve shells and cover each with a square of aluminum foil in lieu of the second shell. Bake 1¼-inch-thick scallops about 13 minutes, as in the recipe; 1-inch-thick scallops need only 11 minutes.

[*Squid and Cuttlefish*] Squid (*calmars* or, in the Basque tongue, *chiperons*) and cuttlefish (*seiche*) are similar animals with long, tubular bodies and tentacles. Both belong to the *cephalopod* family; cuttlefish is the larger animal. The two taste very similar except that the flesh of the cuttlefish, being

larger, is thicker and meatier. It also takes slightly longer to cook. The advantage to using cuttlefish over squid is in dishes that call for squid ink. Cuttlefish have very large ink sacs and their ink is dark in color; squid contain so little ink (the color of which is drab in comparison to that of cuttlefish) that it isn't practical to use it for its ink.

Cuttlefish must be imported from Europe, so it's scarce and expensive. You may be able to find it frozen. But because it's so expensive, it makes more sense to substitute squid in recipes that call for cuttlefish. Cuttlefish ink, processed and packaged in Spain, is sold separately at some gourmet food stores.

[*Octopus*] In Ducasse's kitchens, octopus is frozen overnight before cooking to soften the flesh. Once thawed and cooked, the octopus is skinned and cleaned of viscera. In this country, you're likely to find octopus frozen anyway, and it may also be already cleaned.

The octopus used in the Shellfish Salad with White Beans and Arugula weighs about 1¼ pounds.

Baby octopus, which weigh about 1½ ounces, are very tender—almost the texture of squid and so needn't be frozen before cooking. Squid can be used in place of baby octopus.

MEAT AND POULTRY

Ducasse buys his meats and poultry from all over France. The flesh of the animal tastes subtly different, depending on the land where it is raised and the food it eats. As a general rule, Ducasse keeps meat and poultry as whole as possible: Chickens and ducks are cooked whole and larger animals are cooked in portions for two or more; the meats are carved at the table. This is done in part because the meat tastes better and is moister when it's cooked on the bone. In addition, with larger pieces you have more control over the cooking. For the same reason, chops are cut very thick.

The French butcher meat differently from the way we do, so their cuts are often not comparable to ours. While our butchers cut across muscles, French butchers respect the integrity of the muscle and cut the meat into sections that cook at the same rate.

[*Chicken*] Ducasse uses two kinds of chickens in his recipes: the yellow-skinned *poulets jaunes* from his home region, Landes, and the black-footed *poulets de Bresse* raised near the city of Lyons. The Bresse chickens are used in recipes that call for poaching because, classically speaking, poached birds should be white. There is some difference in taste between the two chickens as well as a difference in shape; Bresse are fatter.

Cockscombs: Cockscombs are used in some of the more elaborate recipes; Ducasse has used them in his cooking for the past twenty years. Cockscombs are quintessential in French cuisine. Their use in Ducasse's cooking pays homage to the roots of classical French cooking and exemplifies Ducasse's notion of re-envisioning French food as a traditional cuisine reinterpreted for today's sensibilities and tastes. The use of cockscombs also speaks to the French tradition of using everything on the animal. Recipes such as the Half-Dried Pasta Tubes with Sweetbreads, Cockscombs, and Kidneys are rich because cockscombs are associated with rich, elegant, aristocratic nineteenth-century cooking. Those recipes usually use the kidneys of the cock as well.

Cockscombs are very mild flavored and gelatinous, more notable for their texture than for their taste. In France, they are sold frozen.

[*Duck*] There are two major commercial varieties of ducks in France, the Nantes and the Barbarie (or Barbary) duck. The latter, also called Muscovy, a small duck, serving only one or two people, represents the majority of the French production. The Nantes is larger than the Barbarie. The moulard, a cross between yet another duck, the Pekin, and the Barbarie duck, is bred in the Southwest for its fattened liver. The legs are used for confit; the large breasts may be used in confit or sold as magret that are traditionally cooked and eaten rare, as one would a steak. The Rouen duck, raised in the region around the city of Rouen, is available only locally. Choose ducks that weigh between 4 and 4¹/₂ pounds.

Foie gras: In France, one can buy both goose and duck foie gras fresh. Goose is reputed to have a finer, more subtle flavor and, because the texture is more fragile, it is usually used for terrines. Duck foie gras has a somewhat juicier texture than goose and is more supple; it is used for sautéing and grilling because it holds up better during these types of cooking. Fattened goose livers may run from 2¹/₂ to 3 pounds, while the duck livers run as large as 1¹/₄ to 2 pounds.

Buying raw foie gras: America produces only duck foie gras. It is graded on the basis of size and amount of veins running through it; the highest grade, A, is assigned to those livers that are large (at least 1¹/₄ pounds and up to 2), smooth, firm, and a good pinkish beige color with few blemishes or bruises. A's have a roundish shape that cuts into well-shaped slices for sautéed foie gras. B's are smaller (weighing ³/₄ to 1¹/₄ pounds), are more oval, and may have some blemishes. Bruising is undesirable because it causes that portion of the liver to melt faster during cooking than the rest. Livers that feel spongy to the touch have a low fat content and may burn during cooking.

The lowest grade, C, can have as good a flavor as the higher grades, but foie gras of this quality is rarely available to consumers.

Foie gras confit: A traditional southwest France preparation in which the fattened duck liver is cooked in duck fat, just as the legs are. Foie gras terrine or raw foie gras may be substituted in recipes that call for foie gras confit.

[*Lamb*] Lamb from three different regions is used in Ducasse's kitchens. Each is distinguished by a slightly different taste and color of flesh. The Atlantic *présalé* is the most different tasting of the three; it feeds on grasses that grow close to the seashore, so the meat picks up the flavor of the salt and the sea. Other than the *présalé,* the restaurants use lamb raised in the Pyrenees and on the plains around Pauillac.

Baby lamb is used in the spring, up until the Easter season, after which time mature lamb is used. Not only is baby lamb smaller than mature lamb but, because the lamb has fed only on milk, its meat is lighter-colored and more delicately flavored. The average size of a baby lamb in France is around 25 pounds. Mature lambs are best between about 33 and 37 pounds. Larger than that and their flavor becomes unpleasantly strong.

To substitute mature for baby lamb in the recipe for Spit-Roasted Lamb with Braised Baby Lettuce and Ricotta Gnocchi, buy the sirloin half of a leg of lamb (about 3 pounds), and one 7- or 8-rib rack (1 to 1$^{1}/_{8}$ pounds). Have the butcher remove the chine bone and french the rib bones; also ask him to bone the leg, then roll and tie it. To roast the leg in the oven rather than on a spit, preheat the oven to 350°F. Brown the leg and the rack in 2 tablespoons olive oil in a roasting pan over medium-high heat. Remove the rack from the pan. Roast the leg in the oven for 25 minutes, then add the rack to the pan and continue roasting until both are medium-rare, about 20 more minutes.

[*Beef and Veal*] Ducasse buys beef from Chalosse both to support his home region and because it is one of the best tasting beefs in France. The particular shape of the animal also gives a cut of rib that is excellent for two people. When the restaurant buys the beef, it has been dry-aged for a week. It is dry-aged a further 2 weeks at the restaurant before using.

Rumsteak: The recipe for Pan-Seared Steak with a Sweet-and-Sour "Condiment Sauce" calls for a *rumsteak*—a steak that is cut from the hindquarter of the beef. The closest cut we have is a round steak, but a sirloin or shoulder steak is tastier for this recipe.

Sweetbreads: Whole sweetbreads are made up of two parts: a compact round piece called the "heart" or, in French, *paume* (because it is the shape of the palm of the hand) and a looser long piece. The hearts are more desirable because they can be cut into more regular, compact pieces; the less desirable half is used in dishes where the shape is unimportant, such as fricassees. Here, where sweetbreads are very often sold vacuum-packed, we're likely not to have a choice. If you end up with one of the less desirable pieces, it can be cut and cooked in the same manner as a "heart"; it just won't look as pretty.

The sweetbreads used in Ducasse's restaurants are from very young, tiny veal; the hearts weigh only about 3 ounces apiece. (The recipe for Sweetbreads Braised Two Ways calls for eight 3- to 4-ounce sweetbreads.) In America, sweetbreads are much larger; buy 1$^{1}/_{2}$ to 2 pounds of sweetbreads and cut them into eight pieces.

[*Pork*] **Crépinette:** *Crépinette* is the French word for caul fat, the lining of the pig's stomach. This thin, lacy tissue is used to wrap sausage meat. It holds the meat together and melts into it when cooked.

Perugina sausages: These small, round, dried sausages made of pork flavored with garlic are used in the stockfish recipe because they are a specialty of the area around Nice.

Poitrine de porc demi-sel: In France, *poitrine de porc demi-sel* (also sometimes called *lard*) is fatty pork belly that is salted but not smoked, and often cut into the small pieces called *lardons*. We don't have a substitute for this in America and have called for slab bacon instead; smoking gives our bacon a very different flavor from that of the French *poitrine*. (Smoked and salted pork belly in France is *poitrine fumée*.) Italian pancetta is salted but not smoked so, although it is less fatty than *poitrine*, it will give you a truer taste. Since pancetta is cured with pepper, adjust pepper in recipes that use pancetta in place of *poitrine de porc demi-sel*.

DUCASSE'S PANTRY

[*Fromage Blanc*] A fresh French-made cheese, becoming increasingly available in the United States.

(See Sources, page 251.) A fresh sheep's milk cheese such as *brébis* or fresh goat cheese such as Montrachet can be substituted for fromage blanc.

[*Olive Oil*] Two different olive oils are used in each of Ducasse's three restaurants. One, the best-quality, cold-pressed extra virgin, is used raw, as a seasoning. A lesser-quality, cold-pressed oil is used for cooking. At the Louis XV, where olive oil is the essence of the cooking, one bottle of extra-virgin oil is set into an ice bucket filled with water and frozen, then kept in the ice bucket and lifted out as needed to finish plates with a final drizzle of oil. The ice makes the oil thick and viscous so that it keeps its drizzled form on the plate.

[*Peppers*] The kitchens use a blend of four different peppers to get a unique marriage of flavors: black pepper, Szechuan pepper, Indonesian pepper, and a long, dried pepper from Java. Indonesian pepper has a somewhat more aromatic and slightly more bitter taste than Szechuan—it's almost closer to allspice than pepper. We can't buy the Indonesian and Javanese peppers here, but one could create an alternative, personal blend using a variety of available peppers.

Espellete pepper is a slender, mildly spicy, red pepper from the town of Espellete in Basque country, used in the recipe for stockfish. The pepper is dried and then ground.

[*Salt*] Sea salt, hand-harvested from the waters around the Guérande Peninsula and the island of Noirmoutiers on the Atlantic coast of Brittany, is used exclusively in Ducasse's kitchens for its flavor (see the photograph on page 123). Because it has not been refined, it has more flavor than standard salt and tastes slightly iodized, like the saltiness of an oyster. Sea salt is gray; refining whitens salt.

There are two grades of sea salt used: the top-quality *fleur de sel* and the *sel de Guérande*, which is used as an all-purpose salt. Both are coarse-grained. The fleur de sel is, literally, the "flower of the salt"; that is, it's that part of the salt that forms above the

water. It is used on raw foods, almost as a condiment sprinkled on before serving. The Guérande salt is used in cooking. When it arrives at the restaurant, it is often slightly damp, so it's first dried; then some is ground in the food processor and passed through a fine sieve (*tamis*) so that the kitchen has both coarse and fine Guérande salt.

Fleur de sel is Ducasse's favorite ingredient: He finds it essential for seasoning.

[*Sour Cherry Vinegar and Nectar*] Sour cherry vinegar and nectar are available by mail-order (see Sources, page 251). Or buy cherry syrup, available at some specialty food stores (particularly those that sell Eastern European foods) and make your own cherry nectar by mixing 1 part syrup to 1 part water. Alternatively, use the syrup from jarred sour cherries, also available at specialty food stores.

For sour cherry vinegar, you can make a reasonable facsimile by combining 1 part sour cherry syrup and 3 parts white vinegar; or substitute raspberry vinegar.

[*Tomato Confit*] *Tomate confite* are seasoned, peeled, and quartered tomatoes baked for two to three hours at a low heat until their flavor is intensified and the flesh is shriveled, but still very moist. These "confited" tomatoes are quite different from sun-dried tomatoes, which are drier and have a heavier, more bitter flavor. Tomato confit can be stored for up to 3 days in the refrigerator.

[*Vinegar*] Two kinds of vinegars are used extensively in Ducasse's kitchens: sherry wine vinegar and an aged balsamic vinegar. The sherry wine vinegar is a relatively acidic vinegar, used in sauces and cooked preparations like the white bean purée served with the roasted cod to add a punch of acidity at the end of cooking. The balsamic, with its rounder flavor, is used in vinaigrettes; it's too sweet to finish a sauce.

[*Doughs*] Ducasse uses a variety of doughs in this book: for ravioli, for sweet tarts, and for savory tourtes. Some must be made by hand, but others are available commercially and it saves time to use them. You may be able to buy uncooked puff pastry dough from a French bakery in town. Frozen puff pastry is available from supermarkets and specialty shops. Look for an all-butter pastry (see also Sources, page 251). Pasta dough is often sold in sheets at stores that make fresh pasta.

TECHNIQUES

[*Vegetables*] Vegetables are handled with extraordinary care and respect in the restaurant kitchens. As the vegetables are trimmed, peeled, and moved about, the movements of the chefs are deliberate and precise. More often than not, each vegetable is handled separately—carrots are not dumped, but placed one by one in a casserole. The tips of the fingers are used to place and arrange the vegetables: There is nothing rough or haphazard in their treatment.

Peeling vegetables: As a general rule, vegetables with tender, easily digestible skins are left unpeeled, or peeled in stripes. So, for example, tiny new potatoes used in vegetable casseroles are cooked in their skins. Black radishes and cucumbers may be eaten unpeeled, or are peeled in stripes. Large round turnips, however, need to be peeled twice because there is a hard, white film underneath the purplish skin that should be removed to expose the more tender flesh.

Vegetables cut *en sifflet*: A *sifflet*, in French, is a whistle. To cut vegetables *en sifflet*, therefore, means to cut them on an angle so that they resemble a penny whistle.

Vegetables cut into *bâtonnets*: Vegetables cut into bâtonnets (as are the salsify in Spit-Roasted Lobster with Caramelized Salsify and Almonds, page 94) are simply cut into thin sticks.

To prepare artichokes: For all varieties, start by filling a bowl half-full with water. Cut a lemon in half, squeeze the juice into the water, and drop in the lemon halves. As you prepare the artichokes, rub the cut edges often with another lemon half to prevent darkening.

To prepare globe artichoke hearts or bottoms: Snap off the outer dark green leaves to expose the lighter-colored, inner cone of leaves. Trim the stem flush with the base. Using a serrated knife, cut off the cone of leaves right above the base to expose the fuzzy choke. Using a sharp paring knife, trim off all the dark green outer skin from the sides and bottom of the artichoke to expose the whitish bottom; trim the bottom to make it smooth and round. Scoop out the choke with a small spoon, and drop the artichoke heart into the lemon water. Cook as directed in the individual recipe, draining well and patting dry if necessary.

To prepare *poivrade* artichokes: Remove the tough outer leaves from the artichoke by snapping (rather than tearing) them off at the base to expose the lighter-colored, inner cone of leaves. Slice off the top third of each artichoke. Trim the stem to ³/₄ inch and peel the stem with a paring knife; as you work, place each artichoke in the bowl of lemon water. Then remove the artichokes one by one from the water and remove the center hairy choke with a small melon baller. Either pat dry and prepare as directed in the recipe or return the artichokes to the lemon water until ready to proceed.

To prepare baby artichokes: Follow the instructions for preparing *poivrade* artichokes, but don't remove the choke.

To prepare asparagus: Asparagus is always peeled to enhance the soft, silky texture of the flesh.

To peel asparagus, first use a paring knife to trim off all the dark green, triangular-shaped, "leaves" that ascend the stalk; this extra step ensures a smoothly peeled stalk. Then, peel the spears one at a time: Hold a spear by the head and lay it on the cutting board. Starting about 1 inch below the bottom of the head, peel the stalk with a vegetable peeler, turning the spear as you go. When all the stalks have been peeled, line them up on the board so that the tops are even, then trim the bottoms of the stalks to the desired length.

To rehydrate dried mushrooms: Dried mushrooms can be used to add flavor to broths. Add dried mushrooms to broth that is hot but not boiling and let infuse for 30 to 35 minutes. Then strain the broth and discard the mushrooms (or reserve for another use).

To roast red peppers: Preheat the broiler. Arrange whole peppers on a broiling pan or cookie sheet, set them under the broiler, about 5 inches below the heating element and broil, watching carefully, until the peppers blacken on top. Turn and let blacken on the other side, then turn to blacken any remaining uncharred spots. When the peppers are completely blistered and blackened, remove from the oven. Immediately wrap the peppers together in plastic wrap, or place them in a large plastic food storage bag and seal; the steam created will make the skin much easier to remove. After 15 minutes or so, use the tip of a small sharp knife to peel off the blackened skin. Remove the stems and seeds. Rinse the peppers very quickly under cold water to remove any remaining blackened bits and seeds and pat dry.

To make a dish of roasted peppers to be served as such, roast and peel red, green, and yellow peppers as above. Quarter them and cook in olive oil over very low heat for 30 to 35 minutes. Drain, add fresh oil to cover, rosemary, and a bay leaf or two and refrigerate overnight.

To bake potatoes: Ducasse places them on a layer of coarse salt that protects them from the heat of the metal baking pan and keeps them moist as they bake.

[*Meat, Poultry, and Fish*] **Cooking with butter:** Butter is used in panfrying to moisten and flavor meat. But because it can't be cooked over high heat—high heat gives butter an unpleasant flavor— it's added in the middle of the cooking process, once the heat has been reduced. So, for example, meats and fish are browned in olive oil, or, very occasionally, when the taste of olive oil isn't correct (as in the recipe for Sautéed Sea Bream with Clams, White Beans, and Girolles), in tasteless grapeseed oil. Once browned on one side, the meat or fish is turned, the heat is reduced to medium, and butter is added to the pan. The melted butter is spooned over the meat as it cooks to "nourish" it.

Butter is used in the same way for making meat or poultry jus; the bones are first browned and then the butter is added. Along with adding flavor to the jus, the butter also serves to deglaze the pan by loosening the browned sugars stuck to the bottom. The one time that butter is used for browning is when the fruits are sautéed. The sugar from the fruit combines with the butter to form a caramel.

To cook cockscombs: Cook in boiling water until tender, about 1½ hours. Then clean any black bits from the cockscombs and remove the cartilage.

To firm the texture of white-fleshed fish fillets, such as cod: Sprinkle the fish with 1 to 2 tablespoons coarse salt and let stand for 30 minutes. Brush the salt off with a towel before cooking.

To soak salt cod and stockfish before cooking: Salt cod is soaked to desalt it; stockfish is soaked to desalt and soften it. Put the fish in a bowl with water to cover. Soak salt cod for 3 days, stockfish for 4, changing the water three times during each 24-hour period.

To clean shucked scallops: Some shucked scallops are sold with a small, crescent-shaped, opaque muscle still attached to the side of the scallop meat. Pull off and discard this muscle; it is fibrous and tough when cooked.

Quadrillage: The technique of marking food, often fish, on a grill with a diamond-shaped pattern. Since *quadrillage* is for presentation, only one side of the food is marked: Place the food on the grill so that it lies diagonally across the rods of the grill grate. After a minute or two, move the food (don't turn it over) so that it lies at a 90-degree angle to its original position. After a minute or two more, the food will be marked and can be turned over and finished on the grill or in the oven.

Resting: After high-heat cooking, meats are allowed to rest on a rack for roughly half their cooking time. (This is a general rule: Very long cooked meats rest for less than half their cooking time.) As meat cooks, it contracts and toughens; resting allows it to relax and soften again. The rack keeps the meat from sitting in its juices, which softens the crust. The rack also keeps the meat from continuing to cook on the bottom.

Reduction: Times given for reduction of liquids are guidelines. Measure liquid every now and then while reducing. If you have too much liquid, reduce further, remembering to adjust salt, as it concentrates as the liquid reduces. Gelatinous stocks, particularly veal stocks, will get gummy if reduced too far.

À *la unilatéral:* The technique by which the fillets in the recipe for Crispy Sautéed Sea Bream with Orange "Beef Daube" Sauce are cooked on one side only; this keeps the fish moist. The fish is panfried skin-side down until the skin is crispy. Then it's removed from the pan and turned over onto a rack on a plate where the residual heat continues to cook the fish completely.

About quantities: Sometimes Ducasse's recipes can't be broken down any further, such as his pasta recipes and his gnocchi recipe on page 45. Extra pasta can be rolled, cut, and stored in a dry place (outside the refrigerator) for a few days. Gnocchi should be shaped, arranged on a baking sheet, and frozen solid; once frozen, they can be transferred to a plastic bag and stored in the freezer until you're ready to cook them.

About the photographs: In Ducasse's kitchens recipes are always evolving; the recipe as it's written captures a moment in time. The photographs sometimes capture another. You may want to incorporate the differences you see in the photographs into the recipes as you cook them. Sometimes, however, the photographs represent the sheer pleasure of the aesthetic.

CONVERSIONS

WEIGHT EQUIVALENTS
The metric weights given in this chart are not exact equivalents, but have been rounded up or down slightly to make measuring easier.

Avoirdupois	Metric
¼ oz	7 g
½ oz	15 g
1 oz	30 g
2 oz	60 g
3 oz	90 g
4 oz	115 g
5 oz	150 g
6 oz	175 g
7 oz	200 g
8 oz (½ lb)	225 g
9 oz	250 g
10 oz	300 g
11 oz	325 g
12 oz	350 g
13 oz	375 g
14 oz	400 g
15 oz	425 g
16 oz (1 lb)	450 g
1 lb 2 oz	500 g
1½ lb	750 g
2 lb	900 g
2¼ lb	1 kg
3 lb	1.4 kg
4 lb	1.8 kg
4½ lb	2 kg

VOLUME EQUIVALENTS
These are not exact equivalents for the American cups and spoons, but have been rounded up or down slightly to make measuring easier.

American	Metric	Imperial
¼ t	1.25 ml	
½ t	2.5 ml	
1 t	5 ml	
½ T (1½ t)	7.5 ml	
1 T (3 t)	15 ml	
¼ cup (4 T)	60 ml	2 fl oz
⅓ cup (5 T)	75 ml	2½ fl oz
½ cup (8 T)	125 ml	4 fl oz
⅔ cup (10 T)	150 ml	5 fl oz (¼ pint)
¾ cup (12 T)	175 ml	6 fl oz (⅓ pint)
1 cup (16 T)	250 ml	8 fl oz
1¼ cups	300 ml	10 fl oz (½ pint)
1½ cups	350 ml	12 fl oz
1 pint (2 cups)	500 ml	16 fl oz
2½ cups	625 ml	20 fl oz (1 pint)
1 quart (4 cups)	1 litre	1¾ pints

OVEN TEMPERATURE EQUIVALENTS

Oven	°F.	°C.	Gas Mark
very cool	250–275	130–140	½–1
cool	300	150	2
warm	325	170	3
moderate	350	180	4
moderately hot	375	190	5
	400	200	6
hot	425	220	7
very hot	450	230	8
	475	250	9

SOURCES

For reservations and information at any of the restaurants of Alain Ducasse, or at the hotels associated with them, contact them directly.

LE LOUIS XV
Hôtel de Paris
Place du Casino, Monte Carlo
MC 98000 Monaco
377–92–16–30–01
fax: 377–92–16–69–21

Hôtel de Paris
Place du Casino, Monte Carlo
MC 98000 Monaco
377–92–16–30–00
fax: 377–92–16–38–50

RESTAURANT ALAIN DUCASSE
59 avenue Raymond-Poincaré
75116 Paris
33–1–47–27–12–27
fax: 33–1–47–27–31–22

Hôtel Le Parc
55–57 avenue Raymond-Poincaré
75116 Paris
33–1–44–05–66–66
fax: 33–1–44–05–66–00

LA BASTIDE DE MOUSTIERS
La Grisolière
04360 Moustiers-Sainte-Marie
33–4–92–70–47–47
fax: 33–4–92–70–47–48

KITCHENWARE

The following kitchen equipment and bakeware supply houses offer a wide range of French cookware, all available by mail order; Bridge also carries the Japanese "Benriner" mandoline slicer, popular in Ducasse's kitchens:

Bridge Kitchenware Corporation
214 East 52nd Street
New York, NY 10022
212–688–4220; catalog information and customer service: 212–838–6746

J. B. Prince
29 West 38th Street
New York, NY 10018
212–302–8611

King Arthur Flour Baker's Catalogue
Box 876
Norwich, VT 05055
800–827–6836

Williams-Sonoma
Mail Order Department
P.O. Box 7456
San Francisco, CA 94120–7456
415–421–4242

Zabar's
2245 Broadway
New York, NY 10024
212-787–2000

FOOD AND SPECIALTY INGREDIENTS

For domestic foie gras, both raw and cooked in a block of confit; fresh ducks, squab, rabbit, venison, and guinea hens; free-range chickens, turkeys, and capons; duck, chicken, and game sausages; and duck and veal demiglace:

D'Artagnan
280 Wilson Avenue
Newark, NJ 07105
800–DARTAGN or 973–344-0565
fax: 973–465–1870

For excellent crème fraîche, fromage blanc, and other specialty dairy products:

Vermont Butter and
   Cheese Company
P.O. Box 95
Websterville, VT 05678
800–884–6287

For a broad range of domestic and imported cheeses, cut to order before shipping:

Ideal Cheese Shop, Ltd.
1205 Second Avenue
New York, NY 10021
800–382–0109 or 212–688–7579

For a wide variety of specialty ingredients, including vanilla beans, Valrhona bulk chocolate, cocoa powder, fine olive oils, tapenade, vinegars, dried herbs, olives, flavored French honeys, French cheeses, tinned foie gras, and much more:

Balducci's
424 Avenue of the Americas
New York, NY 10011
800–822–1444 or 212–673–2600

Dean & DeLuca
560 Broadway
New York, NY 10012
800–221–7714 or 212–431–1691

Joie de Vivre
P.O. Box 875
Modesto, CA 95353
800–648–8854

Maid of Scandinavia
3244 Raleigh Avenue
Minneapolis, MN 55461
800–328–6722 or 512–927–7966

For fleur de sel and sel gris from Brittany's Guérande peninsula; fresh Breton seaweeds; a wide variety of French mushrooms, both fresh and dried; seasonal French produce, such as Cavaillon melons and mâche lettuce; truffles and truffle juice; Arborio rice; baking chocolate; and more:

Marché aux Delices
120 Imlay Street
Brooklyn, NY 11231
888–547–5471; fax: 718–858–5288;
e-mail: staff@auxdelices.com

Urbani Tartufi
29–24 40th Avenue
Long Island City, NY 11101
718–392–5050
fax: 718–392–1704

5851 West Washington Boulevard
Culver City, CA 90302
213–933–8202
fax: 213–933–4235
Urbani products include fresh, flash-frozen, and canned truffles; wild mushrooms of all sorts; truffle juice and other products; tinned foie gras; caviar; etc.

For fine organic stone-ground bread and pastry flours:

Arrowhead Mills
Box 866
Hereford, TX 79045
806–364–0730

Great Valley Mills
687 Mill Road
Telford, PA 18969
215–754–7800

King Arthur Flour Baker's Catalogue
Box 876
Norwich, VT 05055
800–827–6836

ACKNOWLEDGMENTS

This book was a major transatlantic effort on the part of many people. First and foremost, I would like to thank the talented Didier Elena, who for many years has been my right-hand man. It was Didier who put these recipes into written form, who tested each recipe to ensure perfection, and who prepared them to be put in front of the cameras. I am deeply appreciative of the long hours and hard work that Didier gave to this project.

I am grateful as well to Benôit Witz, my chef at the Bastide de Moustiers and another veteran chef from the Louis XV, who also gave many weeks to this project, adapting recipes for the text and also preparing dishes for the cameras. In addition, I want to thank Gérard Margeon, chief sommelier formerly at the Louis XV and now in Paris, who used his years of experience to choose the wines of not only France but from around the world to create the wine suggestions that enrich the recipes.

Other people whose help and participation were invaluable are: Jean-François Piège, my *seconde* in Paris, who chose with unflagging rigor the food for Paris photography sessions and whose standards of perfection and refinement are reflected throughout the Paris dining experience; and Franck Cerutti, my *seconde* at the Louis XV in Monaco. Through their hard work and dedication, they make my ideas and my cuisine come to life. Also, Dominique Potier, the fine manager of the Bastide, and his genial staff, all of whom smilingly put up with two weeks of disruptions in their tranquil, well-organized world when our little team descended on Moustiers for the long days of photography; and Tonya Peyrot, the gifted decorator whose work gave the Bastide its special cachet, and who so generously provided the unique antique elements that made the photographs done in Moustiers so evocative.

My warm thanks also go to Gwenaelle Gueguen, who from the very beginning of this project has been an essential publishing liaison between Artisan, my publisher, and me; my Irish *attachée de presse* in Paris, Marion Walsh, for her time and effort in coordinating communications on both sides of the Atlantic; Leora Laderman, a British-born Monegasque with a passion for food and a translator by profession, who translated, tasted, and participated in the testing of the recipes; Mona di Orio, a *nez* who creates perfumes in Grasse and an amateur cook with a love for gastronomy, whose olfactory capabilities assured a harmony of aromas and flavors in the recipes during the weeks she worked in the Paris kitchen with Didier, Benôit, and Leora developing, translating, and photographing material for the book. Finally, I would like to express my appreciation to and admiration for photographer Pierre Hussenot, whose beautiful photographs capture the spirit and essence of my cuisine in each of our three settings—Monaco, Moustiers, and Paris.

In New York, I am deeply grateful to the talented and professional team at Artisan, who worked so hard and long on my book, and to Linda Dannenberg for getting this project off the ground.

Beyond the parameters of this book, my kitchens are daily enriched by the artisanal farmers, fishermen, poultrymen, mushroom gatherers, sheep farmers, cattle breeders, and many dedicated merchants and suppliers. I thank them all, and my talented colleagues and friends, for the pleasure I derive from their company and the admiration I feel for their work.

ALAIN DUCASSE

The involvement of all the above-mentioned people made this project a truly unforgettable experience for me. I would like to offer my own thanks to the staffs of the Louis XV, the Bastide de Moustiers, and the Restaurant Alain Ducasse—particularly to Franck Cerutti, Benoît Witz, Dominique Potier, Jean-François Piège, and Gérard Margeon—for their many kindnesses. I would also like to express my appreciation to publisher Ann Bramson, editor Deborah Weiss Geline, and art director Susi Oberhelman, as well as to the entire Artisan team, who worked with such diligence over so many months to make this book a reality; to Lin Hansen and Cathy Young for sharing their culinary expertise while this work was in progress; and to Jo Ann Trautmann and Alice Finley for testing and tasting recipes with me. Thanks and love, as always, to my husband, Steve, and my son, Ben, who happily consumed and critiqued many recipes and who were so understanding and forgiving of the countless hours I had to spend away from them.

Finally, I am deeply grateful to my terrific, longtime agents, Gayle Benderoff and Deborah Geltman, for their early enthusiasm and unflagging support throughout the course of this book; to Peter Workman for his commitment to creating a book of this magnitude; and to Leslie Stoker, publisher of enormous talent, with whom I originated this project.

LINDA DANNENBERG

INDEX